ALL ABOUT
DRU&GS
YOUNG PEOPLE

of related interest

A Little Book of Drugs
Activities to Explore Drug Issues with Young People
2nd edition
Vanessa Rogers
ISBN 978 1 84905 304 4
eISBN 978 0 85700 629 5

A Little Book of Alcohol
Activities to Explore Alcohol Issues with Young People
2nd edition
Vanessa Rogers
ISBN 978 1 84905 303 7
eISBN 978 0 85700 628 8

A Little Book of Tobacco
Activities to Explore Smoking Issues with Young People
Vanessa Rogers
ISBN 978 1 84905 305 1
eISBN 978 0 85700 630 1

Working with Drug and Alcohol Users
A Guide to Providing Understanding, Assessment and Support
Tony White
ISBN 978 1 84905 294 8
eISBN 978 0 85700 618 9

Working with Young Men
Activities for Exploring Personal, Social and Emotional Issues
2nd edition
Vanessa Rogers
ISBN 978 1 84905 101 9
eISBN 978 0 85700 282 2

Working with Young Women
Activities for Exploring Personal, Social and Emotional Issues
2nd edition
Vanessa Rogers
ISBN 978 1 84905 095 1
eISBN 978 0 85700 372 0

Understanding Street Drugs
A Handbook of Substance Misuse for Parents, Teachers
and Other Professionals
2nd edition
David Emmett and Graeme Nice
ISBN 978 1 84310 351 6
eISBN 978 1 84642 449 6

ALL ABOUT
DRUGS
YOUNG PEOPLE

ESSENTIAL INFORMATION AND ADVICE FOR PARENTS AND PROFESSIONALS

JULIAN COHEN

Jessica Kingsley *Publishers*
London and Philadelphia

First published in 2014
by Jessica Kingsley Publishers
73 Collier Street
London N1 9BE, UK
and
400 Market Street, Suite 400
Philadelphia, PA 19106, USA

www.jkp.com

Library of Congress Cataloging in Publication Data
A CIP catalog record for this book is available from the Library of Congress

British Library Cataloguing in Publication Data
A CIP catalogue record for this book is available from the British Library

ISBN 978 1 84905 427 0
eISBN 978 0 85700 790 2

Printed and bound in Great Britain

Contents

A   UNDERSTANDING YOUNG PEOPLE'S DRUG USE

B   BE PREPARED

C   DEALING WITH SPECIFIC SITUATIONS

D   THE DRUGS

E   WHERE TO FIND OUT MORE

Acknowledgements

I would like to thank my family and friends, my colleagues in the drug field and the professionals, parents and young people I have worked with, for sharing their knowledge, experiences and ideas with me over the years and for helping to educate me. Special thanks go to Beth Stillings Cohen, Harry Shapiro, Pat O'Hare, James Kay, Ian Clements, Kelly Dyson, Hilary Iredale, Helen Sismey, Jackie Hill, Hugo Edwardes, Jon Davey, Alan Williams and Alan Charnley for helping me to get started and to keep on going.

The Author

Julian Cohen has specialized in work concerning young people's drug use for almost 30 years. He has worked directly with young people, professionals who work with them and with parents as an educator, project leader, trainer and counsellor. Julian is the author of many widely used teaching and training packs, educational games, information pamphlets and books about drugs. Many of these have been published by DrugScope and HIT. He has run training courses about young people's drug use all over the UK and has also lectured, trained professionals and carried out research in America, Australia, Canada, Cyprus, Ireland, the Netherlands, Romania and Spain.

INTRODUCTION

This book is for parents and professionals who work with young people. It gives accurate, up-to-date information to help you to understand young people's use of drugs. I also provide realistic, practical advice to help you respond to young people's involvement with drugs in sensible ways that will help to ensure their safety and well-being.

By 'young people' I mean those aged between 14 and 25 years old, although some of the information and advice I have provided will also be relevant to younger children and those aged over 25.

When I say 'parents', I am aware that some young people do not live with a biological parent and may be cared for by other family relations, including older siblings and grandparents, or by foster parents or care home staff. In some cases parents may also be concerned about, or supporting, a young person who is not their own child.

This book is designed to help anyone who is caring for and supporting young people.

By 'professionals' I mean anyone who works in a paid or voluntary capacity with young people, including school teachers, college and university lecturers, youth and community workers, drug and health workers, counsellors, mentors and advocacy workers, social care and criminal justice workers, including police officers, probation and youth offending team workers, prison officers, magistrates and judges.

Before I outline the contents of the book I want to emphasize what it is not.

It is not a scaremongering treatise about the horrors of drug use. In fact, I go out of my way to make sure that I do not exaggerate the risks and dangers. I do not condemn or condone drug use by young people. Rather, I emphasize that we nearly all use drugs and that, whether we like it or not, and whatever we may do, young people will continue to use drugs. I highlight the need to be realistic and to focus on the safety and welfare of young people.

This book does not focus on the biological aspects of drug use in any detail. I don't mention serotonin or dopamine even once. It also does not analyse or overtly criticize government policy and the laws regarding drug use or propose how they might be changed for the better in future. That is beyond the remit of this book.

I have also tried to avoid using too much jargon. I deplore the many management, business and psycho-babble clichés that have entered the drugs field, and so many other aspects of our lives, in recent years. Many professionals use such language to hide away in a pretended, and often self-congratulatory, objectivity and also to mystify everyone else. Unfortunately, such has become the fate of many professions.

The book is divided into five parts.

PART A: UNDERSTANDING YOUNG PEOPLE'S DRUG USE

This provides background information about the trends in young people's drug use, why they use as they do, where they get drugs from and how much drugs cost. It also considers the 'official' and slang language used to discuss drugs, what determines the effects of taking drugs and how dangerous it is, drug laws and legal obligations and rights and whether you can spot if a young person is using drugs.

Parts B and C are based on my many years of working directly with young people who experience problems with their drug use, and the training, support, advisory and counselling work I have carried out with parents and professionals who work with young people.

PART B: BE PREPARED

This part of the book focusses on practical information and advice about how you can develop your own knowledge, attitudes and skills so that you will be better placed to respond sensibly and effectively to situations where young people are involved with drugs. It includes exercises that you can do by yourself or with other people, including young people, to help you feel more informed, calm and confident.

If possible, I strongly recommend that you read Parts A and B, and work through the exercises in Part B, *before* you are faced with an incident where your own child, or a young person you work with, is involved with drugs in a way that you find difficult to deal with.

PART C: DEALING WITH SPECIFIC SITUATIONS

This provides information and advice about dealing with some of the particular scenarios you could be faced with when young people are involved with drugs. The chapters in Part C are short and to the point and signpost you to information and advice elsewhere in the book that is relevant to the specific situations and issues they address. Part C will be particularly useful for you if you are faced with a situation that is causing you anxiety and that you are finding difficult to manage.

Part C also has an introduction that highlights some of the things parents and professionals should seek to do, and avoid doing, in any situation where young people are involved with drugs.

PART D: THE DRUGS

This contains detailed information about the various drugs that are sometimes used by young people. You may wish to read through the whole of this part, but you can also use it to refer to specific drugs that you want to find more about. For each drug there is information about what it is, street names, a brief history, legal status, availability, extent of use and cost, effects of use and possible harms. I also give harm reduction advice for each drug to use in situations where young people are likely to continue to use drugs, whatever we say to them or do.

Apart from minor tranquillizers, I have not included information about the many prescribed and over-the-counter medicines that can be mood-altering and are sometimes used recreationally, or in a dependent way. Many medicines can be harmful to use, especially in high doses or when combined with use of other drugs. Examples include anti-depressants such as Prozac, codeine-based painkillers and cough syrups, Viagra, stimulants such as Ritalin and cold remedies and decongestants that contain ephedrine, and some diet and travel sickness pills. In addition, paracetamol has been implicated in many fatal overdoses and suicides, including among young people. For detailed information about these, and other, medicines refer to the 'A to Z of medicines' section of the NHS Choices website (www.nhs.uk) or the British Medical Association (2011) book, *New Guide to Medicines & Drugs*.

PART E: WHERE TO FIND OUT MORE

Here I list websites where both you and young people can find more information about drugs, including those from which you can access contact information about helping services in your locality. I have also listed national telephone helplines and recommended books about drugs that you might wish to read.

This book is drawn from my experiences as a professional in the drugs field, father and drug user. I have tried to pass on some of the lessons I have learned. Writing it has been a challenging task for me and I am sure that I have not got everything right. I am still learning and I am interested in any suggestions you may have about how to improve what I have written. I can be contacted at juliancohen@hotmail.co.uk

DRUGS AND DRUG CAREERS

The word 'drug' originates from the Old French word 'drogue', which was later used by the Dutch in the phrase 'droge-vate', meaning 'dry barrels', to refer to the medicinal plants preserved in them.

Dictionaries often define the word 'drug' in a strictly biological manner. I use a broader definition in this book and define a drug as:

> any substance that, when taken, changes not only the way the body functions but also how we feel about ourselves and perceive the world around us.

This means that I focus on drugs that are mood-altering and psychoactive and include a wide range of legal and illegal substances. Some people even say that certain foods, and especially sugars, are drugs that change the way we feel and although I have some sympathy with this idea, I do not explore it in any depth because it is beyond the scope of this book.

A few years ago I was talking with a small group of 16–19-year-olds who were very open about their liking for cannabis, ecstasy, ketamine, LSD and magic mushrooms. They were all very articulate and talented, successful academically and busy producing their own music and all sorts of amazing works of art. They told me they did not drink alcohol at all and looked down on young people who did. During our deliberations one of the group said, and I quote, 'I can't stand those bloody druggies', by which he meant people who use heroin. Another of the group followed with, 'Yeah. But when you think of it, drugs is something other people do.'

On reflection, I found this was a very illuminating way of thinking about drugs. Many of us tend to think of drug use as something that other people are involved with, rather than ourselves, and that it is dangerous, immoral and plain wrong. At the same time, we often go to great lengths to either deny that we use drugs or try to legitimize our own use.

When I point out to people that we nearly all have a lifetime drug career of using mood-altering substances (and that this includes many medicines, caffeine, tobacco, alcohol and, for some of us, illegal and other socially unacceptable substances), they often respond by saying that the substances they use are not really drugs and certainly not very dangerous. If I push them further they often agree with my wider definition of drugs but quickly add that they don't abuse drugs like other people do. We like to cling to the idea that our own drug use is all right, but that other people's use is not. My drug use is OK, but your drug use is not.

It is my belief that, apart from a very few purists, we all use drugs and that the experiences we have had with our own drug use, and that of the people around us, greatly influences our feelings and attitudes towards drugs and the people who use them. Whether we are familiar with certain drugs, or not, will affect how we feel about them. If our experiences of those drugs we have come across have mainly been pleasurable we are likely to have very different views about drug use than if our experiences have been disturbing. If we have had no contact with certain drugs we may well view them with suspicion, even possibly derision, especially if they have had a very bad, and often sensationalized, coverage in the media. We all learn about drug use from a very young age, starting in our childhood homes and neighbourhoods. As with everyone else, my own on-going drug career has been the foundation for the way I view drug use.

Despite this, modern day authors of books about drugs rarely reveal much, if anything at all, about their own drug careers. The exceptions tend to be when ex-addicts tell us in graphic detail about the terrible times they have endured while dependent on drugs. No one tells us about their more 'normal' drug careers and what they have learned from them.

I have decided to break this self-imposed silence by telling you about mine. This should give you some insight into my views about drug use and how I have formed them. Having done this I will explain some of the ways that my work over many years in the drugs field with young people, professionals and parents has also contributed to what I have written in this book.

MY DRUG CAREER

My earliest memories of my own drug use concern alcohol. I was brought up in a lower middle class Jewish neighbourhood in London in the 1950s. My parents rarely drank unless it was for a 'Kiddush' ceremony at our Friday night Sabbath meal, on Saturday mornings as part of the synagogue service or during Jewish festivals. They kept the odd bottle of whisky and sherry in the sideboard cupboard but they hardly ever opened them. When their friends came round for the evening to play cards they served tea and cake, not alcohol. In contrast to current times, not many people in this country drank coffee in those days.

From a very young age, possibly before I was 5 years old, I was included in the Kiddush ceremonies and given a nip of Palwin, a very sweet, sherry-like wine that tasted revolting. I can still smell the aroma and sense the taste to this day. It was many years later that I learned that it is illegal for anyone in this country to give alcohol to a child aged under 5 years old. My parents were never arrested and our home and the synagogue were never raided by the police. I also later discovered that studies of Jews in America found that, although a greater proportion of them drink alcohol regularly, compared to other groups, far fewer of them tend to become alcoholics.

Alcohol use also featured in my early childhood in another way. When I had a toothache my dad would often place a small tumbler of whisky by my bed so that I could dab it on my teeth before going to sleep. I was not given many medicines when I was a child, but I do have some memories of my parents occasionally forcing me to swallow a horrible tasting, pink-coloured syrup that I did my best to resist. In those days medicines were not given to children very often and I was a relatively healthy child anyway.

Tobacco played a huge part in my childhood. My dad was a tobacconist, as was his father and his grandfather before him. Both he and my mum smoked cigarettes and he also sometimes smoked a pipe. I used to work in the family shop from a young age and was given free cigarettes from the age of about 15 years old. My dad died from lung cancer when he was only 56 years old. On his deathbed he still swore that his cancer had nothing to do with smoking.

Despite the way my father died I have smoked cigarettes most of my adult life, with only a few short periods of stopping, and I struggle with staying off them to this day. Somehow or other the trauma of him dying when I was only in my early 20s didn't put me off cigarettes. He intended for me to take over the family business selling cigarettes, pipes and cigars but I turned my back on it and after his death it folded after nearly one hundred years in business.

Poor old dad. He used to work five days a week, leave the house before 7am and was rarely back before 7pm, plus he was always at the shop on Saturday mornings and sometimes went in on Sundays to do the orders and books. He was often exhausted and on a short fuse. But he had a good way of dealing with it. When we used to drive to the shop together he often would stop the car on the way, right outside a chemist shop in Kentish Town. He'd leave the car engine running, walk in to the chemists, pick up one of the small plastic cups that were carefully arranged on the counter, down what he called his 'tonic' in one gulp, stride back out to the car and off we would go again. It all only took a few minutes. Soon he was full of energy and talking like he'd never stop. It was few years later before I realized that my dad was taking amphetamines. They were not controlled as tightly then as they are today. It makes me smile to think that he was so conservative, with both a big and small C, a freemason, held a senior position at the synagogue and vehemently anti-drugs as well.

In my teenage years I didn't use drugs much at all, apart from smoking cigarettes. I hardly drank any alcohol, as was the case with most of the young people and adults I mixed with. Going away to university changed everything, but still alcohol was rarely on my menu. Instead I discovered the delights, and they were delightful experiences for me, of cannabis, LSD, magic mushrooms, mescaline and peyote. I was always a moderate user and very careful about what I took, how much I consumed, where and when I did it and with whom. In the circles I moved in, regular alcohol use was seen as being for losers and careful use of a wide array of illegal drugs was not only accepted, but celebrated.

By my early 20s I had also tried cocaine and opium. I really didn't like cocaine. I felt it made people, including me, too self-centred, too sure of themselves and far too oblivious to others. It always seemed a very Thatcherite drug to me. Opium was a different matter and a real chill-out. The occasional afternoon smoking opium with a group of friends was great but it wasn't something I wanted to do too often. I had far too much to get on with in life and too much opium would stop me doing that.

I have been really drunk only a couple of times in my life and I didn't like it at all. Throughout most of my adult life I have probably drunk alcohol at least twice a week, but always in small quantities. Two pints, three whiskies or half a bottle of wine and then I tend to stop and start on the orange juice. I don't like being around people who are drunk. They get too aggressive, repetitive, insistent or maudlin for me. If people around me are drunk I tend to leave, or if I am with close friends I might hang around with my orange juice to ensure they get home safely.

While I have described my own use of illegal drugs as a delight this has not always been the case for my friends and acquaintances. When I was in my early 20s one friend died from taking a large dose of barbiturates together with alcohol and a few others really 'freaked out' using hallucinogenic drugs. In later years some of my friends have had difficulties resulting in alcohol, cannabis, tranquillizer or anti-depressant dependence and excessive cocaine use. Some of their children have also had problems with drug use, including cannabis, crack and heroin dependence, being convicted of drug offences and one tragically dying in a heroin overdose. But many of us have also experienced difficulties, and sometimes tragedies, that have had nothing to do with drugs and most of my friends, and their children, have had a good time using drugs as I have.

I increasingly realized that the experiences people have with drugs usually have more to do with them as people, their circumstances and how they are in themselves, rather than the drugs per se. But then again, I usually found it much more pleasant to be around people who were smoking cannabis or opium than those who snorted cocaine or drank alcohol like there was no tomorrow. Perhaps our drug use is more a reflection of who we are, where we are in our lives and the situation we are in, rather than a cause of our difficulties.

My drug career continues. I still like the occasional smoke of cannabis. I am a bit nervous about admitting to that in this book. Even though many famous and sometimes respected people, such as cabinet ministers and other senior politicians and public figures, have admitted that they used illegal drugs when they were young, they nearly always tell us it was a big mistake and they did not enjoy it. And they never admit to more recent use of illegal, or other socially unacceptable, drugs. As adults, we often end up lying about our drug use to try to give the impression that we have the right morals. How perverse. Although I am making myself vulnerable by admitting to current illegal drug use, I do not want to lie to you.

Neither have I taken many medicines, prescribed or over-the-counter, as an adult but two instances stand out. My GP once gave me anti-depressants when I was feeling really low. They made me feel less anxious and hopeless but the problem was I didn't feel anything much at all. The lows were not as low but there were no highs at all. After a few weeks of being on a level flatness I threw them away. I have known many people who have been prescribed anti-depressants or tranquillizers. Some have stopped using them for similar reasons to me, but others have become dependent on them and found that dampening down their feelings, and especially painful feelings, for long periods of their life is the only way they can function.

I also recall being prescribed a strong dose of DF 118s to deal with excruciating pain from a tooth abscess. Soon after taking the tablets the pain magically subsided. At the time I was splitting up with my partner and it was very acrimonious between us. Once the effects of the tablets started I found that anything she said or did, that would usually have upset me, was not affecting me at all. I was safely cocooned. DF 118s are opioids and mimic the effects of drugs like heroin. It was a real lesson for me about the attractions of heroin use and the way it kills not just physical pain but emotional distress as well.

Now I take tablets for my blood pressure but they don't really have much effect on how I feel. I sometimes drink vast quantities of coffee, especially while I am writing. And my moderate alcohol use and struggle with cigarette smoking continue, the latter much to my daughter's disgust.

Her drug use has taught me a lot. When she was about 16 years old she drank like a fish. She would tank up on vodka at home or a friend's house and they would then go off, unbeknown to her mum and me, to get drunk at a club in the sleepy, semi-rural town near where we lived. At the time I suspected where she was going and what she was doing but was unsure. I was far from happy and found it really difficult to talk to her about the risks she was facing. It was only later I learned that she had some very close shaves surrounded by violence, very risky sexual behaviour and harassment, and peers collapsing and being rushed to hospital. Soon she moved on to the big city, Manchester, and went to all-night clubs where ecstasy was the drug of choice and alcohol was usually a no-no. In the main the clubs were well run and had a more relaxed environment with little violence or sexual harassment.

By this time I was working in the drugs field and offering harm reduction information and advice to young people. It was much more of a challenge to do the same with my own daughter, but it helped to know that she was, in many ways, safer using ecstasy in city centre clubs, than drinking alcohol just down the road from where we lived.

I had to work hard on myself when she announced that she was going to spend her savings from her Saturday job on a holiday with her friends in Ibiza. I knew that meant two weeks of non-stop ecstasy-fuelled partying, but what could I do? We had quite a few talks about harm reduction and I made sure she had copies of the most up-to-date leaflets. Now she is in her early 30s, and spent the last two years working to develop primary school education in Nepal. While there she was almost tee-total and rarely used any drugs. She has just returned to the UK and has already started to drink alcohol again. It will be interesting to see what happens with her drug use in the future.

That's enough about my drug career and some of the lessons I have learnt from it. I will ask you about yours later in this book.

ME, THE DRUG PROFESSIONAL

I started my professional career as youth and community worker and then as a secondary school teacher and further education lecturer. This work included running some basic drug education sessions for young people and talking and listening to them about drug issues. In 1986 I began working as the co-ordinator of a new young people's drug project in Greater Manchester, one of the first to be set up in the UK.

It soon became clear that drug use among young people had changed a lot since I was young. A much wider range of substances were available to them and their use seemed very individualistic, and possibly more desperate, compared to the more communitarian and self-exploratory drug scene I had been involved with in my late teens and early 20s.

In the area where I worked there were drug-related deaths involving young teenagers using solvents and older, but still quite young, people dying from heroin and alcohol overdoses. Some local estates had vigilante groups who gave heroin addicts and dealers the baseball bat treatment. Rumours that a local teacher might have AIDS led to some parents wanting to remove their children from the school where he taught. Concerns that a surgeon at the local hospital had AIDS led to panic and calls for his dismissal. Many schools had incidents to deal with involving students using and sometimes supplying drugs. A few times a circular was distributed around the local primary schools warning parents that evil drug pushers were tricking young children into using LSD by passing them off as 'blue star transfers', even though this was completely untrue. Locally, the drug squad was very active and sometimes exceptionally heavy handed.

In the late 1980s and early 1990s there was a real feeling of fear and panic in the air about young people using drugs. It was clear that a big part of my role was, together with other workers, to help everyone calm down and respond sensibly. We tried to do this by running large numbers of public meetings and training courses and producing drug information, advice and guidelines for schools, colleges, youth clubs and for parents. We also developed drug education programmes for children and young people and support and counselling services for them and their families.

Despite the claims of the government, the media and many professionals, it was clear that there was no way we were going to stop young people from using drugs. Instead, we focussed on attempting to reduce the harm that young people could face and supporting professionals and parents to educate and support them.

For the last 20 years I have continued with such work, mainly in a self-employed capacity, as an educator and trainer, and author of drug information and education resources, alongside some counselling work with young people and parents and support work with professionals who work with young people.

As well as working all over the UK, I have also lectured, run training courses or carried out research in Australia, America, Canada, Cyprus, Ireland, the Netherlands, Romania and Spain. In other words, I have witnessed how various parts of the UK and a number of other countries deal with young people's drug use.

I have also closely followed the research findings from studies of young people's drug use and about the impact various responses have, and whether or not they are effective. I have read a lot of books about drugs and some of my favourite ones, from which I have learned most, are listed in the Recommended Reading at the end of this book. And I continue to have on-going discussions about drugs with my friends, professionals, parents and young people themselves… and learn from them.

KEY LESSONS AND PRINCIPLES

I have tried to pass on to you the lessons I have learnt from these work experiences, and from my own drug career, in this book. In brief, the following are some of the main things I have discovered:

- It makes no sense to equate 'drugs' only with illegal drugs. We need to also consider the array of legal drugs (particularly alcohol, caffeine and medicines) and other substances that are not illegal but are often socially taboo.

- We nearly all 'self-medicate' and have a lifetime drug career of using mood-altering substances.

- Humans have always used drugs to change the way they feel and they always will.

- The long history of drug use in this country, and in other countries and cultures, can teach us many important lessons to help us understand drug use today and how we can best influence and control it.

- The fact that some drugs are currently illegal, and others legal, has more to do with historical, social, cultural, political and economic factors, than anything intrinsic to the substances themselves.

- Legal drugs, especially alcohol, can be just as dangerous to use as illegal drugs, and sometimes more harmful.

- Although 'drugs do things to people', we need to take account of 'what people do with drugs'. In other words, the particular person using, and their circumstances and the situation they are in, are important in determining the ways they use drugs, their experiences of drug use and the risks and harms they may face.

- People who become heavy drug users nearly all do so in response to having experienced difficult life events. They are often dislocated and do not feel that they fit in with, or can cope with, our society. They use drugs, in the ways they do, to block out difficult emotions and experiences, in an attempt to get through life.

- Drug use, of whatever form, is functional and has meaning and purpose for the people using, even if we may not understand their motives or disapprove of their behaviour.

- The vast majority of young people who use drugs, including illegal drugs, do not come to serious harm and, in the main, enjoy their drug use.

- The dangers of drug use have too often been exaggerated, especially compared to the dangers of other activities, such as outdoor pursuits or sports, that young people are often encouraged to participate in.

- To understand, and respond sensibly and effectively to, young people's drug use we need to take full account of the nature of the society that they live in – that we as adults have created – and the difficulties they face, rather than castigate, demonize or blame them. This involves focussing on them as people and the situations they are in, rather than just on substances.

- There are no simple solutions. In fact many of the solutions that are often proposed, and sometimes acted upon (such as tougher drug laws, trying to scare young people about the terrible effects drug use can have and drug testing them), are not only ineffective, but often counterproductive and make matters worse by isolating vulnerable young people and placing them at greater risk of harm.

- Governments, politicians and the media are often dishonest and/or ignorant in their deliberations about young people's drug use. They are usually more interested in sensationalism, appearing 'tough on drugs' and using soundbites than what is effective in protecting young people and ensuring their health and well-being.

- Our responses to young people's drug use are too often based on fear and ignorance. We need to be better informed, more thoughtful and to keep drug use in perspective if we are to respond sensibly and effectively to young people's drug use.

- Focussing on reducing harm and promoting safety and well-being is much more likely to be effective than thinking that we can stop all drug use.

- We need to be young person centred and focus on facilitating young people's health, safety and welfare. We need to engage young people, especially those who are most at risk, rather than alienate them.

- Professionals and parents can make a positive difference in young people's lives and help them to have relatively safe and healthy, rather than damaging, drug careers.

These are some of the key principles on which this book is based.

UNDERSTANDING YOUNG PEOPLE'S DRUG USE

WHAT ARE THE TRENDS IN YOUNG PEOPLE'S DRUG USE?

YOUNG CHILDREN AND DRUGS

As adults we tend to balk at the idea that young children take mood-altering drugs, but if we include medicines and caffeine, the use of drugs has become a normal part of nearly every child's life. These days most children are given an array of medicines by their parents and by doctors for all sorts of ailments. As most parents and primary school teachers know, this happens to such an extent that young children often ask for, and even demand, medicines if they feel unwell, experience physical pain or cannot easily get to sleep.

The lesson we are inadvertently teaching children is, if you want to change the way you feel, you buy and take a drug. Without being aware of it, we may not only be socializing children into regularly taking medicines throughout their future lives, but also providing them with an apprenticeship in preparation for recreational drug use in later years.

These days many young children also consume large quantities of caffeine, particularly from drinking colas and other soft drinks, and also from eating confectionery, sweets, breakfast cereals, biscuits, cakes and ice creams that contain chocolate or cocoa. Some may be taking so much of this stimulant drug for their body weight that they find it difficult to be still and concentrate and suffer disturbance to their sleep and dietary patterns. This may be connected to the increasing numbers of children being diagnosed as being hyperactive with conditions such as attention deficit hyperactivity disorder, and then being prescribed drugs like Ritalin – an amphetamine-type drug – in an attempt to calm them down and make them more manageable.

There is currently much debate about the role of food and sugar in young children's lives and whether or not they should be regarded as drugs. This has included discussion about the impact of greater consumption of confectionery and processed foods, and the food additives and high sugar content they often contain, on children's health and behaviour. The possibility of children becoming addicted to certain foods, and an increase in childhood eating disorders, such as obesity and anorexia nervosa, has also been highlighted.

Young children are often aware of both legal and illegal drugs to an extent that surprises their parents, school teachers and care workers. The influence of television, films and advertising, and of observing adults and teenagers in their home and local communities, means that few children will be completely unaware of drugs. Many young children already have very stereotypical and negative perceptions of 'drug users' and 'drug dealers' but tend to have much more positive, if sometimes contradictory, views about alcohol.

When I have asked groups of young children to make up a play about 'drugs' the atmosphere always quickly becomes dark and dangerous and the characters they act out are very seedy. It never takes long for at least one of the characters to drop dead. When I have asked the same groups to make up a play about drinking beer and wine they tend to stumble about drunk-like, laugh a lot and sometimes shout and argue and square up for a fight. If there are boys and girls present they often show physical affection and flirt with each other. No one ever dies in the alcohol plays. Young children closely observe our drinking patterns and the way alcohol is portrayed in the media.

I find it both more truthful and useful to think that nearly everyone has a lifetime 'drug career'. Because many drugs cross the placenta, we might even say that most people's drug careers begin prior to birth. During our lifetime we all use a range of mood-altering substances – medicines, legal drugs like caffeine, alcohol and tobacco and also possibly illegal and other socially unacceptable drugs. In this sense nearly all of us are drug users. At some points in our life we may hardly use any drugs. At other times we may use occasionally and in small quantities. At yet other times, and particularly when we are very unhappy or distressed, we may use drugs more frequently and in greater quantities. We nearly all self-medicate throughout our lives.

CIGARETTES AND ALCOHOL

In recent years cigarette smoking has been declining in the adult population, particularly among the middle classes, and also among young people. Some primary school aged children will have tried a cigarette but recent surveys show less than 1 per cent of 11-year-olds can be classed as regular smokers, smoking at least one cigarette a week. A large-scale, long-term national survey of school students in England (Health and Social Care Information Centre 2013) found that the percentage of regular smokers among 15-year-olds was 10 per cent in 2012, a decline from figures of between 24 per cent and 28 per cent in the 1990s. Current smoking rates for 16–19-year-olds have fallen to below 20 per cent from over 30 per cent in 1998, and for 20–24-year-olds have fallen to below 25 per cent from 40 per cent in 1998 (ASH 2013; Health and Social Care Information Centre 2012a).

From the mid-1980s until relatively recently, surveys usually showed a greater percentage of teenage girls than boys as being regular smokers. However, more recent surveys have shown less difference in young female and male smoking rates. There is still a strong link between cigarette smoking and socio-economic class among both adults and young people. People from lower social classes are more likely to smoke.

As with adults, other than medicines and caffeine, alcohol is by far the most common drug of choice among young people. Young children are usually introduced to their first taste of alcohol at home under parental supervision. A recent national survey of 11–15-year-olds attending secondary schools in England found that 12 per cent of 11-year-olds claimed to have ever tried alcohol, rising to almost three quarters of 15-year-olds (Health and Social Care Information Centre 2013). Only 1 per cent of 11-year-olds said that they had drunk some alcohol in the week before the survey, rising to 25 per cent of 15-year-olds. Almost one in five 15-year-olds said they drank alcohol at least once a week, usually at the weekend. Alcohol consumption increases significantly for young people aged over 16 years old, with 16–24-year-olds being more likely to binge drink and become drunk, than any other age group (Health and Social Care Information Centre 2012b).

Overall, the level of alcohol consumption among young people in the UK doubled in quantity over a ten-year period from around 1990 (Department of Health 2009). During this period new 'designer drinks' with high alcohol content (such as strong beers, lagers, ciders and alcopops) were introduced by alcohol manufacturers and specifically targeted at young people. Young people were drinking greater quantities of alcohol and drinking more often, and more were drinking regularly with the aim of becoming drunk. While boys tended to drink greater quantities of alcohol and more often than girls, surveys began to indicate that girls were catching up with boys in their alcohol consumption, particularly with their use of alcopops and spirits, especially vodka. Class differences in alcohol consumption among young people are not as significant as those for cigarette smoking, although social class and disposable income will influence the type of drinks consumed and where drinking takes place, and binge drinking is more likely among young people in more deprived areas.

Young people in the UK remain among the highest consumers of alcohol in the whole of Europe (ESPAD 2012) but there is evidence that their overall level of consumption has decreased over the past few years (Health and Social Care Information Centre 2013). However, this more recent trend may be more indicative of a fall in the number of young people who drink, rather than any significant decrease in the amount of alcohol consumed by the many young people who continue to drink regularly and heavily.

ILLEGAL, AND OTHER SOCIALLY UNACCEPTABLE, DRUGS

Use of a wide variety of mood-altering substances by adults, young people and children has a long history in the UK. However, it was not until the 20th century that governments made the production, possession and supply of some drugs illegal. While there were some moral panics over the use of cannabis, opium and cocaine in the 1920s and 1930s, mainly in London and some other large cities, the period immediately following the Second World War saw little concern about the use of drugs in general or among young people. This changed in the 1960s with the advent of youth culture, the hippies and mods and increased use of cannabis, LSD and amphetamines among young people. Even during the 1960s and 1970s, when British governments joined America in the 'war on drugs' and criminalized many drugs with the passing of the 1971 Misuse of Drugs Act, drug use was not that high on the political agenda.

This situation changed in the 1980s economic recession with a spiralling number of people becoming addicted to the enormous quantities of smokable heroin imported from India and Pakistan. From being restricted to bohemians in London, heroin use quickly spread to poor, working class, inner city areas all over the country and even to many rural areas. For large numbers of young people who were jobless and had little prospects, heroin use became a way of achieving a state of oblivion. A huge increase in heroin use, dependence and drug-related crime followed, accompanied by a switch from smoking to injecting and panic about the advent of HIV and predictions of huge numbers of people becoming infected. Crack, a smokable form of cocaine, also became a cause of great concern in inner city areas with predictions that drug-related violence might escalate and become out of control. Poorer areas also experienced the advent of solvent use, especially glue sniffing, among children and those in their early teens, with annual deaths rising to around 150 in some years.

Alongside the growth of heroin and crack use in the late 1980s and early 1990s, the use of drugs like cannabis, amphetamines, LSD and magic mushrooms increased significantly among a broader range of young people. There was also the introduction of ecstasy and all-night raves and of newer substances such as GHB and ketamine. Surveys showed many more young people were experimenting with a wider range of drugs compared to a few years earlier. Cannabis use spread to the extent that many commentators talked of its use becoming normalized among many young people and in some communities.

The levels of drug use among young people in the UK peaked in the mid-1990s, and then fell slightly, followed by a small upward trend again such that by the late 1990s surveys reported that about a half of 16–24-year-olds claimed to have used an illegal drug at least once. Cannabis was by far the most commonly used substance followed by amphetamines, poppers, ecstasy and LSD, with an increase in use of cocaine by the late 1990s. A lot of this drug use was recreational and based mainly on weekend socializing in clubs and at parties, raves and music events. Although not unproblematic, it was relatively separate from the on-going daily dependent use of many heroin and crack users.

Two large-scale surveys of drug use have been conducted on a regular basis in England and Wales over a number of years and are useful in tracking the trends in young people's drug use over time. The Smoking, Drinking and Drug Use Survey (SDDS) is based on questioning 11–15-year-olds who attend English schools (Health and Social Care Information Centre 2013). The Crime Survey (CS) obtains information from 16–59-year-olds in England and Wales using household samples (Home Office 2013).

These surveys examine the prevalence of drug use by asking people whether or not they have used particular drugs ever, in the past year, past month and more than once a month over the past year. They give some idea about what is happening in the real world, especially as they are repeated over a period of time. However, they do not tell us in detail about frequency of drug use, the amount of drugs taken, when and where people use, the extent to which they may use more than one drug at the same time or about what their experiences of drug use, both positive and negative, have been like.

There are also other limitations with such surveys. Samples may not be sufficiently representative of the population as a whole. Some young people may refuse to participate, especially as they know they will be asked about their drug use. Those young people who are most likely to use drugs (such as school non-attendees and those who do not live at a fixed home address) will not be included. Respondents may have difficulties filling in questionnaires and may not answer questions honestly, particularly when they are reporting illegal activity or are unable to accurately recall their past use.

This means that these surveys should be regarded as an under representation of the true extent of overall drug use among young people.

Both surveys have found a decrease in the numbers of young people who claim to have tried illegal, and other socially unacceptable, drugs since the peak of the 1990s and the relative stable picture in the early millennium.

The SDDS found that the number of 11–15-year-olds who claimed to have ever taken an illegal, or other socially unacceptable, drug in the past year fell gradually each year from 30 per cent in 2003 to 17 per cent in 2012. The numbers claiming to have used such drugs in the year before the survey fell from 21 per cent in 2003 to 12 per cent in 2012. However, this still meant that in 2012, 31 per cent of 15-year-olds said they had ever used drugs and 24 per cent said they had used in the past year. Cannabis was by far the most commonly used substance with almost 19 per cent of 15-year-olds claiming to have used it in the past year.

The CS found the following results for the percentage of 16–24-year-olds reporting use of particular drugs in the past year for 1996, 2006/7 and 2012/13.

	1996	2006/7	2012/13
Amphetamines	11.8	3.5	1.3
Cannabis	26.0	20.9	13.5
Cocaine powder	1.3	6.0	3.0
Crack	0.2	0.4	0.2
Ecstasy	6.6	4.8	2.9
Ketamine	n/a	0.8	0.8
Heroin	0.4	0.2	0.0
LSD	4.5	0.7	0.4
Magic mushrooms	2.3	1.7	0.6
Methadone	0.1	0.1	0.0
Poppers (nitrites)	4.6	4.2	1.2
Steroids	0.5	0.2	0.3
Tranquillizers	0.9	0.6	0.4
Any drug	29.7	24.1	16.3

The CS has thus found that the number of 16–24-year-olds claiming to have used such drugs, in the previous year, fell from around 30 per cent in the mid-1990s to the early 2000s, down to under 20 per cent ten years later, with cannabis again being by far the most commonly used drug.

The figures from the CS for the percentage of 16–24-year-olds reporting having ever used particular drugs in their lifetime were as follows:

	1996	2006/7	2012/13
Amphetamines	18.8	11.2	7.2
Cannabis	39.6	39.5	30.9
Cocaine powder	4.3	10.9	8.4
Crack	1.7	1.4	0.8
Ecstasy	11.7	10.3	7.9
Ketamine	n/a	2.3	3.3
Heroin	0.9	0.7	0.1
LSD	13.1	3.2	2.0
Magic mushrooms	9.8	7.0	3.7
Methadone	0.4	0.3	0.4
Poppers (nitrites)	15.7	13.4	8.1
Steroids	1.5	0.6	0.8
Tranquillizers	3.9	2.3	1.8
Any drug	48.6	44.7	36.7

As can be seen, the CS found a fall in the number of 16–24-year-olds claiming to have ever used such drugs from 48.6 per cent in 1996 to 36.7 per cent in 2012/13. The highest figure recorded by the CS was 53.7 per cent in 1998.

The most recent SDDS and CS have recorded the lowest figures for drug use since they were first conducted. However, the difficulty with regarding them as accurate representations of the true extent of drug use among young people can be seen by comparing the results from the two surveys. For example, in 2012 the SDDS found that 31 per cent of 15-year-olds claimed to have ever used drugs and 24 per cent claimed to have used drugs in the past year before the survey. The comparable figures for 16–24-year-olds from the 2012/13 CS were 36.7 per cent and 16.3 per cent.

We know that many more 16–24-year-olds, than 15-year-olds, take drugs yet this is not reflected in these survey findings. As can be seen, in 2012 the SDDS even found more 15-year-olds claiming to have used drugs in the past year, than the CS found for 16–24-year-olds in 2012/13. This would suggest that the CS, in particular, may be an under representation of the true extent of drug use among young people.

Despite their limitations, these findings from the SDDS and CS, taken together with those from more local surveys and anecdotal evidence, indicate the following trends over the last few years:

- Fewer young people have been using most illegal, and socially unacceptable, drugs.

- Probably only a minority of young people have ever tried such drugs.

- Smaller numbers have used drugs recently or use on a regular basis.

- Cannabis use has decreased but it is still by far the most commonly used illegal drug.

- The number of young people who have used crack or heroin remains relatively small and has declined in recent years.

- The use of amphetamines has declined with the possibility that its use has been replaced by other stimulant drugs such as cocaine and the newly introduced mephedrone – see below.

- Cocaine use increased post-2000 and although numbers using may have since fallen, use is more common now than in the mid-1990s.

- Ecstasy use has declined, although the recent trend to using powder, rather than tablets and capsules, may see its use increase again.

- LSD use has almost died out. Use is very rarely heard of these days.

- The use of GHB and ketamine has increased, although numbers using remain relatively small.

- Solvent use has decreased.

- While use of anabolic steroids remains rare among most young people, in the past few years many local drug projects have reported greater use and increasing numbers of steroid injectors using needle exchange schemes.

- Non-medical use of tranquillizers remains quite rare.

While the available surveys may not be able to give us an accurate picture of the true extent of drug use, currently there are probably well over 12 million people – around one in three 16–59-year-olds – in England and Wales who have tried an illegal, or socially unacceptable, drug at least once and possibly between 2 and 3 million who use drugs on a more regular basis. They fall into two main groups that are relatively separate.

The first group consists of well over 300,000 people who are dependent on heroin and/or crack and are mainly from deprived backgrounds (National Treatment Agency 2013). Their numbers have been falling in recent years but still include possibly 40,000 to 55,000 15–24-year-olds, most of them being over 20 years old.

The second, much larger, group involves many young people aged over 15 years old and consists mainly of recreational users of drugs such as cannabis, cocaine, ecstasy, mephedrone and ketamine and also legal highs. Many of them will also be consumers of large amounts of alcohol.

ARE FEWER YOUNG PEOPLE USING ILLEGAL, AND SOCIALLY UNACCEPTABLE, DRUGS?

While there has been a decline in the number of young people who use certain drugs in recent years, drug use among young people in still relatively high in the UK compared to other European countries (European Monitoring Centre for Drugs and Drug Addiction 2013). The number of young people using amphetamines, cannabis, crack, ecstasy, heroin, LSD, magic mushrooms and solvents may have fallen but there has been an increase in the numbers using cocaine and the introduction of 'new' drugs such as GHB, ketamine and mephedrone.

Recent small-scale surveys and anecdotal evidence have also pointed to the possibility that many dependent heroin and crack users have switched to using medical painkillers, rather than giving up drug use (Wakeman and Seddon 2013).

The last few years have also seen more use of nitrous oxide, a gas that is not illegal and has been used for intoxicating purposes in the UK for over 200 years – see the chapter about nitrous oxide in Part D of this book. The 2012/13 Crime Survey (CS) in England and Wales found that over 6 per cent of 16–24-year-olds claimed to have used nitrous oxide in the previous year.

Although not yet often surveyed, there has also been a significant growth in the use of 'legal highs', substances that mimic the effects of illegal drugs but are not (yet) controlled under the Misuse of Drugs Act. Possession, supply and selling them remain legal. For more information about legal highs see Part D. The 2102/13 CS in England and Wales found that just over 1 per cent of 16–24-year-olds claimed to have used Salvia, a short-acting, hallucinogenic legal high, in the previous year. However, the survey did not ask respondents about their use of other, possibly more commonly used, legal highs.

Mephedrone burst into the headlines in 2009 as a new legal high and use among young people was suddenly reported all over the UK. Its use has continued, despite the government making it an illegal drug in 2010. Since then, the annual CS surveys in England and Wales have found between 1.6 per cent and 4.4 per cent of 16–24-year-olds claiming to have used mephedrone in the year prior to being asked.

Many other legal highs have also recently become available to young people, through dealers who also sell illegal drugs, the many and growing number of headshops in cities and larger towns, other retail outlets and by purchasing with a credit card over the internet. As I explain in Chapter A3, the internet is being increasingly used to buy both legal highs and illegal drugs. This is changing the drugs market and making it easier for young people to access drugs without any direct contact with dealers or even friends and acquaintances who might supply them.

While there may have been a decline in the numbers who are using certain drugs, many young people are still using them and they now have access to, and are selecting from, a broader repertoire of drugs, both illegal substances and other socially taboo drugs.

ARE THOSE WHO DO USE DRUGS USING IN GREATER QUANTITIES?

Another question that arises is whether those young people who take drugs are using in greater quantities and more frequently than young people have in the past. We know that more young people in the UK use drugs – be it illegal drugs, legal highs or alcohol – than those in most other developed European countries (EMCDDA 2013; ESPAD 2012). Both young people and adults in the UK have also gained a reputation for not being as moderate with their alcohol and drug use as our European counterparts. We tend to consume greater quantities when we do use to 'get out of our heads'.

There is no clear evidence about whether or not binge and dependent drug use – see Chapter A2 – have increased among young people in this country. Surveys of young people's drug use rarely ask respondents for detailed information about their frequency of drug use or about the quantities they consume (apart from with alcohol or cigarettes) or the extent to which they may combine use of more than one drug.

The Crime Survey in England and Wales found that the percentage of 16–24-year-olds claiming to have taken an illicit drug more than once a month, on average, in the year prior to being asked (frequent drug use) fell from 12.4 per cent in 2003/4 to 5.1 per cent in 2012/13. Again, cannabis was, by far, the drug most commonly used on a frequent basis. However, as I stressed before, if asked about their levels of consumption many people find it difficult to remember how much they have taken and how frequently over a time period. Also, when asked, those who can remember may be reluctant to admit to drug use and how much they use, especially when it comes to reporting an illegal activity.

In contrast to this finding, anecdotal evidence (such as from local drug projects and youth services and from small surveys of clubbers and internet-based polls) points to a possible rise in binge drug use among young people, that may be in response to the increasing difficulties, insecurity and stress many young people are facing these days. Binge use of alcohol, cannabis, ecstasy, cocaine, GHB, ketamine, mephedrone, nitrous oxide and of legal highs has been highlighted, together with many young people engaging in polydrug use by taking some of these drugs in combination.

Similarly, there is no conclusive evidence about whether or not increasing numbers of young people are becoming dependent on drugs. We know that in recent years fewer young people have been using heroin or crack, and becoming dependent on them, and that the group of people who are dependent on these drugs has become older, with most now being over 30 years old. As I explained before, some of these heroin and crack users may have switched to using medical painkillers, rather than giving up drug use. However, this is only part of the story regarding young people being dependent on drugs.

In recent times between 20,000 and 24,000 young people who are aged under 18 years old have been recorded as accessing specialist drugs services each year (National Treatment Agency 2012). Two thirds of them have been males and the main substances that have been causing these young people difficulties have been cannabis and alcohol. We do not know what percentage of these young people have been judged by professionals, or themselves, as dependent drug users. In addition, drug services have been reporting that they are now being approached by more young people who have problems with their use of cocaine, ketamine, legal highs and mephedrone, including those who say they have become dependent.

By no means all young people who are dependent on drugs will approach helping services. However, as with binge use, anecdotal evidence suggests that more young people may have become dependent on certain drugs in recent years, especially alcohol, cannabis, cocaine, mephedrone and also possibly some legal highs and medical painkillers.

We also know that more young people, especially young women, are being prescribed anti-depressants by their doctors to treat depression, often on a long term basis, and that large-scale prescribing of tranquillizers, for anxiety and problems with sleeping, continues.

GEOGRAPHICAL, CLASS, ETHNIC AND GENDER DIFFERENCES AND TRENDS

Consistent availability of a wide array of drugs will usually be greater in cities and larger towns, rather than in more rural areas, but accessibility still varies between localities and over time. At a particular point in time a certain drug may be freely available and used in one area and not in another, but this situation can change quickly. However, more recent changes in drug markets, and especially the advent of use of mobile phones and emails to access and buy illegal drugs and the internet to buy both illegal drugs and legal highs (see Chapter A3), means that where people live is not as big a factor in drug availability as it once was.

Much of young people's drug use crosses geographical and social class boundaries. While heroin, crack and solvent use have tended to be concentrated in poorer areas, among the disenfranchised, the use of other drugs by young people has been more widespread. However, surveys show that those using more frequently, and experiencing problems with use of drugs, are more often from poorer and deprived backgrounds (Home Office 2013). This is not to say that drug use is not prevalent, or sometimes excessive, among the middle and upper classes. It is usually more hidden, and less visible, in their communities and neighbourhoods.

If account is taken of social class, there seem to be few differences in drug use between young white people and those of African-Caribbean origin. In general, young people of Asian origin are less likely to be involved in drug use but the trends indicate that they are beginning to catch up their white and African-Caribbean peers (UK Drug Policy Commission 2010).

Surveys usually show more young males than females have tried various drugs and that males use more often, in greater quantities and are more likely to become dependent. However, in recent years females have been catching up with males when it comes to use of illegal drug use and alcohol. It is now possible that a snapshot of drug use among 14–16-year-olds will find more females than males have used drugs like cocaine and ecstasy, even though overall numbers will be small at this age. This may have to do with the fact that, unlike boys, girls of this age group can sometimes get into clubs and music events where these drugs are often available and used and that they often mix with males who are quite a bit older than themselves.

Another important trend has been the increased use of stimulants by some young women because of the appetite suppressing qualities of these drugs. Heavy caffeine consumption (low calorie colas and other soft drinks, strong black coffee, energy drinks like Red Bull and tablets like Pro Plus), cigarette smoking (nicotine being a stimulant), use of amphetamines (from which slimming pills are often made) and use of ecstasy, cocaine, mephedrone and stimulant legal highs may have added attraction for young women who are determined to keep their weight down, and have been connected to cases of anorexia nervosa.

BECOMING ADULTS

Most young people decrease their use of alcohol and either moderate, or completely stop, their use of illegal drugs by their mid-20s when they take on adult responsibilities, such as regular employment, a mortgage, a committed relationship, having children and so on. Many move from being 'burnouts to straights'. The task of professionals and parents might be seen as a holding operation and supporting young people through their teens and early 20s until they settle down and change and moderate their drug-using behaviour.

However, there is evidence that many young people, and possibly a growing number of them, continue with regular, and sometimes heavy, alcohol use and use of illegal drugs into their late 20s and early 30s, albeit usually less often and in smaller quantities. The trend is that a greater number of parents of young children will not only have used illegal drugs like cannabis and cocaine in the past, but that more continue to use longer term.

The on-going recession, together with high levels of youth unemployment and increasing levels of poverty and marginalization, are resulting in a significant and growing number of young people who have to wait longer to take on adult responsibilities or never manage to do so. These young people are much more likely to continue with more chaotic lifestyles, with attendant excessive use of alcohol and other drugs.

We should also be aware that drug use, and especially what might be called over-medication, is increasingly common among the growing numbers of elderly people in our society. In this country we are living longer and this is partly due to the vast array of medicines that are prescribed to the elderly on an on-going basis to keep them alive and relatively healthy. These days most of us do not want our elderly parents living with us (and they may not want to live with us either) and increasing numbers are confined to old people's homes. To make them more manageable, and some might also say to lessen the cost we have to bear for their care, an array of mood-altering medicines are prescribed for the elderly, especially sedatives. As I emphasized earlier in this chapter, in current times, our drug careers usually begin before birth. They also often continue until our dying days.

WHY DO YOUNG PEOPLE USE DRUGS AND IN WHAT WAYS DO THEY USE THEM?

The reasons that young people use drugs are similar to the motivations we have as adults to use mood-altering substances. Humans have always wanted and found ways to change the way they feel, and have used drugs to enhance pleasure and relaxation, and to reduce pain and distress. Throughout history many people have used drugs to feel more energetic and alive, to be able to work and concentrate for long periods and to aid socializing and communicating with other people and to celebrate key life and religious/spiritual events. Some people have also used drugs to explore different states of consciousness and ways of experiencing the world and to deal with the boredom, monotony and suffering of everyday life.

The underlying reasons that young people use drugs are based on comparable, existential human needs, although the specific motivations for using drugs will depend on the particular desires, needs and circumstances of each individual.

The reasons for drug use can be best understood by appreciating that there are different ways that drugs are used – experimental, recreational, binge and dependent – and usually different motivations for each form of use.

EXPERIMENTAL DRUG USE

Experimental drug use is novice use, where people try a particular drug for the first few times. It will often involve young people but adults may also be experimental users if they are new to using a particular drug. Experimental users may be relatively ignorant about the drug they are using and not know what to expect from using, how much to take, how to take the drug and so on. Experimental drug use can be dangerous for these reasons. Being shown how to use by a more knowledgeable person can make drug use safer.

There are a range of possible reasons that young people start to experiment with using drugs. Particular drugs may become freely available for some young people and be given a good press by friends, acquaintances and/or siblings, the media and through the internet. Use may be based on curiosity about what the experience of using drugs will be like. In this sense using may seem a very ordinary and natural thing for young people to do.

Some young people may begin to use drugs because they believe it will help them to feel part of a particular group or social scene that is appealing to them. They may use partly because they are bored and feel there is nothing much else of interest to do. Life right now, and in the imagined future, may feel monotonous and drug use can seem exciting in comparison. It can be fun and interesting to change the way you feel and experience the world and it may be even more appealing for some young people if the adults and authority figures around them say drugs are very dangerous and they should not touch them. In this way young people may see drug use as a protest against oppressive social norms. Sociologists have adopted the term 'deviancy amplification' to denote the process whereby adults criticizing the use of drugs by young people may, in itself, give drug use added meaning and legitimacy for many young people.

Most of these reasons for using drugs are relatively normal aspects of being an adolescent, growing up and beginning to experience the world as an independent person. They do not indicate any significant social or psychological problems. Indeed, we often actively encourage young people to try out new experiences, to take risks and break out beyond normal boundaries. A good example is the way we promote outdoor pursuits and extreme sports to young people, the irony being that these activities may often be more dangerous than using drugs, and statistically more likely to result in injuries and fatalities. I discuss this in more detail in Chapter A5. At this point I wish to emphasize that while we, as adults, may see risky behaviours such as drug use in a bad light, young people may see such activities as attractive *because* they are risky. Engaging in risky behaviours can be a thrilling experience, especially for young people.

For many people the first try of a drug is not a good experience. The first time people smoke a cigarette often makes them cough and choke and feel dizzy. The first taste of alcohol is usually an unpleasant experience. Many people say the first time they use cannabis either nothing much happens or they feel disorientated or fall asleep. The first time people try heroin they are often sick. Some people find these initial unpleasant experiences are enough to put them off ever using drugs again but many will try again because they hear from friends and peers and observe that drug use can be a rewarding experience. It usually takes time to learn how to use drugs effectively – to know how much to take, how to take it, where best to use, what to expect, how to avoid unpleasant effects and so on, and to know how to steer the drug experience to advantage.

Many adults believe that the main reason young people start to use drugs is peer pressure. While there may be some peer influence to use drugs, in the sense that drug use is acceptable among certain groups of young people and friends may encourage each other to experiment, actual overt peer pressure to start using is not very common. Young people are rarely forced or threatened to take drugs when they do not really want to. In fact the only time most of us are ever made to take drugs against our will is when we are children and our parents force us to take medicines by using physical force, threats or rewards. Rather than talking of peer pressure it is usually more accurate to talk of peer preference. Young people choose their friendship networks partly on the basis of which drugs are, and are not, acceptable and the ways they are used. These groups may include friends who do not use alcohol or cigarettes at all, those that use alcohol moderately, others that regularly drink to become drunk, some that accept cannabis use but refuse to have anything to do with other illegal drugs and those that use a wider range of illegal drugs.

We should also appreciate that there can be a lot of quite overt peer pressure to not use certain drugs. For example, most young people look down on their peers who become involved with heroin and crack and will not want anything to do with them. There is also sometimes actual pressure from peers to drink alcohol. It can be difficult to go out with friends who are drinking alcohol and not drink yourself. Friends will often buy you a drink even when you say you do not want one. And adults are probably more involved in such peer drinking games than young people.

Peer pressure is an overused concept that usually conceals the real motivations for drug use. However, young people themselves, and their parents, often adopt peer pressure explanations when trying to explain initial involvement with drugs. If caught with drugs young people often adopt peer pressure explanations because they can then put the blame on other people for their own drug use. Many parents like to blame the person who has supplied drugs to their child and talk of their child getting into the wrong crowd. Their child is never seen as being part of the wrong crowd. Peer pressure explanations can allow people to avoid taking responsibility for their own actions and to blame someone else instead.

RECREATIONAL DRUG USE

Recreational drug use may be occasional or relatively regular, but is not everyday, compulsive drug use. For young people it usually takes place alongside activities such as socializing with friends, attending pubs, clubs, music gigs and festivals, dancing, watching films, playing computer games, playing or watching sports and relaxing into sexual situations. Commonly, recreational drug use is a weekend and holiday activity.

Recreational users are more experienced drug users than experimenters and are more likely to know what they are doing. Many recreational users are relatively discerning about their drug use and take care over exactly what they take, how much they take, how they take it, where they are, who they are with, when they do it and what they have to do the next day. Most adults are recreational alcohol users and take similar care with their drinking. A lot of young people use illegal and other socially unacceptable drugs in this relatively controlled way.

Reasons for recreational, more regular, use of drugs, may include some of the reasons for experimenting in the first place. However, with recreational drug use, people tend to feel they get something of special value from use of drugs. In particular, they may feel that drug use can give them a lot of pleasure, help them to relax, feel more confident and be great fun. Recreational drug use often enhances communication and social bonds between people. Drug use can also help young people – and adults – to feel less inhibited and self-conscious and make it easier for them to feel at ease in social and sexual situations.

For some young people the appeal of drugs is to help them explore different states of consciousness and to find out more about themselves and the world around them. And drug use can give a very much needed and appreciated temporary relief from the worries and stresses of everyday life. In this sense it can give people a break and be a treat to oneself.

Another common motivation for recreational drug use may be to increase energy, alertness and performance. Many adults have used drugs like amphetamines to help them work for long periods or travel long distances. Many young people use stimulant drugs for similar reasons and to stay awake overnight to go clubbing and dancing or to revise for examinations.

It should be noted that recreational drug use is often a social activity that takes place in pairs or small or larger groups. This is in contrast to a lot of dependent drug use – see below – that often occurs as a solo activity. In this sense recreational drug users tend to benefit, safety wise, from the presence of other people since they can look after each other if something goes wrong.

Whatever adults may think, a lot of young people see drug use in this positive way. Some young people even say they prefer illegal drugs such as cannabis over alcohol because it is cheaper, helps them to relax and unwind, aids socializing and does not lead to a hangover or to people becoming violent.

Most young people enjoy taking drugs and do not come to much harm. Many don't fear or are not convinced by the messages they receive about the harm drug use will bring. Drug taking, especially for youngsters who are new to it, can be an extraordinary, thrilling experience. It may also unite them with their peers with whom they can make common cause against a disapproving adult world.

BINGE DRUG USE

Binge drug use involves taking a large quantity of drugs in one session. This is particularly common when young people drink alcohol with the definite aim of becoming really drunk. It also happens with use of other drugs and through taking more than one drug at the same time to 'get out of our heads'. Binge use can involve one-off sessions but may also occur on a more regular basis for some young people. And of course many adults, including professionals and parents, binge with alcohol and sometimes other drugs. It is common for both adults and young people to binge at the weekend, especially on Friday nights, possibly as a way of delineating 'their time' from 'my time'. It seems people are more likely to socialize with their partners on Saturday nights and this tends to have a moderating influence on their drug use.

The motivation for binge use often has to do with young people being fed up and wishing to drown their sorrows and 'get wasted' in an attempt to escape from the monotony, predictability and stress of their everyday experiences of school, college, home and family life, work, unemployment or life in general. Binge use may also involve groups where there are peer and cultural expectations to consume large quantities of drugs. Occasional binge use may exist alongside recreational drug use, while more regular binge use may be a precursor to dependent use.

DEPENDENT DRUG USE

I describe the physical and psychological aspects of drug dependence in Chapter A4. Dependent drug use is where someone has already taken drugs on a regular basis for a time and has developed a strong compulsion to keep taking them, usually on a daily basis. We sometimes use the term addiction to describe this. Dependent users feel that they cannot get through life without using drugs. Many dependent users may have a drug of first choice but if it is unavailable they will use other substances. Their drug use may be very chaotic and they may go to great lengths to make sure that they have a constant supply of drugs. They may also mostly use alone, rather than with other people.

The reasons that a small minority of the young people who use drugs become dependent tend to be different from the other forms of drug use, although some of the motivations may be similar to those involved in binge use.

Being continually under the influence of drugs can block out deeply ingrained emotional distress and allow people to mask negative feelings about themselves, other people in their lives and the world around them. We know that a disproportionate number of dependent users have experienced significant loss in their life or suffered physical, emotional or sexual abuse or neglect as children.

For some young people life can seem of little purpose with no hope for the future. This is particularly the case in areas of high unemployment, poor housing and poverty where life may be hard and opportunities may be very limited. It can also be true of young people from more privileged backgrounds who do not want to take on the roles that their families have assumed for them. Constant drug use and being 'out of your head' can help people escape from their feelings of helplessness and a world they experience as hostile.

Following the work of the Canadian author, Bruce Alexander (2008), dependency can be viewed as a 'poverty of the spirit' and results from people becoming psychologically, socially and/or economically 'dislocated' from mainstream society.

Dependent drug use can itself give meaning to an otherwise relatively empty life. The daily hustle to obtain money, procure drugs, prepare and take them, avoid the police and be part of a drug scene with other people can provide some structure and purpose for users, and result in what might even be seen as an alternative career.

Rather than being an illness or disease, dependent drug use usually signifies an attempt to find an on-going escape from significant social and/or emotional problems. In lieu of other ways of dealing with their difficulties, some people may find that constant drug use is the only way of dealing with their predicament. As with other forms of drug use, dependent drug use is functional. Despite the many risks and possible problems involved, it may provide relief and purpose and a meaningful activity for young people who have very little going for them and feel very negative about themselves, their prospects and the world in general.

Dependence on heroin is instructive. It is a very effective pain killer. It is used medically for people who are in a lot of physical pain, such as after major operations or for those who are terminally ill with cancers. Heroin also kills emotional pain. You don't have to feel anything. No one can hurt you when you are on heroin. It gives users a warm, cocooned feeling that protects them from unpleasant emotions and situations. Being dependent on heroin requires planning and forethought. You have to get out of the house, obtain money to buy drugs, meet the dealer and get the heroin, prepare it for smoking or injecting, take it and try to make sure you avoid the police. A whole new social scene is created out of the necessary drug-related relationships. For some particularly vulnerable young people the question may not be 'Why keep using?' but 'Why not?'

Dependence on other drugs, and indeed on non-drug activities (such as computer games, gambling, sex, viewing pornography, religion, exercise, sports, outdoor pursuits, work, obtaining money, eating food, shopping, beauty treatments, a relationship with another person and exercising power over others) may function similarly to enable people to escape from, and push aside, feelings and situations they find difficult to deal with and also provide them with a definite meaning and purpose to their life, even if we may be bemused by their behaviour.

It is important to appreciate that dependence on drugs is not necessarily something that young people will experience for the rest of their lives. In time they may be able to moderate their drug use or stop using the drugs they are dependent on altogether, even though many people may replace drug dependency with another dependency that may be more socially acceptable. In the right circumstances and with opportunities to find a place for themselves in more mainstream society, together with good on-going support from people around them and sometimes help from specialist services, they will often be able to deal with the underlying issues that they have been facing and make positive changes in their drug-using behaviour and life in general. For more information about behaviour change see Chapter B3.

I am aware that this discussion of dependence is very short and that it is a very contentious issue for some people, especially for those who, unlike myself, regard dependence and addiction as diseases or illnesses, see them as being due to genetics and people having fixed 'addictive personalities' or believe that certain drugs, such as crack, are instantly addictive. It is not the purpose of this book to address such issues in depth. For more detailed consideration of the definition, nature, causes and treatment of addiction and dependence, and the mythology that often accompanies their discussion, see the books in the Recommended Reading section on pages 290–291 and especially those by Bruce Alexander (2008), John Davies (1997) and Stanton Peele (1977, 1985, 2007).

RISK AND PROTECTIVE FACTORS

As I have already emphasized, the context within which young people live can greatly influence the likelihood that they may become heavily involved with drug use. By context I mean a young person's past and current physical, social, economic and emotional environment. We know that young people who have experienced poverty, homelessness, sexual or physical abuse, childhood neglect, family breakdown or mental health difficulties and those who truant from school, have few educational qualifications, have been unemployed for longer periods or have been in trouble with the law are more likely to have problems with their drug use. These are sometimes referred to as risk factors. Young people who have such experiences may feel that they are powerless to create a better life for themselves and are sometimes referred to as vulnerable.

On the other hand, there are also protective factors that make it less likely that young people will become heavily involved with drugs. These are the converse of the risk factors and include a more stable and loving home environment, adequate access to material goods and fulfilling employment opportunities, positive relationships with adults, educational achievement and a positive image of oneself and of possibilities for the future. Young people who have been brought up and live in such environments tend to feel that they have the power to create fulfilling lives for themselves.

I am not saying that young people from more deprived backgrounds always get into problems with drugs or that those from more fortunate backgrounds do not. In many cases risk factors can be outweighed by certain protective factors, such as when a young person receives on-going care and support from a particular adult or discovers that they have a particular talent that they are encouraged to develop. What may, on the surface, seem like a more fortunate background may also involve a young person having had very troubling, and possibly damaging, experiences. Examples may include emotional neglect, physical or sexual abuse, loss of a parent or sibling or experience of other traumatic events. In addition, we live in a society where insecurity, unrealistic expectations and stress are commonly experienced across a wide range of social classes.

Those young people who have relatively positive feelings about themselves – high self-esteem as it is sometimes called – are not less likely to have used drugs, but they are more likely to use them in more moderate and controlled ways. Those young people with more negative feelings – low self-esteem – are more likely to use drugs excessively in an attempt to block out their sometimes very disturbing emotions. Risk and protective factors are not associated so much with whether young people use drugs but with *how* they use them.

We live in a society that has become very individualist and tends to blame individuals for their actions and expect them to change to fit in with current social norms. However, we should not forget the wider context and the risk and protective factors that will influence how young people feel and the various ways they may use drugs. Excessive drug use will often be more a symptom of already existing difficulties that young people are facing, rather than a direct cause of them, even if it may sometimes also lead to further problems.

DRUG USE IS ALWAYS FUNCTIONAL

It is important to appreciate that drug use, in whatever form, is functional for the people who engage in it. It is an activity that has meaning and purpose for the person using, even if we may not appreciate or understand what they get out of it. People return to drug use when it is successful in achieving the outcomes that they want or need and they cannot find other ways of getting through life.

WHERE DO YOUNG PEOPLE GET DRUGS FROM AND HOW MUCH DO THEY COST?

LEGAL DRUGS

Before considering illegal substances it is important to remember that many young people have easy access to a wide, and increasingly diverse, range of drugs that are legal.

Caffeine is available to children from a very young age in their own homes through drinking colas and other soft drinks, and also from eating confectionery, sweets, breakfast cereals, biscuits, cakes and ice creams that contain chocolate or cocoa. Tea and coffee are usually added to the menu by the early teenage years. Caffeine energy drinks, tablets, chewing gums and mints can be purchased by young people from a wide range of shops. There are no legal age restrictions on sales although some vendors may be reluctant to sell energy drinks and tablets to under 16s.

Most young people are given their first alcoholic drink by their parents or another family member. Rather than buying alcohol directly, most of the younger age range obtain it from friends and older siblings and by asking people to buy it for them. Despite the advent of checks through proof of age cards, once into the later teens many young people will be able to pass for 18 years old and buy alcohol in pubs and clubs, although they may still find it difficult to buy it from shops and supermarkets and have to rely on other people to get it for them from these places. Young girls may sometimes have easier access to alcohol than boys, both because they often look older than boys of the same age and often mix with boys and young men who are older than themselves.

The increase in age at which shopkeepers can sell cigarettes to young people from 16 to 18 years old will have made access to smoking more difficult for younger teenagers. However, younger ages can often obtain cigarettes via older friends and siblings and the illicit markets that provides cheap supplies in many, and especially poorer, localities.

If young people want access to solvents they may well find a range of products that can be inhaled in their own homes. They will also have few problems buying solvents from a wide range of shops despite the legislation that attempts to restrict their access to them. Few of the younger age range will be able to buy poppers from sex shops or at clubs but they may find it relatively easy to get them from some tobacconists and fashion and clothes shops aimed at the younger age range. Young people aged over 18 years old will be able to buy poppers from all of these sources.

And young people have plenty of access to both prescribed and over-the-counter mood-altering medicines through visiting their doctors, buying medicines from pharmacies, supermarkets and other shops and from the many unused medicines that we often store in our homes.

These days both adults and young people have increased access to prescription-only medicines through making purchases over the internet and having them delivered by post. In recent years there has been an increase in the number of people buying mood-altering medicines in this way, without obtaining a prescription from their doctor, even though it can be deemed illegal to do so. These medicines have included Prozac and other anti-depressants, anti-anxiety and sleeping tablets such as tranquillizers, codeine-based painkillers, Viagra and stimulant drugs such as Ritalin and various diet pills.

LEGAL HIGHS

Although not completely new, the increased availability of a wide range of legal high drugs that mimic the effects of illegal substances has provided young people with a much broader menu of mood-altering substances from which to choose – see the information about legal highs in Part D for more details. Legal highs may be available to young people through friends and acquaintances and older siblings, and sometimes directly from drug dealers, in a similar way to obtaining illegal drugs. More commonly they are purchased from the increasing number of headshops that now exist in many cities and sizeable towns and through purchase over the internet. Some legal highs are also now being sold from other retail outlets, including petrol stations, tattoo parlours, take-aways, newsagents, sex shops, market stalls and even at car boot sales.

A headshop is a retail outlet specializing in selling legal highs, drug paraphernalia used for growing and using cannabis and other drugs, and sometimes also counterculture art, magazines, music, clothing and home décor. Many headshops sell a wide range of different legal highs under all sorts of brand names. Most say they only cater for people aged over 18 years old but under-18s who do not look too young should have few problems purchasing from headshops and also may have older, or at least older-looking, friends who can buy for them.

The other way to access legal highs is through the internet and online mail order businesses. There are a small number of major importers and retailers of legal highs and a much larger number of small traders who deal in smaller purchases, often sourced from the majors. Some of these businesses will be the same as the headshops found in cities and larger towns but many will be based in small warehouses or even people's own homes. The best way to see what is available and how it works is to do a bit of research yourself. If you carry out an internet search of 'buy legal highs' or 'headshops', you will have the choice of hundreds of sites to explore. As you will see, a very wide range of different legal highs is available under a boggling variety of brand names. All you need is a credit card and your purchase will be delivered to your door very soon by normal postal or courier services. And orders can be placed at any time, 24/7.

The wider availability of legal highs has seen the advent of a different type of drug dealer, with entrepreneurs seeing 'legitimate' business opportunities while substances remain legal. Many suppliers, and especially small-scale ones, may not have had previous involvement in the illicit drug trade and just want to make some quick money. This has included young people who have set up their own businesses with websites that sell on a national basis and also those who supply to local student populations at colleges and universities. Some of these young entrepreneurs may advertise on student notice boards, websites and social networking sites, distribute business cards and run a telephone and/or internet ordering service with deliveries to the customer's door, much like a pizza delivery service.

ILLEGAL DRUGS

The illegal drug economy is a huge worldwide business that has been estimated to be worth 7 to 8 billion pounds a year in the UK alone. It is so large that it is not a wholly illicit economy and may be more accurately seen as a grey window economy in which we all, knowingly or not, are in some ways involved. The illegal drugs trade is often integrated with other aspects of illicit trade at a local level but is also part of the 'legitimate' global economy as shown by the many cases of mainstream banks being involved in, and sometimes prosecuted for, laundering drug monies.

The nature of illegal drug markets varies between different areas and over time but in the main there are two relatively separate illicit drug markets. Heroin and crack tend to be used and sold in more deprived areas. In these localities drug dealing may be conducted on the streets, in parks, from known houses or flats or be delivered to users after they place an order by a mobile telephone call, text or email. Suppliers will mainly be local small-scale dealers at the bottom of the chain who may sell drugs partly to fund their own drug use. Young people who live in such areas are more likely to come across, and possibly be involved with, larger-scale dealers and associated criminal violence. It could include a teenager delivering drugs on a bike or acting as a lookout. In recent years about a quarter of people convicted of supplying Class A drugs have been aged 21 years or under and there has been a rise in number of teenage dealers arrested, charged and sent to prison (Ministry of Justice 2013).

In most cases the market for drugs like cannabis, cocaine, ecstasy, ketamine and mephedrone tends to be separate from that for heroin and crack, although there can be an overlap, especially for cocaine. While these drugs will be available from dealers at party venues, clubs and music events and festivals, much of the trading in them operates in a relatively private and low key way through on-going direct personal contact. Most young people obtain illegal drugs from friends and acquaintances who purchase on their behalf sometimes at no, or very little, profit. Not many young people will have direct contact with large-scale drug dealers.

Many small-scale dealers and suppliers will specialize in only one or two drugs, and particularly cannabis, with occasional access to other drugs. They may be contactable by mobile phone and often all that is needed to place an order is a phone call, text or email. The purchaser may go to the supplier's home or meet them at a pub, café or on the street to pick up the drugs or the supplier might come to their home. With dealers, the drugs may be delivered to the doorstep within half an hour, sometimes by someone on a bicycle or motorbike and without the customer necessarily seeing the dealer they have been in contact with. Again it can be compared to ordering a pizza for home delivery. This is very common in cities and towns and particularly those that have colleges or universities, where dealers may even advertise to students on noticeboards and via the internet.

Some young people who become involved in drug dealing may see it as a way to make a living, or at least a good sum of money quickly, in much the same way that young people are encouraged to be entrepreneurial and start up their own businesses with legal products. There have been stories of some students becoming drug dealers as a way of paying their university fees and expenses. For some, small-scale dealing will be seen as a way of supplying themselves with drugs for free. For others it may also be a way of becoming popular among their peers.

There are many internet forums where users, and often young people, discuss various illegal drugs, their experiences of using them, the effects and dangers and where to buy them. Such discussions also take place on more general social networking internet sites. While these forums may sometimes provide young people with useful information, some of what they read may be inaccurate, especially when it is written by people who are heavily involved in drug use and/ or supplying drugs.

There is also a growing trade in internet sales of illegal drugs that has been compared to eBay. Illegal drugs can be ordered online 24 hours a day and are delivered by post direct to the customer's door. One internet site, Silk Road, was set up so that law enforcement agencies could not trace the computers of sellers or buyers. Transactions used the digital currency, Bitcoin. Silk Road was recently shut down following action by the American FBI, but was soon up and running again. Other sites using anonymous transactions to buy illegal drugs, such as Black Market Reloaded and Sheep, have now closed, but some, such as The Market Place and Pandora, may currently be growing.

Other internet sites that sell illegal drugs work in a traditional way using credit cards. They often use coded listings for drugs hidden among job adverts, private sales and suspiciously cheap properties to let. So an advert for cocaine might say something like 'Flat for rent – £60 – ask for Charlie'. Use of such sites by young people puts them at risk of being apprehended by the police. While internet sites selling illegal drugs are not nearly as common as those selling legal highs, they may well become an increasing part of the distribution network for illegal drugs in future years.

DRUG DEALING MYTHS AND STEREOTYPES

When it comes to illegal drugs the popular image is of the evil drug pusher plying innocent and unsuspecting children with dangerous drugs. In its most scary form the shady drug dealer is at the school gates and tricks or forces children to use drugs or offers the first deal free and then gets them hooked. However, the demon drug pusher as an alien figure waiting in the shadows to corrupt the nation's youth is mostly a figment of the imagination. In 2006 the UK government changed drug laws to increase penalties for drug use or supply in the vicinity of schools and, to date, I don't think a single person has been convicted of such an offence.

Other than buying from dealers at clubs and music events and festivals, most young people obtain illegal drugs in relatively small quantities from their friends, older siblings or acquaintances and regard it as a favour when they do. They often seek out and request drugs. Often one young person gets hold of some drugs, or knows where to get them from, and others will ask to be supplied, possibly pooling their money to make the purchase. Small-scale local drug supply may be an interaction between friends and not involve any profit.

Large-scale surveys have found that people who have used illegal drugs most commonly obtain them from domestic circumstances such as their own home or from someone else's home. Studies exploring where young people get cannabis from have found that they nearly all access it via a friend or someone they already know. A study of 11–19-year-olds found only one in 20 obtained cannabis from an unknown dealer (Duffy *et al.* 2008). Half of the young people surveyed had purchased cannabis for a friend or sold small quantities of it.

Drugs being deliberately sold that contain dangerous poisons may happen very occasionally but its occurrence has often been greatly exaggerated. Drugs are often supplied to young people by friends, acquaintances or siblings and they do not want to poison the people they supply to. In fact they will want them to have a good time using drugs and not to come to harm. Professional dealers also rarely want to damage their customers because they want them to come back for more.

Most people who supply illegal drugs will also avoid selling to younger age groups because they will regard the young as unreliable and irregular customers who are unlikely to have a regular source of money and are not worth doing business with. In my experience many users and dealers of illegal drugs also believe it is immoral to sell to very young people and do not want them to start using at such a young age.

The use of the term drug pusher exacerbates the misconceptions and stereotypes that surround drug dealing. Drugs are much more commonly 'pulled', rather than 'pushed'. There cannot be supply without demand. Some adults find it difficult to face the fact that there is a demand for drugs among many young people, especially when it comes to their own children or young people they work with, know and respect.

Some young people even complain of being pressurized or harassed by their friends and acquaintances to obtain drugs for them. I have been consulted by some schools over drug incidents where it was found that students who supplied drugs had been bullied by their peers into doing so. Professional dealers may also sometimes threaten young people to sell drugs for them, especially if they are owed money.

Many people wrongly believe that all illegal drugs are imported into this country from abroad. Drugs like cocaine and heroin are imported but some illegal drugs are manufactured in the UK, as well as being imported. For example, illicit laboratories in the UK have produced amphetamines, ecstasy, LSD and mephedrone. In addition, herbal cannabis is commonly grown in this country on both a large-scale commercial basis and on a smaller scale for an individual's own consumption and supply, and possible sale, to friends and acquaintances.

There is little truth to the commonly heard gateway or slippery slope theories that young people are given cannabis by drug dealers who then give them heroin to get them hooked on drugs. Apart from the fact that the markets for cannabis and heroin are usually relatively separate and operated by different dealers and in different ways, most heroin users have tried cannabis but most cannabis users never try heroin and regard it with fear and derision. There are millions of people in the UK who have smoked cannabis and the vast majority have never had any interest in trying heroin, even once. In fact early use of legal substances, such as alcohol and tobacco, is a much stronger indicator of later use of illegal drugs and problematic use (Lloyd *et al.* 2000).

When the police do manage to intercept a large quantity of illegal drugs and remove them from the open market we tend to assume that this is a wholly good thing with no negative consequences. However, life is not that simple. For example, if heroin becomes scarce in a particular locality people who are dependent on it do not stop using. The price of heroin is likely to increase resulting in more drug-related crime, especially break-ins and theft, because users need more money to buy drugs. The heroin that is available is more likely to be bulked with other substances to make it go further and be more adulterated, leading to more overdoses and hospital admissions. If users cannot get hold of much heroin they may use other drugs instead, such as tranquillizers or medicinal painkillers, which can be particularly dangerous to take, especially if injected. And, in many cases, within a few weeks fresh supplies of heroin will probably hit the streets and everything will be back to normal.

There are many other examples of where a decrease in the availability of a particular drug has resulted in increased use of other drugs. I have worked in areas where a crackdown by the police on alcohol use among young teenagers led to a surge of solvent use. Some commentators say that one of the main reasons for the rise in use of mephedrone and legal highs in recent years has been because of the decline in the availability and quality of ecstasy and cocaine. Similarly, the decrease in solvent use among young teenagers may have been due to increased availability of alcohol and cannabis to the younger age range.

HOW MUCH DOES IT COST TO USE DRUGS?

This is a difficult question to answer because the cost of drug use will depend not only on which drugs people use but also how much they use, and how often, and variations in prices over time between localities based on availability. However, one thing is clear. Drug use, and particularly occasional experimentation, or even more regular recreational use, is not as expensive as many adults assume.

Regular alcohol use or a binge session may be expensive but alcohol consumption can be relatively cheap. It may involve high strength but low cost lagers and ciders bought in large bottles or in packs containing a quantity of bottles or cans. Cheaper brands of spirits can be purchased, sometimes in large bottles and make getting drunk less expensive. Many young people will drink alcohol at home before going out to drink in pubs and clubs or at parties. Happy hours and other special offers at pubs and clubs can also make alcohol relatively cheap.

While smoking 20 cigarettes a day purchased from a shop now costs a lot of money many young people may smoke fewer and some may buy cheaper brands or, as with alcohol, they may obtain cigarettes locally on the black market at a fraction of their full retail price.

Caffeine-based drinks, tablets, chewing gums and mints are inexpensive. Many inhalable, solvent-based products may be available in the home and are very cheap to buy in shops. Nitrous oxide balloons may cost as little as £1.50 to £3 each. Poppers usually retail at between £4 and £6 for a 10ml bottle.

The increase in use of legal highs over the last few years has been partly explained by them being cheap compared to illegal drugs. A few pounds will buy pills, powders or smoking mixtures that will give at least one, and possibly more, drug use sessions of a few hours' duration and possibly longer.

In the last few years the street price of many illegal drugs has hardly changed, despite inflation in the rest of the economy, meaning use of many drugs has become cheaper, in real terms, over time.

Average street prices in 2013/14 for some of the illegal drugs that young people are most likely to use were as follows:

Amphetamine costs about £10 per gram, which may come as one or two 'wraps', enough to keep a user alert and speeding for a good few hours.

Cannabis costs, per quarter ounce, about £25 to £30 for resin, £30 for standard herbal cannabis and £35 to £50 for sinsemilla/skunk. £10 will buy enough cannabis for a few joints, sufficient for a small group to have a few hours of being stoned.

Cocaine costs about £40 to £50 per gram but more if it is high quality. £10 will buy a few lines of cocaine powder – enough for a few snorts, each of short-lived effect. A longer session might cost anything between £20 and £100.

Crack costs about £10 per rock, enough for one or two smokes, each of short-lived effect. Sustained use will obviously cost a lot more.

Ecstasy costs about £3 to £5 per pill, up to £10 for the best pills and about £30 to £40 per gram for powder/crystal. Many users will use two or three ecstasy tablets or a quarter gram of powder for an all-night session, but some will use more.

GHB may cost £10 to £15 for a bottle (enough for a few doses) but only a few pounds for a capful of liquid.

Heroin costs about £35 to £60 a gram and is often sold in £5 and £10 bags. A small bag of heroin can be enough for one person to have a smoke or to inject but many users will take more, especially if they are dependent.

Ketamine costs about £20 per gram. Users may take anything between half a gram and three or four grams for a session.

Mephedrone costs about £15 to £20 per gram. Prices were nearer £10 a gram before it was made illegal in 2010. Users may take anything between half a gram and three or four grams a session.

WHAT DOES ALL THIS DRUG LANGUAGE MEAN?

This chapter considers the 'official' language that is often used by professionals to describe various aspects of drug use and the street language used by drug users.

THE 'OFFICIAL' LANGUAGE

All emerging professions develop their own language, concepts and terminology and the drugs field is no exception. While this is to be expected, and in some ways welcomed, there is also sometimes a downside as well. Overuse of specialist language can confuse and mystify and restrict dialogue and discussion to a small clique. With regard to drugs it can exclude the general public rather than aid wider understanding.

The language used to explain various aspects of drug use can seem strange and be difficult to understand for many non-drug professionals, for parents and the wider public. Below is a short glossary of terms that drug specialists often use and definitions of them. Do read through them and check to see which you have heard of and compare what you think they might mean to the definitions I have given.

If a professional uses a drug term that you do not understand, do ask them what they mean. Don't be too shy to ask. And do be careful about the language you use when talking with young people. Check with them that they understand the terms that you are using and what you are saying and, if necessary, ask them to clarify what they mean by any words or phrases they use that you do not understand.

Abstinence, as with abstain, means not using drugs.

Addiction is a term that is commonly applied to drug use but is also increasingly used with regard to many other human activities and behaviours that become everyday, compulsive and habitual and people find difficult to stop. The fact that it is often used inappropriately and in ill-defined ways, and that terms like addict, and particularly drug addict, have very negative and stereotypical connotations has led to many people preferring the less emotive term **dependence**.

Analgesic refers to a drug that reduces physical pain.

Binge drug use is where someone takes a large amount of a drug in one session with the aim of 'getting out of their head'. Binge drinking of alcohol is the most common example.

Controlled drugs are substances that are subject to the Misuse of Drugs Act (see Chapter A6, page 71) and illegal to be in possession of and/or to supply.

Decriminalization differs from **legalization** in that while drugs may remain illegal in some senses, certain offences such as personal possession of small amounts, would no longer be criminal offences or result in a criminal record. The term has most commonly been used with regard to cannabis possession, with some people suggesting this should be a civil offence incurring a warning or small fine, but not a criminal record.

Dependence, like **addiction**, is everyday, compulsive drug use that people find difficult to stop. It can have both physical and psychological aspects.

Physical dependence happens when someone has taken certain drugs regularly for a time and if they stop they feel physically ill. This can happen with **depressant** drugs like alcohol (alcoholism), heroin and tranquillizers when people experience **withdrawal symptoms** if they stop regular use – shaking, sweating and vomiting like a bad dose of flu. A form of physical dependence can also happen with **stimulant** drugs such as amphetamine, cocaine, crack and mephedrone when everyday users feel tired, depressed and lacking in energy if they stop regular use. In this sense, mild withdrawal symptoms may be experienced by everyday caffeine, cigarette and cannabis users when they try to stop using. Dependence also always has a strong psychological side.

Psychological dependence is when someone feels they need to keep taking a drug in order to feel OK and get through life. It can happen with many drugs, including cannabis and cigarettes. Being repeatedly under the influence of drugs can relieve, and shield people from, emotional and existential pain and the difficulties they face, at least for a time. It may also make it difficult for people to positively address their underlying pain and problems. People can also become psychologically dependent on many other activities including computer games, gambling, sex, viewing pornography, religion, exercise, sports, outdoor pursuits, working, obtaining money, eating food, shopping, beauty treatments, a relationship with another person and exercising power over others. The activity they are dependent on becomes such an essential feature of their life that they feel they cannot do without it for long and become very stressed at the thought of not doing it on an on-going basis.

Dependent drug users often experience:

- increased **tolerance** to the drug(s) they are using so that they begin to consume greater amounts to get the same or desired effect

- **withdrawal symptoms** when drug use is not repeated

- a fear of having to face and experience life without using drugs

- lone drug use, rather than mostly in social situations

- seeking, obtaining, preparing and using the drug becomes central to their thinking, life and everyday behaviours.

Dependence is discussed in more detail in Chapters A1 and A2. Information about dependence on different drugs is given in Part D of this book.

Depressant is a drug which depresses and slows down body functions and usually makes people feel more relaxed and, in large doses, sleepy. Examples include alcohol, GHB, heroin, ketamine, methadone and tranquillizers. Depressants are also sometimes called downers.

Detoxification is the process of stopping or coming off drugs after being dependent so that drugs are cleared from the body and the user is drug-free. It often involves a gradual reduction in the amount of drug taken over a period of time. For some drugs it may involve use of a substitute drug, such as methadone or Subutex for people who are coming off heroin.

Drug refers to a substance that has a marked physiological and/or psychological effect when taken into the body. In other words drugs are substances that when consumed change the way the body works and how we feel and perceive things. This means they can include medicines and legal substances such as caffeine, nicotine and alcohol as well as **controlled drugs**.

Drug abuse is a social, legal and medical term. Legally the use of any **controlled drug** can be seen as abuse. Medically, the use of medicines in a manner not prescribed 'correctly' by a doctor or regulatory instructions can be seen as abuse. Socially, using certain substances that are not accepted by wider society, or using in ways that are not condoned, can be seen as drug abuse.

Drug career is a term used to denote the history of a person's use of drugs over time. It could be applied to a particular person's use of a certain drug over the specific time period that they use the drug. It could also be applied to us all and our use of mind-altering substances, both legal and illegal, in our lifetime.

Drug misuse implies that drug use is harmful or not carried out in the proper manner. Like abuse, misuse is often used in a blanket way to indicate that use of a certain drug, in itself or in large quantities, is bad or wrong. However, what one person thinks is drug abuse or misuse another person may not.

Dual diagnosis is used to describe a situation where someone has been diagnosed with having a mental health problem and a drug problem and there is a relationship between the two that makes it difficult or impossible to tackle the two independently. It is also sometimes called COD, co-occurring disorders. It is a disputed term because of the difficulties of defining what is meant by mental health problems and the question as to whether they can be distinguished from drug problems. The use of the term dual diagnosis may have something to do with competition, and attempts at co-operation, between different professions.

Experimental drug use is novice use, where people are trying a particular drug for the first few times. It will often involve young people but adults may also be experimental users if they are new to a particular drug.

Hallucinogenic refers to a drug which affects the senses to the extent that people experience the world, and especially see and hear things, very differently. Examples include LSD, magic mushrooms and ketamine, to a lesser extent ecstasy and strong types of cannabis. Hallucinogenic drugs are sometimes called mindbenders and all-rounders.

Hard drugs is a term often used to describe what are regarded as the most dangerous drugs such as heroin, crack and cocaine. It is not a very helpful term to use. In reality the dangers of drug use vary depending on how much is taken, how it is taken, the person using, the environment and so on. This means that heroin, crack and cocaine could be used relatively safely and drugs like alcohol and cannabis could be very dangerous to use.

Harm reduction/minimization are terms used to describe strategies that drug users can adopt to keep themselves as safe as possible while taking drugs. The terms are based on the fact that there are safer and more harmful ways of taking drugs. Reducing and minimizing harm are particularly important in situations where drug users are determined or likely to carry on using, no matter what other people say to them or do.

Intravenous literally means introducing a drug into the veins and is used generally to mean injecting drugs.

Legal highs are drugs that do not fall under the Misuse of Drugs Act and are sold as legal alternatives to illegal drugs, usually by dealers, headshops and through the internet and mail order suppliers. See the information about legal highs in Part D of this book.

Legalization is a term used in the debate about whether controlled drugs should be made legally available on a similar basis to drugs like alcohol and cigarettes. It is most commonly discussed with regard to cannabis, but some people have advocated the legalization of all drugs.

Maintenance means to cause or enable a state of affairs to continue at the same level or rate and/or to provide people with the necessities for life or existence. In the drugs field the term has often been used to describe the prescribing of methadone to heroin addicts on an on-going basis, rather than in reducing amounts in an attempt to get users completely off drugs. In this way maintenance has been seen as a way of stabilizing heroin users until they reach a time where they are better able to actually stop using.

Narcotic derives from a Greek word meaning 'to numb'. It is sometimes used to refer to drugs such as cocaine and heroin as well as to describe drugs that have a hypnotic, numbing and sleep-enhancing effect such as some **depressants**.

Normalization is the process by which behaviours that have previously been regarded as deviant become accommodated and accepted into wider society and integrated into otherwise normal lifestyles. In recent years many commentators have talked about the normalization of alcohol, cannabis and sometimes dance drugs like ecstasy into youth culture.

Overdose (OD) is what it says – taking more than the suggested dose of a drug such that the experience can be very disturbing and possibly dangerous to the extent that the functioning of the vital organs of the body are endangered. Fatal overdose may particularly result from taking large doses of depressant drugs such as alcohol, heroin and tranquillizers, and is more common if more than one drug is taken at the same time. Paracetamol is also a drug that can, relatively easily, result in fatal overdose.

Polydrug use is the use of more than one drug at the same time. People may be under the influence of more than one drug at the same time, including alcohol and medicines.

Problem drug use refers to drug use that has a negative impact on the user's life, such as experiencing social, financial, physical health, psychological or legal problems that occur as a result of their drug use. It is also sometimes used as a phrase to describe a situation where a person's drug use has an adverse effect on other people. The government and drug services commonly use 'problem drug use' to refer to people who are dependent on heroin and/or crack and especially injecting users. However, the term can also be used to refer to other drugs and other forms of drug use. The difficulty with the term problem drug use is that what some people see as a problem, other people, and especially users themselves, may not.

Psychedelic was first used in the 1950s to describe the effects of LSD. It literally means 'soul manifesting' and has come to be used in a similar way to **hallucinogenic**, although it also tends to imply that the drug experience acts as a catalyst to further, and often new, feelings and thoughts.

Recovery is a term that has come into more common use over the last few years to describe people who are getting over a period of drug **dependence**. Strictly speaking the word recovery means a return to a normal state of health, mind or strength after a period of illness or trauma or the process of regaining control of something stolen or lost. The difficulty with applying the term recovery to people who experience serious drug problems is that few will want to go back to where they were before becoming dependent. Instead, they are more likely to want to move on to somewhere better, both in terms of the situation in which they are living and how they feel about their life and themselves.

Recreational drug use may be occasional or relatively regular, but is not every-day, dependent drug use. It is usually concerned with recreational activities such as socializing, dancing, listening to or playing music, watching films, playing computer games, playing or watching sports, relaxing into sexual situations. Recreational users are more experienced drug users than experimenters and are more likely to know what they are doing. Many recreational users are relatively discerning about their drug use and take care over exactly what they take, how much they take, how they take it, where they are, who they are with, when they do it, what they are planning to do the next day and so on.

Rehab refers to rehabilitation and particularly to centres and programmes where drug users are treated and helped to overcome being dependent. It usually involves users completely stopping use of the drug(s) they are dependent on. Rehab is also often used to refer to residential treatment facilities.

Route of administration refers to the way that a drug is taken. Possibilities include taking drugs orally (swallowing by mouth), snorting up the nose, smoking and injecting.

Sedative is similar to **depressant** and refers to a drug that depresses and slows down the central nervous system to the extent that a large dose will send people to sleep and a very large dose may result in fatal overdose. Examples include alcohol, GHB, heroin, ketamine, methadone and tranquillizers.

Self-medication describes the way people consciously take drugs in an attempt to make them feel and perform better. Most people do this with medicines, caffeine and alcohol. Many people add illegal, or other socially unacceptable, drugs to their menu.

Soft drugs is a term sometimes used to describe drugs like cannabis that are regarded as not particularly harmful. Like the term **hard drugs**, it is not a very helpful term because depending on how much drug is taken, how it is taken, the person using and the situation, soft drugs can lead to people experiencing serious problems.

Stimulant is a drug which speeds up body functions and makes people feel more alert. Examples include caffeine, nicotine, amphetamine, cocaine and crack, ecstasy and mephedrone. Stimulants are sometimes called uppers.

Tolerance refers to the adaptation of a person's body chemistry to tolerate increased amounts of certain drugs if they are taken on a regular basis. This means larger doses may be needed to get the same or desired effect. This is likely to happen more easily with some drugs (including alcohol) than other substances. See Part D for information about the potential tolerance from using various drugs.

Twelve steps are the 12, quasi-religious, principles of Alcoholics Anonymous (AA) and Narcotics Anonymous (NA) that form the basis to their approach to dealing with alcoholism and drug addiction. AA and NA see **addiction** as a lifelong disease where addicts need to be **abstinent** and not use at all, rather than able to use alcohol or other drugs in more moderate and controlled ways.

Withdrawal symptoms are the unpleasant physical and psychological symptoms which can result from stopping long term, dependent use of drugs. See **dependence** above.

STREET LANGUAGE

Drug users often use their own language and jargon. Street language is the slang names users give to different drugs, paraphernalia used to prepare and take drugs, different ways of taking drugs and specific effects and dangers of taking drugs.

Street language can seem very obscure and difficult to understand for those who are not part of a drug scene and not used to it. It may not be immediately obvious what 'dropping love doves' (taking ecstasy tablets) or 'cranking smack' (injecting heroin) means unless you are in the know. And that is the point about street language. One of its main purposes is to exclude non-users, and especially professionals and parents, from knowing what is going on.

The street names that are used can vary over time and between different geographical locations. Once certain slang names become more commonly known they have a nasty habit of going out of use, especially when professionals and parents become familiar with them. Some street language has been in use for ages but some terms go out of fashion soon after they come into use.

Some slang terms can have more than one meaning and can refer to various things at different times and in different places. For example, 'Have you got any dope?' could refer to cannabis, heroin or sometimes any illegal drug, as well as referring to information in general.

It is not just adults who may be confused by slang terms. Young people themselves may use terms in ways that are inaccurate and not usually used. This happens especially when they are new to particular drugs and may be trying to impress their peers and/or us about how much they know.

Some common street names associated with different drugs, and ways of using them, are listed in the Part D of this book. However, there is no guarantee that the names I have given will be the ones used by young people in your locality. They may use street names that are not listed in this book.

Some words of advice regarding street language. Take care with your own use of street language. There is nothing worse than an adult trying to use street language in an attempt to impress young people when it is clear to them that you don't really know what you are talking about and are trying to appear hip.

Wherever possible it is best to use the 'proper' names for drugs, paraphernalia and ways of using drugs, rather than using street jargon.

If a young person uses a slang term that you do not know or understand, ask them what they mean by it. Most young people will be more than happy to explain it to you.

WHAT ARE THE EFFECTS AND HARMS OF DRUG USE AND HOW DANGEROUS IS IT?

This chapter focusses on the potential effects and harms of drug use, the factors that influence them and how dangerous drug use actually is. I have attempted to explain these things in general terms. More detailed information about the effects and potential harms of particular drugs can be found in Part D of this book.

EXAGGERATION OF RISKS AND HARMS

If we believed everything we read in newspapers and saw on television we might conclude that drug use by young people is exceedingly harmful and that many of them are in serious danger of becoming addicted to drugs, or even worse, dying from a drug overdose. Sensationalist reporting, and exaggeration of risks and harms in the media have been the order of the day for a long time and made us very fearful of drugs.

How dangerous is drug use in reality? Straight away, I wish to emphasize that in the vast majority of cases use of drugs by young people does not lead to them experiencing serious problems. In fact most young people have a thoroughly good time using drugs and few come to serious harm. While drug use can lead to serious harm the chances of that happening are relatively rare.

A lot of young people only try particular drugs a few times and then decide not to use again. Many use drugs only occasionally. Of those who use regularly the majority take care about what they take and how much, when, how, who they are with and where they are. There are young people who get into serious health, social, financial and/or legal problems through drug use but they are a small minority of those who use.

Drug use can certainly be dangerous and particular drugs, and ways of taking them, are potentially more harmful than others. In England and Wales an annual survey is carried out of drugs mentioned on death certificates. This does not give a totally accurate picture of drug-related deaths because certificates may not always record cases accurately or take account of when more than one drug is involved. However, it does give us an indication of the number of drug-related deaths.

The number of people recorded on death certificates as dying each year, over the past five years, from using controlled/illegal drugs has been between 1496 and 1941 in England and Wales (Office for National Statistics 2013b). Most of these deaths have been following use of heroin, morphine and/or methadone and many involve use of more than one drug, with alcohol also often being implicated. Around one in five of these deaths involves 20–29-year-olds. Few involve young people aged under 20 years old.

In total, there have been over 300 ecstasy-related deaths in the UK, many involving young people, since the drug first appeared in the mid-1980s, but annual deaths have fallen in more recent times (ACMD 2009). Over the last five years the annual number of fatalities recorded on death certificates, in England and Wales, as following ecstasy use has been between eight and 31 a year (Office for National Statistics 2013b). The same survey found that, in 2012, 139 deaths in England and Wales were recorded as being associated with cocaine use, 97 were associated with use of amphetamines and 20 were associated with use of the ecstasy-type drugs PMA and PMMA. The annual number of deaths associated with mephedrone and legal highs rose from 29 in 2011 to 52 in 2012.

Solvent deaths have commonly involved young teenagers and in the 1990s annual deaths were as high as 150 a year. In more recent years figures have fallen to below 50 deaths a year (Ghodse et al. 2012).

It is instructive to compare these figures to those for deaths involving legal drugs. Tobacco-related deaths have fallen in the UK but still run at 80 to 90 thousand a year (Health and Social Care Information Centre 2012a), although these will not be young people. Direct deaths through cirrhosis of the liver, other diseases directly associated with heavy alcohol use, poisoning and overdose stand at around 9000 a year in the UK (Office for National Statistics 2013a). These do not include the many deaths involving alcohol-related accidents and violence, road traffic accidents involving drunk drivers and diseases where alcohol may have been a contributing factor. Other than cirrhosis of the liver and other specific alcohol-related diseases, a significant number of alcohol-related deaths occur among young people.

In the last five years, between 613 and 752 deaths a year have been recorded in England and Wales, as being from use of tranquillizers or anti-depressants (Office for National Statistics 2013b). Between 182 and 260 deaths each year have been recorded as paracetamol-related (some of which have involved young people committing suicide) and in 2012, 175 deaths were associated with use of Tramadol painkillers.

While many drug-related deaths involving young people who have used illegal, and other socially unacceptable, drugs are prominently reported in the media, this is not nearly as common when legal drugs are the cause. Some high profile cases of young people dying after using illegal drugs have also been inaccurately reported. The death of Leah Betts was said to be because of ecstasy but later found to be due to her drinking excessive amounts of water and also possibly the effects of drinking alcohol. The death of Rachel Whitear was reported as being due to heroin injecting but subsequent pathology reports did not find a sufficient quantity of drugs in her bloodstream to kill her and the cause of her death remains a mystery. More recently, two young men were assumed to have died after taking mephedrone and a huge media campaign followed that led to mephedrone being made illegal by the government. Subsequent pathology reports found the two young men had taken methadone and been drinking alcohol, but that they had not taken mephedrone. It has been very rare that the media has corrected their initial sensationalist and inaccurate reporting of such deaths. In fact, in all three cases graphic images of the young people involved have been used as the basis for hard-hitting anti-drugs campaigns against ecstasy, heroin and mephedrone in schools and in the media.

There are deaths involving young people using drugs, especially when they have, often without knowing, taken too much or taken more than one drug at the same time. Some may also have particular health conditions, possibly unknown to themselves, that make them more susceptible to the effects of drugs.

Every death of a young person is a tragedy but drug-related deaths need to be kept in perspective. To do this the relative risk of drug use can be compared to the risk of possible death and injury from other causes and activities.

For example, in 2009 Professor David Nutt conducted a careful analysis of the comparative risk of using ecstasy and of horse riding in his academic paper, 'Equasy – an overlooked addiction with implications for the current debate on drug harms' (Nutt 2009). He compared the two activities on a nine-point scale of harm that included acute and chronic harm to the person, potential physical and psychological dependence, harm to society and cost to society. Regular participation in horse riding, or Equine Addiction Syndrome as Professor Nutt calls it, was found to be statistically more dangerous than regular use of ecstasy.

Our society has double standards regarding attitudes towards risk. We encourage young people to engage in certain activities which are statistically very risky and often far more dangerous than drug use, such as outdoor activities and extreme sports, to the extent that people who excel in them are often portrayed as role models for the young. We tend to ignore, or at least downplay, the risks of such activities and assume that the thrill of being involved is more important. At the same time we tend to exaggerate the dangers of drug use, especially when it involves illegal, and socially unacceptable, drugs.

WHAT HARMS CAN RESULT FROM DRUG USE?

This is not to say that drug use cannot be very dangerous. Far from it. Depending on the drug used, the amount used and way it is used, the characteristics of the person using and the situation they are in, drug use can lead to a wide range of significant harms for young people.

Drug use can lead to serious physical health problems short of death. Regular use of many drugs may lead to dependence and the many problems that can be associated with it – see Chapter A2, page 41.

Taking large doses of stimulant drugs can cause serious and sometimes life-threatening problems, especially if users already have heart or blood pressure problems. Smoking drugs can lead to breathing and respiratory problems. Regularly snorting of drugs can damage the nasal passages. And getting heavily into drugs can lead to serious dietary problems, disturbance of sleep patterns and generally people not caring well for themselves. Although few young people inject drugs, those that do so can cause great damage to their bodies through infections and abscesses and are in serious danger of contracting HIV and hepatitis if they share injecting equipment with other users.

Lack of co-ordination, slower reaction times and increased impulsivity, while under the influence of drugs, may all increase the risk of serious accidents, especially if young people are driving, operating machinery or using drugs in dangerous environments. Drug-related violence, crime and debt are possible, especially among those who binge or are dependent on drugs, including alcohol.

While drug use is unlikely to be the cause of mental health problems for people who have not previously experienced them, in some cases it may make existing conditions worse. There has been much recent debate, and exaggeration, about the impact of cannabis use on young people's mental health and this is dealt with in some detail in the section on the drug in Part D.

Young people may become paranoid and very anxious and scared while on drugs. Some get into conflicts in their relationships, especially with their family, friends and partners through their drug use. Many may have unsafe sex while under the influence of drugs, be it legal or illegal substances, and do not use condoms. They, and especially young women, may also be more likely to be victims of non-consensual sex. A recent internet survey of young people who used drugs found that one in five had been 'taken advantage of sexually' after they had been drinking alcohol or taking other drugs (Global Drug Survey 2013).

For young people drug use may lead to problems with attendance and performance at school, college or work. Some may be excluded from school or college, or sacked from work, because of their involvement with drugs. Regular drug use can also lead to lack of motivation to do anything constructive with their life, being convicted of a drug offence and receiving a criminal record, social exclusion and isolation.

Professor David Nutt has worked with a number of drug experts to develop a comprehensive list of 16 criteria of potential harm resulting from drug use. In his book, *Drugs Without the Hot Air* (Nutt 2012), he divides these into nine possible harms to individual users and seven types of harms to people other than the user. The harms to individual users were:

- *Drug-specific mortality*: Death by poisoning.

- *Drug-related mortality*: Death from chronic illness caused by drug taking, such as cancers, and associated behaviours and activities such as injecting.

- *Drug-specific harm*: Physical damage short of death such as alcohol-related cirrhosis, tobacco-related emphysema, damage to the nose from snorting cocaine or to the bladder from ketamine use.

- *Drug-related harm*: Damage from drug-related activities and behaviours short of death such as viruses and infections and accidents, including road traffic accidents, while under the influence.

- *Dependence*: How easy it is to become dependent on different drugs.

- *Drug-specific impairment of mental functioning*: How far intoxification impairs judgement that may lead to risky behaviours such as unsafe sex or drink/drug driving.

- *Drug-related impairment of mental functioning*: This refers to psychological effects that may continue once the drug has left the bloodstream and the user is no longer intoxicated. This might include psychotic symptoms, depression, anxiety, memory loss, aggression, etc.

- *Loss of tangibles*: Losing your job, income, possessions or home.

- *Loss of relationships*: Losing friends and/or family.

The harms to other people – social harms – were:

- *Injury*: Injuring others while being intoxicated such as road traffic accidents or domestic violence.

- *Crime*: Acquisitive crime to fund a drug habit and crime committed when judgement is impaired while under the influence.

- *Economic cost*: Lost workdays, police time spent dealing with associated crime and cost to health and support services.

- *Impact on family life*: Including negative effect on family relationships and functioning and child neglect.

- *International damage*: Caused by the drugs trade, War on Drugs, brutality of drug barons and carbon emissions and other environmental effects.

- *Environmental damage*: Pollution through drug production, dereliction and lack of safety in areas where drugs are used and sold.

- *Decline in reputation of the community*: Where particular social groups become stigmatized and certain neighbourhoods become no-go areas.

Looked at in this way drug use can seem very dangerous and scary. But how dangerous are the various drugs that young people may use, how likely is drug use to lead to harm and what factors contribute to harm?

HOW HARMFUL ARE DIFFERENT DRUGS?

David Nutt's panel of drug experts went on to rate 20 drugs according to these 16 criteria using official government statistics and a range of research data. While acknowledging that rating different drugs for some criteria, and particularly social criteria, was far from objective the panel went on to develop a system whereby each of the drugs could be given a total harm score out of 100.

Overall the most harmful drug was alcohol with a score of 72 out of 100, followed by heroin with 55, crack 54, cocaine 27, tobacco 26, amphetamines 23, cannabis 20, GHB 19, ketamine and tranquillizers 15, methadone 14, mephedrone 13, solvents 11, steroids 10, ecstasy and khat 9, LSD 7 and magic mushrooms 6.

It is instructive that this list of relative harm bears little relation to whether or not drugs are illegal in the UK and the way they are ranked as Class A, B and C under the Misuse of Drugs Act. The six most harmful include four Class A drugs but also include alcohol and tobacco. Ecstasy, LSD and magic mushrooms, all currently Class A drugs, come out as some of the least harmful drugs in relative terms.

With regard to young people's drug use a case might be made that the harms to individuals are more important than the social harms to others. Again the findings of David Nutt and his colleagues are instructive. Regarding harm to individuals, on a score out of 100, crack scored highest with 80 and heroin scored 73. Alcohol scored 56, more than cocaine powder on 43, amphetamine on 41 and GHB on 38. Tobacco also scored 38, ahead of ketamine, mephedrone and cannabis which all scored between 25 and 30 out of 100 and ecstasy, LSD and magic mushrooms which scored under 20 out of 100.

However, while different substances may have greater or less potential to cause harm there are always other factors involved, especially the amount of drug taken, the frequency and method of use and also the characteristics of the person who is using and the situation they are in.

THE IMPORTANCE OF DRUG FACTORS, SET AND SETTING

We often talk of drugs having particular effects and harming individual users, their families and local communities and even wider society as though inanimate substances can, in themselves, do things to us. It may be more accurate to say that rather than drugs doing things to people, people do things with drugs that can have consequences – both potentially positive and negative – for them and other people. In this sense it is important to realize that the person and the situation they are in are central to understanding the potential effects and harms of drug use.

Of course the effects and possible harms of drug use will depend on the specific substances people use but we also know that the same drug, and even the same amount of the same drug, can have very different effects and dangers depending on the person taking it and their situation. In other words it is important to understand that, as well as the drug used, personal and environmental factors are very important in determining the effects and dangers of drug use.

Following the work of Zinberg (1984), we can call these inter-related aspects drug (factors), set and setting. *Drug factors* are everything to do with the substance used. *Set* refers to the person who is using drugs. *Setting* refers to the environment in which the person is using drugs. I will look at each of these in turn, starting with the *drug factors*.

Drug factors

Obviously the type of drug used and its particular properties will partly determine the effects and dangers of drug use.

Stimulant drugs such as amphetamines, cocaine, crack, khat and mephedrone speed up heart and pulse rate and tend to make people more alert and energetic. They can lead to people experiencing anxiety, panic attacks and possibly paranoia, especially if taken in large quantities. They may also be particularly dangerous to people who already have high blood pressure or heart problems. In some cases this may include caffeine.

Depressant drugs like alcohol, GHB, heroin, ketamine and tranquillizers have a sedating effect and slow down heart and pulse rate. Smaller doses tend to relax people but larger doses have a numbing effect that impairs co-ordination, meaning they may contribute to accidents from people falling over or being unable to operate machinery safely or drive properly. These depressant, downer drugs can also lead to a fatal overdose if consumed in large quantities, especially if taken in combination, while other drugs such as cannabis cannot directly kill, no matter how much is taken.

Hallucinogenic drugs such as LSD and magic mushrooms, and to some extent ecstasy, ketamine and stronger forms or doses of cannabis, can change the way the senses work to the extent that the world is perceived very differently. People may have very disturbing experiences using them and become paranoid. Their behaviour may become very erratic and possibly dangerous, especially if they are already feeling anxious and unstable.

Some drugs may be easier to become dependent on than others. The depressant group of drugs, including alcohol, are more likely to lead to a definite physical dependence if enough is taken over a period of time. Body chemistry changes so that more of the drug is needed to get an effect – increased tolerance – and physical withdrawal symptoms, similar to a strong dose of flu and tremors, are experienced if drug use is stopped.

With stimulant drugs people may also become dependent with regular use but the withdrawal symptoms are likely to be experienced in different ways such as lack of energy, anxiety, restlessness and sleep problems. Certain stimulant drugs (such as cocaine, crack, nicotine and also sometimes mephedrone and some stimulant legal highs) may also be easier to become dependent on because they are relatively short-acting and tend to be 'more-ish', with users often quickly repeating the dose to maintain the effects.

Many people become dependent on caffeine or cigarettes and feel vulnerable and anxious if they cannot use on a regular basis. People who become dependent on cannabis may have similar, but possibly more intense and disturbing, experiences if they try to stop using.

The fact that some drugs are legal to use, and others are not, also affects possible harms. Unlike legal substances, illegal ones, and also legal highs, are not subject to quality control. It is more difficult to know how strong a dose is and whether any other substances, which themselves may be dangerous, are also present. Being involved with illegal drugs is more likely to involve contact with shady characters and other illegal activities. Being found guilty of possessing or supplying illegal drugs may lead to young people getting a criminal record, with the possibility of limited access to jobs and restrictions on international travel as a consequence. They may also receive a hefty fine and could find themselves sent to prison.

How much of a drug is taken, and how often, are also obviously important in determining the effects and dangers of drug use. Many fatalities occur when people overdose because they have taken a large amount of a drug, sometimes without realizing how much they have consumed. This seems to be increasingly a problem with the advent of new drugs and legal highs, where users may not know what the safe dose level is or even which drug they have actually taken.

Illegal drugs and legal highs are commonly bulked with other substances that may be dangerous to take, although stories of drugs being cut with things like rat poison, strychnine and brick dust tend to be untrue. Unless a dealer has a score to settle, it is not in their interests to have customers dropping dead from deliberately contaminated drugs. More often, drugs contain other substances the user is not expecting to be present such as glucose, caffeine, ephedrine or paracetamol.

Many people are also take more than one drug at the same time (including alcohol, prescribed medicines and over-the-counter drugs) and this polydrug use can lead to chemical interactions that are unpredictable and sometimes dangerous. Many fatal overdoses have involved users taking more than one drug, sometimes while being unaware of the likely consequences.

The route of administration – how a drug is taken – is also an important determinant of drug effects and possible harms. Injecting means a drug gets into the bloodstream very quickly. Snorting or inhaling the fumes from a drug also tends to bring on effects quickly. Effects from smoking drugs tend to take longer to arrive. The user may be better able to control how much they take. Swallowing a drug usually means effects are delayed longer but may happen very abruptly, especially if a large amount of drug has been consumed. Snorting may damage the nasal passages, smoking may lead to respiratory problems and injecting is often the most dangerous way to take a drug with the possibility of abscesses, greater risk of overdose because of taking a full dose in one go, and risk of hepatitis and HIV if equipment is shared.

Set

Set refers to the person who is using drugs. Drug use is a very personal and individual experience. The meaning and purpose of using, and the effects and possible harms, vary from person to person. If someone has an existing physical health condition, such as heart disease, high blood pressure or asthma, use of particular drugs may be much more dangerous. If users are feeling unwell or run down at the time of use they may be putting themselves at greater risk. If they are feeling angry, anxious or depressed when they use they are likely to have a very different experience than if they are feeling calm and relaxed. And if people have mental health difficulties, drug use may sometimes help them temporarily feel better but it may also lead to disturbing experiences and exacerbate their problems. How we feel about ourselves, our lives and the world about us impacts on how we use and experience drugs.

Body weight and gender are also important determinants. Heavier people can usually consume a greater quantity of drugs than those of lower body weight without experiencing adverse effects. The different way that fat is distributed in the body means that men can usually metabolize and break down drugs quicker than women of the same body weight.

How long people have been using drugs and whether they are a novice or an experienced, more knowledgeable user are also important in influencing what effects and harms drugs have, as is why they are using drugs, what they want from their use and what they expect to happen. In some cultures, and sub-cultures, certain forms of drug use are acceptable, even expected, but in others are not.

Those young people who feel relatively good about themselves, and their lives, are likely to use drugs in relatively controlled and moderate ways. Those who are experiencing emotional and/or social difficulties may be more likely to use drugs excessively in an attempt to escape such feelings and problems and be more likely to become dependent on drugs. For more information about dependence see Chapter A2.

Setting

Setting refers to the environment in which the person is using drugs. How people experience their use of drugs, and the possible dangers they may face, will vary depending on where they are and what they are doing at the time. Are they using at home, at school or work, in a club or pub, at a festival, in a park or on the streets? Is their use part of a religious or cultural event? Who else, if anyone, is around and what is going on? Are they driving a car, operating machinery, playing sport, involved in outdoor pursuits, in a sexual situation, dancing, going swimming, having a bath or doing nothing much at all? How relaxed, threatening or dangerous is the environment? All these things can have an important bearing on how young people use drugs, the experience they may have and the dangers they may face.

KEEPING DRUG EFFECTS AND HARMS IN PERSPECTIVE

All this means that we need to take care not to exaggerate the harms that can follow from young people using drugs. We need to avoid scaring ourselves and not project our own anxieties on to young people.

To really understand the possible effects and harms of drug use we need to take account of the specific drug, set and setting factors involved for a young person who is using. Guidance about how to do this and make a careful assessment of a young person's drug use, and the possible risks and harms they may face, is given in Chapter B5. Detailed information about the potential effects and harms of particular drugs is given in Part D of this book.

In addition, I want to emphasize that many children and young people face difficulties associated with drug use other than their own. This may include them being concerned about, and sometimes detrimentally affected by, the drug use of their parents, siblings, other family members, partners, friends or school, college or work colleagues. I have discussed this further in Chapter C11.

WHAT DOES THE LAW SAY?

There are many drug laws in the UK and they are sometimes unclear. Recent UK governments have continually changed the law and made more drugs illegal, often without much, if any, parliamentary or public debate, and sometimes against the advice of its own expert panel, The Advisory Council on the Misuse of Drugs.

I have tried my best to provide you with accurate, up-to-date information about UK drug laws but by the time you read this book I am sure that more changes will have been made. For the latest information about UK drug laws I suggest that you try the Release website (www.release.org.uk) and the Frank website (www.talktofrank.com).

However, do be aware that these websites are not necessarily completely up to date. Despite the advent of the 'Information age', unfortunately there is currently no one site on the internet that has detailed, accurate and up-to-date information about all our drug laws.

THE MISUSE OF DRUGS ACT 1971 (MDA)

The MDA is the main law that regulates what are called controlled or illegal drugs. It divides drugs into three classes as follows: Class A drugs are treated by the law as the most dangerous and Class C as the least dangerous.

Class A

These include cocaine and crack (a form of cocaine), dimethyltryptamine (DMT), ecstasy, heroin, LSD, magic mushrooms that contain psilocin, mescaline, methadone, methamphetamine (crystal meth, ice), morphine, NBOMe (N Bomb), opium, pethidine, phencyldine (PCP), paramethoxyamphetamine (PMA), 2CB and any Class B drug which is injected, such as, for example, amphetamines.

Class B

These include amphetamines (not methamphetamine which is Class A), 5 and 6-APB (Benzo Fury), barbiturates, cannabis, codeine, ketamine, mephedrone, methoxetamine (Mexxy, MXE), methylphenidate (Ritalin), naphyrone (NRG1), various synthetic cannabinoids (cannabis-like drugs such as Annihilation, Black Mamba and Spice) and 2-DPMP (Ivory Wave).

Class C

These include anabolic steroids, benzylpiperazine (BZP), buprenorphine (Subutex), phenazepam (Bonsai, Supersleep), GHB, GBL, khat, Tramadol painkillers and minor tranquillizers (Ativan, Rohypnol, Temazepam, Valium, etc.).

When new drugs become available

As new substances, especially 'legal highs', have become more widely available, the current government has made more drugs illegal under the MDA. In 2011 it also introduced 'Temporary Class Drug Orders' (TCDOs) to make it easier to ban new drugs that were causing concern. Under these orders drugs are banned for one year while the health risks are considered. During this period a drug that is subject to a TCDO is illegal to supply but not illegal for individuals to be in possession of, if small quantities are involved. However, the police can confiscate the drug from individuals and dispose of it. So far the government has issued TCDOs for methoxetamine (Mexxy, MXE), 5 and 6-APB (Benzo Fury) and NBOMe (N Bomb), with more legal highs probably to follow. These three drugs have all now become controlled drugs under the MDA. The government is currently exploring alternative ways of controlling legal highs. See the information about legal highs in Part D of this book for more about their legal status.

Offences under the Misuse of Drugs Act

These can include:

- *Possession of a controlled drug*: This means being in possession of a relatively small quantity of a drug for personal use. It can also involve past possession (if someone admits to it or there is evidence), joint possession (involving more than one person) and attempted possession (where someone obtains what they believe to be is a controlled drug and it turns out to be something else).

- *Possession with intent to supply another person*: This involves being in possession of a larger quantity of a drug and/or having the drug divided up in ways that indicate it is going to be supplied to other people. Any evidence of intending to supply, such as having scales or paraphernalia used to package up drugs, may be taken into account.

- *Supplying a controlled drug by either giving or selling drugs to someone else*: This can include supplying friends at no profit. It is also an offence to offer to supply another person with a controlled drug or to be involved in supply, such as acting as a lookout.

- *Production, cultivation or manufacture of controlled drugs*: Most commonly this involves growing cannabis plants.

- *Import or export of controlled drugs.*

- *Allowing premises you own, occupy or manage to be knowingly used* by other people for the production, use or supply of controlled drugs – see pages 78–80 for details.

There is no offence of actually using controlled drugs. It is also not illegal to be under the influence of controlled drugs, unless in charge of a motor vehicle and being unfit to drive.

SPECIAL CASES

The law is complicated by the fact that some drugs are treated in an exceptional way under the Misuse of Drugs Act (MDA).

Certain controlled drugs, such as amphetamines, barbiturates, cocaine, heroin, methadone, morphine, pethidine, Ritalin and minor tranquillizers can be prescribed by doctors in some circumstances. People who have a legitimate doctor's prescription for such drugs are not committing a possession offence, although it is illegal for them to supply their prescribed drugs to another person. Drugs such as cannabis, ecstasy and LSD have a history of being used medically but UK law does not currently allow doctors to prescribe them for their patients. One current exception is Sativex, a cannabis-based nasal spray that is sometimes prescribed for people who have multiple sclerosis.

Anabolic steroids are controlled under the MDA as Class C drugs but the possession offence is waived in most cases, so that it is not usually illegal to be in possession of them without a prescription. It is illegal to sell or supply them to another person. People can also be prosecuted for possession with intent to supply if they have large quantities of steroids without a prescription for them. Most steroids that are used in the UK are manufactured abroad. It is legal for people to go abroad and bring back steroids to the UK but it is illegal to import them into the UK through mail order or courier services. This means that, in most cases, steroids are illegal to purchase over the internet or from mail order companies based abroad.

Minor tranquillizers (benzodiazepines) are controlled under the MDA as Class C drugs. Until recently, possession was not an arrestable offence if people did not have a prescription, except in the case of Rohypnol or temazepam tranquillizers. More recent changes in the law mean that the police can now arrest people who are in possession of any minor tranquillizer and cannot show a legitimate prescription for them.

PENALTIES

Unlawful supply, possession with the intent to supply, production and import or export are defined in law as trafficking offences.

Maximum sentences under the Misuse of Drugs Act (MDA) are as follows:

	Possession	*Trafficking*
Class A drug	7 years and/or fine	Life and/or fine
Class B drug	5 years and/or fine	14 years and/or fine
Class C drug	2 years and/or fine	5 years and/or fine

In most cases people found guilty of offences under the MDA receive sentences which are less than these maximums. As well as the type and amount of drug and nature of the offence, any past offences and any mitigating circumstances will be taken into account when courts decide about the exact sentence to be given.

Buying a relatively small quantity of drugs, especially Class A drugs, for friends could result in a custodial sentence, but this would be rare. A person who tells the police, 'I was just getting some drugs for my friends' may end up in more trouble than if they say that the drugs were for their own use. However, new sentencing guidelines have now made a distinction between social dealers who supply drugs to friends and family and those who deal for profit. The latter are more likely to receive stiffer sentences, including prison.

In recent years about a quarter of the people convicted of supplying Class A drugs have been aged 21 years old or under and there has been an increase in the number of teenage dealers who have been convicted and received prison sentences. Young people who are involved in drug dealing, especially involving heroin and crack in poorer areas, are likely to be at bottom of the chain and operating as direct suppliers and lookouts but may still be prosecuted for supplying drugs. In fact they are more likely to be caught and prosecuted than their bosses who trade in large quantities of controlled drugs.

The maximum penalties under the MDA apply to Crown courts where offenders are tried by a jury and sentenced by a judge.

Less serious cases are usually tried at a magistrates' court, or for children and young people aged 10 to 17 years old, a specialist youth court, where there is no jury and magistrates preside.

Maximum penalties at a magistrates' court are:

- Six months' imprisonment and/or a £5000 fine for possession of a Class A drug or trafficking in a Class A or B drug.

- Three months' imprisonment and/or a £2500 fine for possession of a Class B drug or trafficking in a Class C drug.

- Three months' imprisonment and/or a £1000 fine for possession of a Class C drug.

Maximum penalties at a youth court for 10–17-year-olds are a £1000 fine, for which parents are responsible in cases involving young people aged under 16 years old. Those aged 12 to 17 years can be subject to a Detention and Training Order of up to 24 months' duration, with the first half spent in custody and the second half spent in the community.

These maximum detention periods can be extended for serious offences, when magistrates' or youth courts refer cases on to Crown courts.

Between 2007/8 and 2011/12 drug offences in the UK fell for Class A drugs from 20,103 to 15,585 for possession, from 8104 to 6959 for possession with intent to supply and from 10,428 to 7253 for supply (Hansard 2012). In contrast, over the same period the number of offences for Class B drugs rose significantly from 28,300 to 47,979 for possession, from 3828 to 7286 for possession with intent to supply and from 1225 to 2212 for supply. This reflected cannabis being reclassified from a Class C to Class B drug in 2009. The number of offences for Class C drugs was much smaller and remained at similar levels over the five-year period.

CANNABIS POSSESSION

Special procedures are adopted by the police in relation to cannabis possession offences. For first offences involving adults (aged 18 years old and over) and small quantities, police will confiscate the cannabis, issue a Cannabis Warning and record the incident. If it is a second offence the police will usually issue a Penalty Notice for Disorder and a £80 on-the-spot fine. Being subject to a Cannabis Warning, or paying the fine for a Penalty Notice, does not result in a criminal record. For a third, or subsequent, possession offence the police will usually arrest the offender and prosecution will follow. If the offender is found guilty a fine and criminal record will result. If there are aggravating factors, such as possession near a school or playground, the responses can be escalated, even for a first offence.

For a first possession offence involving young people aged under 18 years old, the police will confiscate the cannabis and issue a reprimand. A second possession offence will usually result in the young person receiving a final warning and being referred to a youth offending team for assessment. To receive a final warning the young person has to admit that they are guilty of the offence. Reprimands and final warnings are not regarded as convictions and do not constitute having a criminal record. However, they are recorded by the police and may influence the response of the police and courts to any future offending. A third or subsequent possession offence involving a young person aged under 18 years old will usually result in arrest and prosecution, as with adults.

Supply of cannabis, or possession with intent to supply, will usually result in arrest and prosecution, whatever the offender's age.

It is not illegal to be in possession of cannabis seeds but it is illegal to grow cannabis plants from them, even if the plants are not harvested or used.

DRUG TESTING ON ARREST

The police have powers to drug test people over the age of 18 years old who are arrested for 'trigger' offences. These offences include possession or supply of Class A drugs such as heroin, cocaine or crack as well as theft, robbery, burglary or fraud which is thought by the police to be for funding use of these drugs. The test is usually made using an oral swab and carried out by a police officer or staff employed by the police. If people test positively for Class A drugs they have to attend an assessment and participate in drug treatment. Failure to agree to be tested or to attend assessment or treatment sessions are, in themselves, offences.

THE MEDICINES ACT 1968

This Act regulates the production and distribution of medicinal products. It divides medicines into three categories. The most restricted – prescription only – can only be sold or supplied by a pharmacist on receipt of a doctor's prescription. The least restricted – general sales list – can be sold without a prescription by any shop. The remaining drugs – pharmacy medicines – can be sold without a prescription but only by a pharmacist.

Various medicines, including those available over-the-counter without a prescription, are sometimes used recreationally, or in a dependent way. Many can be dangerous to use, especially in high doses or when used in combination with other drugs. Examples include tranquillizers and anti-depressants such as Prozac, codeine-based painkillers and cough syrups, Viagra, stimulants such as Ritalin and cold remedies and decongestants that contain ephedrine and diet and travel sickness pills. Also, paracetamol has been implicated in many accidental fatal overdoses and suicides, including among young people.

DRUGS THAT ARE NOT COVERED UNDER THE MISUSE OF DRUGS ACT

Alcohol is not illegal for anyone aged over 5 years old to consume away from licensed premises. It is an offence for a vendor to knowingly sell it to an under-18-year-old. A 14-year-old can go into a pub alone but not consume alcohol. A 16-year-old can buy and consume beer, port, cider or perry, but not spirits, in a pub if having a meal in an area set aside for that purpose. In some areas there are by-laws restricting drinking of alcohol on the streets at any age. Police also have powers to confiscate alcohol from under-18s who drink in public places.

Poppers (mainly butyl nitrite) are not covered by the Misuse of Drugs Act and are not illegal to possess or buy. They are often sold in joke and sex shops and also in some pubs, clubs, tobacconists and sometimes music or clothes shops used by young people.

Solvents (glues, gases and aerosols) and also nitrous oxide are not illegal to possess, use or buy at any age. In England and Wales it is an offence for someone to sell such products to an under-18-year-old if they know they are to be used for intoxicating purposes. It is also illegal for shopkeepers to sell lighter fuel (butane) to under-18s, whether or not they know it will be used for intoxicating purposes.

It is not an offence for people of any age to smoke cigarettes or use other tobacco products. It is an offence for a vendor to sell tobacco products to someone they know to be under 18 years old. Since July 2007 smoking in public places has been banned in the UK.

DRUG USE AND DRIVING

It is an offence to be in charge of a motor vehicle while unfit to drive through drinking of alcohol or having taken drugs. As with alcohol, the police can detain people they suspect of being unfit to drive through the influence of drugs. They can take blood, urine and/or saliva to test for drugs. If the test is positive and a conviction follows, offenders will be banned from driving for a minimum of one year, subject to a fine of up to £5000 and be deemed to have a criminal record.

The UK Government is about to change the law with regard to driving while under the influence of drugs and set specified limits for various substances in a similar way to what is done for alcohol. For certain controlled drugs, including cannabis, cocaine, ecstasy, heroin, ketamine, LSD and methamphetamine, it will be illegal to drive with relatively small amounts present in the body. It will also be an offence to drive with larger, and again specified, amounts of medically prescribed drugs in the body, including methadone, morphine and various minor tranquillizers, such as diazepam and temazepam.

LEGAL OBLIGATIONS OF PROFESSIONALS AND PARENTS

If professionals or parents know that young people have been using or supplying illegal drugs they do not have a legal obligation to inform the police or anyone else, even though this may sometimes be the best course of action. This is also the case for housing and hostel workers and pub and club owners and managers. Guidance for professionals about confidentiality and informing parents if their children are involved with drugs is given in Chapter B6 of this book.

Many organizations have their own drug policies and guidelines and these may contractually oblige professionals to pass on information to certain people, especially line managers. Failure of staff to follow the policy or guidelines of their own organization is unlikely to result in legal proceedings but could result in disciplinary action being taken against the member of staff.

If professionals or parents find, or are voluntarily given, what they believe to be a controlled drug there are two possible, legally permissible, courses of action open to them. One option is to call the police and hand the drug over to them. Be aware that the police may ask you who you think the drug belongs to. Alternatively, it is legally acceptable to dispose of the drug without informing the police. This might be done by flushing the substance down the toilet or disposing of it in a bin. Whatever action is chosen it should be done soon. It is not a good idea to have a controlled drug in your possession for too long because the police could surmise that the drug was for your own use. For professionals, wherever possible, a colleague should be present to witness what has been done so there can be no insinuation that the drug was kept for personal use by staff. A written report should be made of what has been done and a line manager should be informed about the situation.

Under Section 8 of the Misuse of Drugs Act it is an offence for a person to *knowingly* allow premises they have responsibilities for, or own, to be used by any other person for:

- the administration or use of a controlled drug which is unlawful to be in possession of (however, this is currently unclear in UK law – see below)

- the supply of any controlled drug

- the production or cultivation of controlled drugs, such as growing cannabis plants.

Professionals can be prosecuted if they knowingly allow any of these things to occur on work premises. Premises can include normal work buildings, buildings used during day-trips or residentials and possibly adjacent grounds such as front steps, yards and outbuildings. Similar legal arrangements apply to parents if they knowingly allow their children, or other people, to use, supply or produce controlled drugs in their own home.

It is not a legal offence for professionals or parents to allow the use or supply of drugs that are not controlled under the Misuse of Drugs Act. This includes alcohol, cigarettes, legal highs, poppers and solvents. However, the policy and practice of most organizations that work with young people bans all, or most, of these drugs, being allowed on their premises.

The law requires that if people become aware of the use, supply or production of controlled drugs on premises they have responsibilities for or own, they must take reasonable action to prevent these activities continuing. For professionals this may include young people being requested to leave the premises or being asked to voluntarily hand over the drugs. Where young people refuse to comply with such requests the police may have to be called. In such situations it is advisable for staff to inform their line manager as soon as possible and to make a written report of what has happened and what actions have been taken. Parents also have to be seen to take reasonable action to stop their children's involvement with controlled drugs at home if they want to avoid breaking the law themselves. 'Reasonable action' for parents is not clearly defined in law but they must, at minimum, be seen to condemn and challenge such behaviours by their children.

Section 8 has been a contentious part of the Misuse of Drugs Act and aspects of it are still to be clarified. Strictly speaking it is not an offence for professionals and parents to knowingly allow other people to use most controlled drugs on premises they have responsibility for or own. The letter of the law only applies to the smoking of cannabis or opium, but not the use of other controlled drugs. Some parents have been prosecuted for allowing their children to smoke cannabis in their own home. However, this aspect of the law is unclear and it is probably best for professionals and parents to assume that it may apply to the use of all controlled drugs. It should be emphasized that under Section 8 there is no confusion about the supply and production of controlled drugs. They definitely apply to all controlled drugs.

There is also confusion about what 'reasonable action' is when trying to curtail other people using, producing or selling drugs. A case involving an agency for homeless people led to the manager and another member of staff being prosecuted for allowing the premises to be used for supply of heroin and given stiff prison sentences. On appeal they were released from prison early, even though their convictions were upheld. The jury in the case was not convinced that the staff had taken sufficient action to curtail heroin dealing. The prosecution argued that the staff should have informed the police about the clients who were suspected of involvement and given them access to confidential client information. The staff felt that this would have been a breach of client confidentiality and resulted in many of their most vulnerable clients deserting the project. The case shocked staff that work in hostels, with the homeless and heroin users, and owners and managers of clubs where illegal drugs are commonly used and supplied. Calls for the government to clarify professional obligations regarding premises have so far not been acted upon.

The police have rights of entry to search work and private premises if professionals or parents give consent or if they have a search warrant. It is also legally permissible for police to enter and search without a warrant or consent in certain situations. These include, to arrest someone for an offence, to avoid a breach of peace, to catch someone who is illegally at large or if the premises are in the immediate vicinity of an incident of supply of controlled drugs.

Professionals and parents are usually under no legal obligation to answer police questions or to give information about young people to the police. Exceptions, which are very rare, include where a court instructs an agency to release information about a client or where the Prevention of Terrorism Act applies. Most professionals are under a contractual, rather than strictly legal, obligation to pass on information about child abuse or neglect to their designated safeguarding member of staff, social services or the police.

It is an offence for anyone to obstruct the police by, for example, hiding controlled drugs or by helping a young person to avoid arrest. If asked to give a statement to the police, professionals and parents can request that this is done at the police station rather than on work premises, their own home or at the scene of an incident.

LEGAL RIGHTS OF YOUNG PEOPLE

The police have powers to stop and search people and to arrest them where there is evidence that they may be in possession of controlled drugs, supplying them or where they are in the vicinity of an incident involving drug supply. They can arrest people who are suspected of driving while under the influence of various drugs, not just alcohol, and those who are acting is disorderly ways or causing a breach of the peace. The police are also allowed to confiscate alcohol from under-18s who drink in public places.

It is important that professionals and parents are aware of the legal rights of young people in such situations. Young people also need to know their rights.

Children can be convicted of a criminal offence from the age of 10 years old in England and Wales and from 12 years old in Scotland. These are among the lowest ages of criminal responsibility in Europe.

Many of the legal rights that apply to young people are the same as those for adults but some special protective measures apply to those aged under 17 years old.

Legal rights for young people include:

- If questioned by the police people have the right to remain silent and not answer questions. However, doing so could count against them later. If people have a defence against a charge, and do not tell the police, this can harm their defence once they get to court.

- Before stopping and/or searching people for drugs the police should have reasonable grounds for suspecting them of an offence. People's age, gender, appearance, clothing or skin colour are not reasonable grounds.

- If the police wish to search someone they should explain why they want to do so. Strip searches (removing more than just outer clothing) and intimate searches (examining within body orifices) should only be carried out by an officer of the same sex in a private place where no one else can see.

- If people are arrested, the police should only use reasonable force and should explain to the person why they are being arrested.

- The police should not take people to a police station unless they have arrested them first or the person agrees to go voluntarily. However, heavily intoxicated people can be taken to a police station as a place of safety.

- If a young person aged under 17 years old (or under 16 years old in Scotland) is arrested, the police should contact their parents or guardians to tell them why the young person has been arrested and where they are being held. If people of any age are arrested they have the right to ask the police to notify a friend or relative. These rights can be waived if the case involves a serious offence (such as supply of a controlled drug) or where a senior police officer has reasonable grounds for believing that informing a particular adult will lead to interference with evidence, physical injury to other people, alert other people who are suspected of being involved but have not yet been arrested, or will hinder recovery of proceeds resulting from drug offences.

- The police should not question, take a statement from or strip or intimately search a young person aged under 17 years old (under 16 years old in Scotland) without their parent, guardian or another appropriate adult being present. An appropriate adult can be a professional who works with the young person.

- If people are arrested and held at a police station or interviewed by the police they are entitled to legal advice. If they know a solicitor they can ask to phone them. If they do not know a solicitor they can request one through the Criminal Defence Solicitor Call Centre, which provides free legal advice. If people have asked for legal advice, in most cases the police should not question them further until they have spoken to a solicitor.

- Reprimands, warnings and cautions imply an admission of guilt and are entered on a record that can be held against offenders if they break the law again. Young people should only accept a reprimand, warning or caution if they are admitting that they are guilty of an offence.

- If people are arrested and taken to a police station they can be held for up to 24 hours (36 hours for serious offences such as supplying controlled drugs) without being charged. After that time the police should either let the person go, charge them with an offence or have a court warrant to hold the person for longer without charging them. During the time of detention a police inspector should periodically review how the enquiry is proceeding and whether or not the person should be released or held longer.

Please be aware that police powers and legal rights can change over time. For up-to-date and more detailed information access the Release website (www.release.org.uk) or that of the Children's Legal Centre (www.childrenslegalcentre.com).

THE IMPLICATIONS FOR YOUNG PEOPLE OF HAVING A CRIMINAL RECORD

Each year thousands of young people are convicted of drug offences under the Misuse of Drugs Act or other legislation and receive a criminal record. Depending on their age, the nature of their offence and their circumstances, they may receive non-custodial sentences, be fined or sent to prison. There can be serious implications for them.

Previous convictions can be cited in subsequent criminal proceedings leading to stiffer sentences if people reoffend. A conviction can also severely restrict employment and travel opportunities. A spell in prison for a young person may become an apprenticeship in crime and increase the likelihood of further criminal behaviour on their release.

There are government guidelines regarding when a criminal conviction becomes 'spent' after a period of non-offending and rehabilitation. For up-to-date information about this go to the website www.justice.gov.uk and search for 'rehabilitation of offenders'.

Employment applications commonly ask applicants whether they have a criminal conviction or record. A conviction for a drug offence does not always bar an offender from employment within a particular field. An employer can exercise their discretion but in a period of high youth unemployment and where there are often many applicants for each post, a conviction will often go against a young person who applies for a job.

Applicants who do not disclose unspent convictions, when asked to do so, can be dismissed on the grounds of having deceived the employer and can even possibly be prosecuted.

When applying for jobs in certain occupations, and in particular public offices, people are expected to declare their convictions, even if they are spent. These include:

- jobs involving working with under-18-year-olds such as teachers, school caretakers, youth and social workers, nursery workers and childminders

- jobs that involve working with vulnerable adults, such as the elderly, disabled, people who have mental health problems, the chronically sick and people who are experiencing alcohol and/or drug problems

- jobs in the health field (doctors, dentists, nurses, pharmacists, etc.) and criminal justice system (police, lawyers, probation, youth offending, traffic wardens, etc.)

- senior managers in banking and financial services

- jobs where national security may be an issue, including the armed forces.

Having a criminal record may also restrict travel abroad. Many countries, including the US, enquire about criminal records when people apply for travel visas or work permits.

CAN YOU TELL IF YOUNG PEOPLE ARE USING DRUGS?

You will know that a young person is using drugs if they themselves tell you or if you see them actually using drugs. You may suspect that they are using if they behave in an intoxicated manner, you find what you think is a drug or paraphernalia used to take drugs, or another person, who you consider to be a reliable source of information, tells you so and can provide some sort of evidence.

But can you really be sure if a young person is using drugs? This chapter examines three possibilities – spotting signs and symptoms of drug use, drug testing and the use of sniffer dogs – and asks how effective these methods are and what issues their use involves.

SPOTTING SIGNS AND SYMPTOMS

In many cases it will be obvious if a young person is actually under the influence of drugs. They may be behaving in an uncharacteristic way and, depending on which drug(s) they have taken, how much they have consumed and how they have been feeling, they may be unsteady on their feet, sleepy, very energetic and talkative, disturbed or paranoid or even very quiet. However, it is important not to jump to conclusions. In some instances these sorts of behaviours could be due to a reaction to legitimate use of medicines or a response to an illness, or a traumatic experience, that does not involve drugs.

Some publications list possible signs and symptoms of drug use on the assumption that, even if you never see young people using drugs or intoxicated, you may be able to spot whether they are using by observing changes in their behaviour and appearance. The lists often include things like:

- marked and uncharacteristic changes in mood

- aggressive or apathetic behaviour

- anxiety or paranoia

- truancy from, and lateness for, school, college or work

- deterioration of personal hygiene and dress

- sudden and marked changes in interests and friends

- suspicious behaviour, vagueness and lying

- lack of motivation and purpose

- excessive borrowing of money

- stealing or selling of property

- use of drug slang

- deterioration in performance and concentration

- poor appetite, weight loss or eating binges

- regularly complaining of not feeling well and lacking energy

- spending more time away from home

- excessive sleeping and disturbed sleep patterns.

There are problems with using such lists. In most cases, unless you are with a young person while they are using or clearly intoxicated, there may well be no signs and symptoms that they have been using. Many of the listed signs and symptoms may be relatively normal aspects of a young person's behaviour and development, at least for a period of time, especially if they are rebellious. Any of the items on the list could be happening for reasons that have nothing to do with actually using drugs.

A danger of using lists of signs and symptoms is that we can jump to the wrong conclusion, start accusing young people and end up being in conflict with them. It may also mean we fail to find out about or understand the real difficulties that young people may be experiencing. If you notice marked changes in a young person's appearance or behaviour, and are concerned about them, the best approach is to talk to them sensitively and check out how they are feeling and what is going on for them. It may take time to gain their trust and for them to actually tell us what has been going on.

Another possibility is that you find what you think looks like a drug such as a powder, some pills or capsules, a herbal mix, a small block or a bottle or ampoule of liquid. You might have some idea about what it could be but, depending on how much you know and what drugs you have seen before, both in the real world or in pictorial form, you may not have much idea at all.

It is important to appreciate that the same drug can often come in various forms and that different drugs can have very similar appearance, especially when they are in powder, pill or capsule form. This has been compounded in recent years by the introduction of so many new drugs, particularly legal highs, that may look like illegal drugs but may be something else. Indeed, many regular drug users have ended up buying powders, pills, capsules or smoking mixtures which are not the drug they thought they were purchasing, have had other drugs mixed in as well or no active drug in them at all. These days it is easy to find photos of different drugs on the internet (see the websites listed at the end of the book) but this does not necessarily mean you will be able to identify exactly which drug you have found. You may not even be sure that a substance you have found is a drug at all or that tablets or capsules are not medicines that have a legitimate use. The only sure way of knowing what you have found may be to have it analysed in a laboratory but that is costly and takes time.

It can sometimes be difficult to identify cannabis because of the many different forms it can take. The most commonly used form is herbal and consists of crushed leaves, but also sometimes buds, stalks and seeds of the plant. The colour may vary between green, brown and almost yellow. The texture may vary depending on the exact type of cannabis and where and how it has been grown. Some may be softer and fluffier, some may be more stringy, Some may be sticky, some very dry. Even regular users have sometimes been caught out and bought mixtures of dried-out everyday herbs with no cannabis in at all. In addition there are also some legal high smoking mixtures that look like herbal cannabis but have no cannabis in. Cannabis also comes in resin form as a block that may look a bit like a stock cube and can vary in size and shape but also in colour from light golden, to greenish brown, dark brown to black. It can feel light and be dry and crumbly but it can also feel heavy and be oily and hard. And occasionally cannabis can come as a dark oil, a bit like a runny treacle. In recent years a wide range of smokable legal highs have also become available which may look like cannabis but are actually made from other substances. So cannabis can come in many forms, some of which could be mistaken for other things and some substances that look like cannabis may not be cannabis at all.

Another possibility is that you find drug paraphernalia: items that are used to prepare and consume drugs. These could include many different objects depending on which drug is being used and how. For example, to make and smoke a cannabis joint, people may use tobacco (or not), cigarette papers (often three of normal size stuck together or one of the larger-sized papers), small pieces of card to make a 'roach' or filter, a cigarette lighter and/or matches. Many young people use pipes or 'bongs' to smoke cannabis, rather than joints, and there are many different types. Some are commercially purchased but some are home-made. Some involve drawing cannabis smoke through water, to cool it, but many do not. Some have filtering systems but others do not. And the cannabis itself might be kept in a special tin, little self-sealing plastic bags (like money bags used in banks), cellophane, cling film, tin foil and so on and so forth.

Smoking heroin involves heating the powder on tin foil or a metal spoon from below, using a cigarette lighter or matches, until it vaporizes and gives off fumes that are then drawn up into the mouth and/or nose through a straw or rolled up paper tube. Snorting cocaine often involves chopping the powder with a razor blade, sometimes on a small mirror so it is visible and none is lost, and using a straw or small roll of paper to draw the powder up the nose. There is often a lot of paraphernalia involved in injecting drugs, other than the actual needle and syringe. Heroin injectors often use water, lemon juice, citric acid, cigarette filters or pieces of tampon (to trap any chalk or other impurities in the solution), a rubber tube or strap as a tourniquet (to prepare veins for injecting), metal bottle tops and spoons (in which to 'cook' up the mixture) and so on.

Supply of drugs may be indicated by finding a number of small packages with drugs in, potential packaging material such as cellophane, cling film or tin foil, small packets such as bank coin bags and weighing scales.

Finding the objects described above, and especially more than one item together, could be indicative of involvement with drugs, but many of the items also have everyday uses that have nothing to do with drugs.

As well as actually finding what you think may be drugs or drug paraphernalia, you may sometimes be tempted to search young people, their clothes, bags, bedrooms and/or storage lockers. This is rarely a good idea, especially if attempted without a young person's consent or knowledge, because it is likely to lead to a breakdown of trust.

If someone else has told you that your child, or a young person you work with, is involved with drugs decide whether you think they, and what they have said, is reliable. They may have got it wrong. They could even be exercising a grudge or trying to divert attention away from themselves and attempting to put the blame on someone else.

For practical guidance about what you can do if you suspect that a young person is using drugs see Chapter C1.

DRUG TESTING

Drug testing has become much more widespread in recent years particularly in industry for jobs such as airline pilots and train drivers, in some public services such as the armed forces and police, and in professional sports. Drivers who are suspected of being under the influence of drugs are often tested and prisons often drug-test inmates.

In the UK, people aged over 17 years old can also be made to take a drug test if they have committed offences that are thought to be associated with funding a drug habit – see 'Drug testing on arrest' on page 76 for details. Some schools, and particularly private ones, have also introduced random drug testing of their students and a number of companies now advertise drug testing kits that parents can buy to use on their children at home.

There are different sorts of drug tests that can be carried out. They include blood, urine, breath, saliva, sweat and hair tests. Many tests, including those that can be commercially purchased and used at home, give almost instant results and can show whether a drug has been used, and if so, which drug or drugs. Some tests are for specific drugs but some test for a number of drugs from one sample. More accurate verification, and more detailed results about the amount of drug in the body and timing of use, usually requires blood or urine samples to be sent to laboratories for analysis.

There are a lot of practical and ethical problems involved in drug testing young people. The results of drug tests, and especially those used at home that do not involve further laboratory analysis, are not always accurate. There can be false positives (a positive result where there has been no drug use) and false negatives (a negative result where there has been drug use). Certain medicines, such as some cold remedies and cough syrups, can produce a positive result. Hair tests can give positive results from traces of drugs that are smoked. This can include situations where drugs such as cannabis, crack and heroin have been absorbed through smoke in the air where other people have been using drugs but the person being tested has not.

Detection periods vary with different drugs, the amount of drug consumed and the type of test. Hair tests, possibly the least accurate of all test methods, can often detect drug use for up to 90 days after use. For other types of tests the detection period for alcohol is about six to 24 hours after use and for many illegal drugs is about two to four days after use. However, the nature of cannabis, and the way the body metabolizes it, means detection periods are longer and may be two to seven days after use and up to one month for someone who has been using heavily for a long period of time. In some institutions that have used random drug testing, such as prisons, this may have led to people switching from cannabis to use of more dangerous drugs, such as heroin, in an attempt to avoid detection.

Some companies target advertisements at parents and suggest they should buy test kits to use on their children. This has included hair tests where parents take a lock of their child's hair, possibly while they are asleep. Testing young people for drug use is unlikely to provide information that will be of any use in ensuring their safety. Testing without active consent is likely to destroy trust with young people. The danger is that imposing drug testing on young people is likely to make it more difficult for parents, teachers and other professionals to build open and communicative relationships with them. As found in professional sports, where testing has been forced on people, they have sometimes found ways around being detected, despite their drug use.

SNIFFER DOGS

The police sometimes use sniffer dogs at music events and festivals and at the entrances to some clubs. Some schools have also brought in sniffer dogs in an attempt to detect drugs on site and to deter drug use by students. Headteachers are within their rights to invite the police or private companies to bring sniffer dogs on to school premises.

However, use of sniffer dogs has led to a number of serious concerns. Dogs can pick up traces of certain drugs in the hair and on clothing. They may focus on young people who have not actually used drugs but may have been around other people who have been using, especially smoking drugs like cannabis. Dogs may also sometimes identify students who are taking prescription medicines. There have also been cases reported of dogs focussing on girls who have been menstruating. The use of dogs may also be a very sensitive issue for some Muslims and Buddhists who regard dogs as unclean. And, in schools, dogs might also pick out members of staff, as well as students.

As with drug testing, use of sniffer dogs raises issues of privacy and civil liberties. It may create mistrust and damage relationships between staff and students. Some people suggest that there are unresolved legal issues about whether or not parents have to give consent for their children to be subjected to sniffer dogs and also drug testing. The issues arise of what the school will do if particular students or parents do not consent and what action they will take if dogs identify specific young people or staff as possibly having used drugs.

According to the Association of Chief Police Officers in their 2006 guidance document for police working with schools and colleges, extreme caution should be exercised when considering the use of drugs (sniffer) dogs without a warrant and 'drugs dogs should not be used for searches where there is no evidence for the presence of drugs on school premises. Demonstration and educational visits should not be used as a covert detection exercise' (ACPO Association of Chief Police Officers of England, Wales and Northern Ireland 2006, p.48). I could not put it better myself.

B

BE PREPARED

BE INFORMED – LEARN FACTS, NOT MYTHS

You don't have to have an encyclopaedic knowledge of drugs to understand young people's drug use. In fact, it is probably more important to be able to empathize with young people and take account of what life is like for them and how they may be feeling. However, it is important to not fall for the many myths and stereotypes that surround discussion of drug use, particularly in the media.

In my experience adults often know more about drugs than they realize. Sometimes, and particularly when faced with a difficult situation where a young person is involved with certain drugs, parents and professionals tend to panic, fear the worst and forget that they do know something about drugs. Young people, especially teenagers who may be new to drug use, sometimes know less about drugs than they realize. They think that because they know a bit of street language they are knowledgeable.

This chapter contains a couple of simple exercises that you can use to further your understanding of drug use and also suggests ways you might avoid drug mythologies and develop your knowledge of the facts and reality of drug use. Chapter B8 discusses ways you can help young people to become better educated about drugs.

DRUG KNOWLEDGE QUIZ
Decide whether the following statements are TRUE or FALSE. Then look at the answers at the end of the chapter.

1. Alcohol use has been increasing among young people over the last few years.

2. Amphetamines are stimulant drugs that give an energy boost.

3. It is illegal for shopkeepers to sell caffeine tablets to under-18s.

4. Some forms of cannabis are much stronger than others.

5. Cocaine and crack are sedative drugs that relax people and slow them down.

6. Ecstasy always comes in the form of tablets or capsules.

7. It is particularly dangerous to take GHB while drinking alcohol.

8. Heroin use mostly occurs in poor, deprived areas.

9. Ketamine is used as an anaesthetic for operating on children and animals.

10. Khat is commonly used in African-Caribbean communities.

11. Legal highs tend to be a lot safer to use than illegal drugs.

12. In recent years there has been an increase in the use of LSD.

13. A magic mushroom trip usually lasts for up to one hour.

14. Mephedrone is usually smoked.

15. Nitrous oxide has been used for pleasure in the UK for over 200 years.

16. Poppers give people a short-lived rush of energy.

17. It is illegal for shopkeepers to sell butane gas to under-18s.

18. A lot of body-builders inject anabolic steroids.

19. In recent years cigarette smoking has fallen among adults, but not young people.

20. Many adults are dependent on medically prescribed tranquillizers.

You might also ask a friend, work colleague or your partner to try the quiz and discuss their answers with you. If appropriate, try the quiz with your own child and/or a young person you work with.

DRUG MYTHS EXERCISE
Look through the list of drug myth statements below. They are all untrue yet commonly held views about drugs.

General myths about drug use

- Drug use only happens in poor, inner city areas.

- It is easy to recognize different drugs by looking at them.

- All illegal drugs are imported from abroad.

- Illegal drug use is always very expensive.

- Most young people obtain illegal drugs from professional dealers.

- Many young people are forced into drug use by dealers.

Myths about people who use drugs

- Many people go through life without using drugs.

- Children and elderly people do not use drugs.

- Most young people use illegal drugs.

- Most drug use involves young people rather than adults.

- Drug use among young people is a new phenomenon.

- There is something wrong with people who use drugs.

- Many young people are pressurized into using drugs.

- Very few adults used illegal drugs when they were young.

- Middle class people do not use illegal drugs.

- It is easy to recognize if someone uses illegal drugs.

- Addiction is inbred and caused by genetic make-up.

Myths about the effects and harms of drug use

- Most young people who use illegal drugs come to serious harm.

- The same drug has the same effect on different people.

- Drug use is always very dangerous.

- Illegal drugs are always more dangerous to use than alcohol.

- One try of some drugs and you become hooked.

- Once you are addicted to drugs you are addicted for life.

- Cannabis is a very dangerous drug.

- Cannabis is a completely safe drug.

- Legal highs are not as dangerous as illegal drugs.

- Most drugs users commit crimes to get money to buy drugs.

- Many drugs users are very violent when high on drugs.

Myths about what we can do about drug use

- Tougher laws will stop young people using drugs.

- Shocking young people about the dangers of drugs will stop them using.

- Giving young people the facts about drugs will stop them using.

- Telling young people to 'say no' to drugs will stop them using.

- Talking to young children about drugs will encourage them to use.

- If we give young people more to do they will not use drugs.

- There is no help for people who have drug problems.

Questions to consider

1. Which, if any, of the myths do you tend to think are true?

2. What evidence is there for the statements being true or not?

3. Which of the myths might professionals, parents and young people believe to be true? Why might this be the case?

4. What other commonly held drug myths are there, other than those listed above?

If you still think some of the statements are true read more of this book, especially the chapters in Part A. Also have a look at some of the books by other authors that I recommend at the end of the book.

You might also discuss the myths with a friend, work colleague, partner or other family members. If appropriate, talk to your own child and/or a young person you work with about the myths.

LEARNING MORE

There are a number of ways that you can learn more about drug use. Part A of this book covers a wide range of drug issues. Chapter B8 focusses on drug education and its impact on young people. Part D gives information about a wide range of different drugs. You might also read some of the drug books I have recommended and look at some of the websites listed in Part E.

You may be able to attend drug training courses in your locality. Contact your local drug service – see Part E for information about how to find them – and see what training is available. Both professionals and parents may be able to attend training courses and local agencies may be able to put on training sessions for particular professional and/or community groups when requested.

If you want to learn more about drugs talk with other people; friends, work colleagues, your partner and other family members, but most of all, young people themselves. We can learn a lot from talking to each other.

DRUGS KNOWLEDGE QUIZ ANSWERS

The answers are as follows:

- TRUE: 2, 4, 7, 8, 9, 15, 16, 17, 18, 20.

- FALSE: 1, 3, 5, 6, 10, 11, 12, 13, 14, 19.

How well did you do? Have a look at Part D of this book, which provides information about all the drugs in the quiz, to find out more.

BE AWARE OF YOUR OWN USE OF DRUGS, YOUR FEELINGS AND ATTITUDES

We all have a lifetime career of using mood-altering substances, be they medicines, legal or illegal drugs. We have also all directly experienced, or heard about, situations where other people have been using drugs, be it our own parents, siblings, partners, children, other family members, friends, neighbours or work colleagues. Some of these experiences may have been pleasurable and even great fun. However, some may have been very distressing and stressful for us.

Our own use of drugs, that of others close to us and the way drug use is reported in the media all have a big bearing on our feelings and attitudes. They also affect how we respond to situations in which young people are involved with drugs. We do not all share the same feelings and views towards drugs. Professionals or parents will often respond to similar situations where young people are involved with drugs in very different ways. We always bring ourselves, and our past experiences and our particular feelings and views, with us. It is important to stop and reflect on where we are coming from and why.

This chapter contains two exercises to help you reflect on your own drug career and your feelings and attitudes towards drug use and the ways these could affect how you might respond to young people who are involved with drugs. It also suggests ways you might explore your feelings and attitudes in more depth.

YOUR DRUG CAREER

Look through the following list of drugs.

Alcohol, amphetamine, anabolic steroids, caffeine, cannabis, cocaine, crack, ecstasy, GHB/GBL, heroin (and other opiates and opioids), ketamine, legal highs, LSD, magic mushrooms, mephedrone, nitrous oxide, poppers, solvents, tobacco, tranquillizers and other medicines that have mood-altering affects such as anti-depressants.

Consider the questions below and write down your answers on a piece of paper.

1. Which of these drugs have you ever used?

2. What other mood-altering drugs have you tried that are not on the list?

3. Which did you try when you were young and why did you try them?

4. Have you enjoyed using them? If so, in what ways?

5. Have you had any difficult or unpleasant experiences with any of them? If so, in what ways?

6. Which of the drugs have you used in recent years and what has your experience of using them been like?

7. Which of the drugs have been used by other people you have been close to and how has their use of them affected you?

8. What does all this tell you about yourself, and how may it have influenced your feelings and attitudes towards young people using drugs?

You might also try plotting yourself a 'Drug Career Graph'. Take a sheet of A4 paper and work on it in landscape format to make a graph. Use the X axis (along the bottom) for your age from birth (0 years) to your current age. Use the Y axis (vertical) to start with 'not used at all' and to move up to 'moderate, occasional use', 'more regular use' and at the top 'everyday use'.

Choose a few drugs that you have used to focus on. Alcohol, particular medicines, tobacco and caffeine are good ones to start with. Plot on the graph how your use of these drugs has changed over the years. Then think about what was going on in your life at various times, especially when you have used particular drugs a lot or very little, and what this might tell you about your drug use and your motivations to use in particular ways.

If you have used any illegal, or other socially unacceptable, drugs you might also include these on your graph. If relevant, you can also pinpoint times in your life when the drug use of other people around you has impacted, positively or negatively, on you.

Finally reflect on what your own drug career might tell you about young people's use of drugs, their motivations to use, how drug use may change over time and your own attitudes to young people's drug use.

It can be very useful to do this exercise with your partner, a family member, a trusted friend or work colleague. You can help each other to learn from your own, and each other's experiences. If they are willing, and feel it is appropriate to share information about their own drug careers, parents may find this a useful activity to conduct and discuss with their own children.

Professionals should think carefully before trying the exercise with young people they work with because it may be inappropriate to discuss their own drug use with their young clients and this could be frowned upon by managers and possibly put them at risk. For more advice about telling young people about your own drug use see page 112.

YOUR FEELINGS AND ATTITUDES ABOUT DRUG USE

Try this exercise to help you think more about your feelings and attitudes towards drugs.

Do you AGREE or DISAGREE with the following ten statements? Record your answers and then look at the scoring system below.

1. I am a drug user.

2. A lot of young people are forced or tricked into using drugs when they don't want to.

3. Alcohol causes a lot more problems than illegal drugs.

4. There should be tougher penalties for using and supplying illegal drugs.

5. Most young people who use drugs have a good time and come to little harm.

6. We should shock young people about the terrible effects drugs can have.

7. Most drug problems involve adults rather than young people.

8. There is something wrong with young people who use illegal drugs.

9. People have always used drugs and they always will.

10. We should work towards a drugs-free society.

For your answer to each statement score yourself either +1 point or −1 point, as shown below, and then add up your total score. For example, if you score six +1s and four −1s your total score will be +2.

Statement	1	2	3	4	5	6	7	8	9	10
AGREE	+1	-1	+1	-1	+1	-1	+1	-1	+1	-1
DISAGREE	-1	+1	-1	+1	-1	+1	-1	+1	-1	+1

Place your total score on the continuum below.

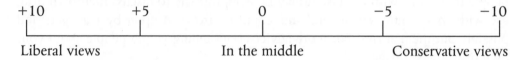

Liberal views   In the middle   Conservative views

Think about where you are on the continuum and why, and what this says about your views about drugs and their use by young people.

Try the exercise with friends, work colleagues, your partner and other family members. How do their feelings and attitudes compare to your own? If you disagree with them, why is this so? And, ask your child or young people you work with to do the exercise with you. How in, or out, of tune are your views, compared with these young people and why?

EXPLORING YOUR FEELINGS AND ATTITUDES FURTHER
As with learning more about drugs, there are a number of ways that you can explore your feelings and attitudes about drug use in more depth. Part A of this book covers a wide range of drug issues and may challenge your attitudes. You might also read some of the drug books I have recommended and look at some of the websites listed in Part E.

You may be able to attend drug training courses in your locality. Contact your local drug service – see Part E for information about how to find them – and see what is available. Both professionals and parents may be able to attend training courses and local agencies may put on training sessions for particular professional and/or community groups when requested.

Most of all talk and compare views with other people; friends, work colleagues, your partner and other family members and especially young people. We can learn a lot from them.

BE REALISTIC ABOUT
WHAT CAN HAPPEN

When we first discover that our own child, or a young person we work with, is involved with drugs, especially illegal drugs, we are often shocked and want them to stop using straight away. We may feel that their drug use is a dangerous and possibly very serious problem, but they may not. Even if they agree that they have been getting into difficulties we often want them to change their behaviour and put matters 'right' without delay. In such situations we may become angry with them, shout, try to force them to agree to what we want or threaten them with punishments or loss of privileges.

Such actions on our part are unlikely to have a positive effect on young people and may even make matters worse. They may say they agree to our demands only for us later to discover that they have not carried them out. They are unlikely to change their behaviour unless they really want to.

Further consideration about what we mean by a drug problem is given at the start of Chapter B5 of this book. Drug rules, and sanctions for breaking them, are dealt with in Chapter B7.

At this point I want to emphasize that we cannot expect young people to make big changes in their behaviour straight away. We need to be realistic. This means we will need to be patient, understand that behaviour change can be difficult and take time and focus on, and appreciate, small changes that may fall short of what we would ideally wish for.

BEHAVIOUR CHANGE

The cycle of change model is one of the most influential pieces of thinking about behaviour change, particularly in the field of drug treatment for people who have become dependent, and is useful in helping us to think about what may be involved if young people are going to change their drug-using behaviours.

The model developed from the simple observation that people cannot simply be divided into two categories: those who are motivated to change and those who are not. It takes account of the fact that people may have a range of feelings at different times about their risk taking and that it may take more than one attempt for them to change their behaviours.

The model is drawn up in various ways but is normally seen as having six stages. These are:

1. *Pre-contemplation*, where the person has not (yet) started to think that there are problems associated with their behaviour and may not even be experiencing any.

2. *Contemplation*, where the person has started to acknowledge that they are experiencing problems, is thinking about the possibility of changing their behaviour but has not yet made up their mind to do so. They may feel it is too difficult to change or see little point in changing.

3. *Preparation*, where the person is becoming ready to change their behaviour, has started making plans to change but has not yet started to do so. They may have set a date to change, been working on strategies to handle anticipated problematic situations and formulated some plans to help get them through the most difficult parts.

4. *Action*, where the person has actually made the change. They may be preoccupied with the changes they are making and find it hard to think about anything else. There may also be issues to do with cravings and a yearning for their old behaviours and lifestyle.

5. *Maintenance*, where the change is now integrated into the person's everyday life so that they can start to think about other things, as well as drugs. For some people the change may become long term or permanent. For others, lapse or relapse may still be an issue and they may find temptations are still there, especially when life is going either very well or very badly for them.

6. *Lapse or relapse*, where people fall back into their old patterns of behaviour and will have to try again if they are to succeed in making more permanent changes.

This model is useful to help us understand that changing established behaviours can be very difficult and take time. It also shows that people may need to go through a number of stages before they are in a position to actually change their behaviour.

At the same time, research has found that the cycle of change model is not always a good predictor of the way people actually go about making changes in their drug-using behaviour in the real world. The six stages are not always separate and discrete and some can overlap. People do not always go through all of the stages or in the order given in the model.

In addition, we know that the possibility of someone making changes in their life is not just down to them as individuals and their own motivation and actions. It is also often about their circumstances and what is happening around them. Changes in their environment, which facilitate them to change their behaviour, may occur because of the actions of other people and sometimes through sheer chance. As has often been said about, and by, people who are dependent on drugs, 'Getting off drugs is relatively easy, but staying off is much more difficult', especially when they return to the same situation they were previously in that contributed to them being dependent in the first place. Having opportunities, resources and support to make a new and meaningful life for oneself are often crucial.

If young people are going to alter their drug-using behaviour don't expect the changes they make to be big or carried out quickly. You will need to be patient. Agreeing sensible targets, and a timescale in which they might be achieved, can be useful but it is important that proposed changes are manageable and realistic. Take it step-by-step and acknowledge and praise any positive changes they make, even if they fall short of what you would ideally want of them.

To help you to understand the processes and issues that may be involved in changing behaviour, try this exercise. You may like to write down your answers on paper.

1. Think about a particular difficult change you have made in your life. What was it?

2. How did you feel when faced with the situation?

3. What made it difficult for you to make the change?

4. What helped you to make the change?

5. How did the way you went about making the change compare to the cycle of change model?

6. What bearing might this all have on you understanding young people changing their drug-using behaviours?

7. What might you need to do, or avoid doing, to help your child, or a young person you work with, to change their drug-using behaviours, rather than hinder them doing so?

You might try this exercise with your partner, another family member, a friend or work colleague and compare notes. In some situations it may also be appropriate to discuss it with your own child or young people you work with.

THE IMPORTANCE OF HARM REDUCTION

If a young person will not stop taking drugs and is likely to continue using, we may feel that we are powerless to do anything constructive. If we are not careful we may end up in constant conflict with them. This does not have to be so. We can help to ensure their safety and keep them healthy by focussing on harm reduction.

Harm reduction is based on the fact that there are safer and more dangerous ways of taking drugs. It involves being able to develop good and honest communication with young people and checking that they are using drugs as safely as possible. This means exploring and discussing the 'drug, set and setting' factors outlined in Chapter A5 with them. These can include which drug or drugs they use, how much they use and how often, the method of drug use, whether they use more than one drug at the same time, when they use, where and who with and what they are doing at the time.

Common harm reduction guidelines include:

- Find out as much as you can about the drug or drugs you are taking.

- If you are unsure how strong the drug is, or you are new to using particular drugs, start with a small amount and do not take any more for at least an hour.

- Don't take too much or use too often.

- Reduce the amount of drug you take and/or how often you take it.

- Avoid using during the day.

- Don't use last thing at night or first thing in the morning.

- Have drug-free days.

- Don't use more than one drug at the same time, including use with alcohol and medicines.

- Don't use if you feel unwell or are very anxious or troubled.

- Take special care if you have an existing health problem, such as with your blood pressure or heart or if you have asthma or epilepsy.

- Don't use alone or in dangerous places where accidents are more likely.

- Don't drive, operate machinery or go swimming while under the influence.

- Try to ensure you have a good diet, sensible sleep patterns and do regular exercise.

- Avoid friends and acquaintances who use drugs and places where they are used.

- Don't become isolated. Get out, meet friends and engage in non-drug activities.

- Ensure that you have condoms, or another form of contraception, with you if you think you may have sex.

- Don't inject, but if you do, don't share injecting equipment with other people and use a needle exchange service.

- Keep a diary of your use and feelings and monitor how you are doing.

- If you are having difficulties, talk to other people about it and, if necessary, seek specialist help.

You can find more detailed harm reduction advice for specific drugs in Part D of this book.

Some people see harm reduction as encouraging or condoning drug use. However, rather than this being the case, harm reduction can literally be a life saver if a young person continues to use drugs, as many parents and professionals have discovered. It can also be a key to enable us to develop trust and communication with a young person who is using drugs, rather than having no productive discussion with them at all.

HOW REALISTIC ARE YOU?

You may not be able to make a young person behave in ways you want them to. But if you cannot change them, you can change the ways you behave in order to improve your relationship with them. The next chapter, B4, looks at how we can communicate effectively with young people, but first it may help you to reflect on how realistic you are.

Try this exercise:

1. On a continuum of 1 = very patient, up to 10 = very impatient, how patient would you say you were?

2. On a continuum of 1 = very calm, up to 10 = very anxious, how calm or anxious would you be if you found out that your child or a young person you work with was involved with drugs in a way that concerned you?

3. What could you do to make yourself more patient and less anxious?

4. On a continuum of 1 = very unhappy, up to 10 = very happy, how happy do you feel about using a harm reduction approach with your child, or a young person you work with, when discussing their drug use with them? Why is this so?

5. What could you do to feel more comfortable about using a harm reduction approach with them?

You might try this exercise with your partner, another family member, a friend or work colleague and compare notes. In some situations it may also be appropriate to discuss it with your own child or young people you work with.

KNOW HOW TO LISTEN AND RELATE TO YOUNG PEOPLE

It can be difficult for us to listen and relate to young people in many situations. It can be particularly difficult when it comes to their involvement with drugs. We may be unsure whether or not they are involved and, if they are, to what extent. We may be shocked by what they are doing and feel angry with them and upset. The danger is that we will rush in and give them a real 'talking to' and they will either say very little or get into an argument with us.

I am well aware of these pitfalls from my many years of being a father and as counsellor in the drugs field. It is not easy to develop an open, trusting relationship with a young person when it comes to drugs. However, if we want to know and understand what is really going on, and ensure the safety of our children and the young people we work with, we need to first look at ourselves and be aware of how our own behaviours might facilitate and hinder the way we communicate.

This chapter focusses on ways of communicating effectively with young people but before doing so I explore how we can better understand young people by putting ourselves in their shoes.

PUT YOURSELF IN THEIR SHOES

I am 60 years old and I am glad that I am not a young person living in this country today. Life for young people is a lot more difficult and stressful than when I was young. Individualism and privatization have triumphed over community values. Consumerism and economic aspiration are rife, as is intense competition and the cult of celebrity. The advent of the internet and social networking may have resulted in some benefits but has also made young people more image conscious and vulnerable to social pressures and self-doubt.

There is a lot more pressure on young people to succeed in life but, at the same time, we are in a deep economic recession where poverty and inequality is increasing in the UK and elsewhere and unemployment, especially youth unemployment, has risen dramatically. Traditional pathways to adulthood, through regular and secure employment and housing, have been disappearing for both the working class and middle class, especially for young men. Increasing numbers of young people are having to delay becoming independent adults and rely on their parents to provide housing and money, if they have it, well into their 20s. Many of our young people are living in environments that are increasingly insecure with no sense that things will change for the better in the future There is very little discussion of the bigger picture and the possibility of working together to make the world a better place for everyone in which to live.

All this has had, and will continue to have, a strong bearing on the ways that young people use drugs, especially the need to 'get out of one's head'.

I have found that, if I am going to relate effectively with young people, I need to keep reminding myself about what their worlds may be like, rather than assuming that life for them is similar to when I was young. I strongly recommend that you do the same.

Below are some important questions for you to think about. You may find it useful to write down your answers on paper and then review what you have written once you have answered all of the questions.

1. What was life like for you as a young person? What were the good things about being young then? What was not so good?

2. What is life like today for your child and/or the young people you work with? How does it compare to the life you had when you were young? In what ways might life be better for them and in what ways might it be more difficult?

3. What particular pressures and difficulties do young people, and particularly your own children and/or young people you work with, face today?

4. How might this contribute to and affect their use of drugs?

5. What, in particular, do they need if they are to have a fulfilling life?

6. What might you be able to do to help them to obtain what they need?

7. In what ways might you act to prevent them from having what they need?

You might discuss these questions with other adults you know such as friends, work colleagues, your partner or other family members. And it will also help you to understand young people if you also discuss these issues with them.

COMMUNICATION SKILLS

In my experience there are a number of golden rules about how best to relate to, and communicate with, young people, especially when it comes to talking with them about their drug use. We can act in ways that facilitate good and open communication with them. I call these helping behaviours. But we can also act in ways that hinder and block good communication with young people. I call these hindering behaviours.

Helping behaviours

Helping behaviours include the following:

- Listen carefully.

- Use open body language.

- Ask open-ended questions.

- Take and allow time.

- Be realistic.

- Take their ideas and feelings seriously.

- Be honest about how you feel and why.

- If you don't know, say so.

- Help them to reach their own decisions.

- Start what you say with 'I', rather than 'you'.

- Show empathy.

- Clarify confidentiality and boundaries.

- Allow silences.

- Be positive.

- Put yourself in their shoes.

- Explore, and take account of, your intuition.

- Help them find their own way forward.

- Check that you understand each other.

- Be aware of, and question, your own judgements.

- Be aware of your own strengths and limitations.

- Refer them on to specialist services, if needed.

- Get support for yourself, if you need it.

Hindering behaviours

Hindering behaviours include the following:

- Shouting.

- Rushing.

- Accusing.

- Assuming.

- Jumping to conclusions.

- Patronizing.

- Threatening.

- Putting them down.

- Talking too much.

- Lecturing and talking at them.

- Interrupting and talking over them.

- Telling them what they should feel.

- Telling them what they must do.

- Asking too many (closed) questions.

- Asking rhetorical questions.

- Asking 'why?' too often.

- Exaggerating dangers.

- Giving inaccurate information.

- Making out you know things when you don't.

- Using jargon.

- Revealing too much personal information about yourself.

- Overuse of street language.

- Making promises you can't keep.

- Overestimating what you can do.

- Underestimating what you can do.

To find out about how you are likely to communicate with young people try this exercise. You will either have to write on this book, photocopy the lists of helping and hindering behaviours or write them down.

1. Have a good look through the two lists.

2. Start with the helping behaviours. Put a tick next to behaviours that you feel you are good at using when talking with young people (your own child and/or young people you work with), especially when it comes to talking with them about their drug use. Put a cross next to those behaviours you feel you are not very good at using.

3. Now focus on the list of hindering behaviours. Put a tick next to those behaviours you feel you tend to not use and are good at avoiding. Then put a cross next to behaviours that you feel you do tend to use when talking with young people.

4. Look through the behaviours in both lists that you have ticked. This should give you a good idea of where you are strong in communication skills. Try to remember to use these skills when talking with young people.

5. Now look at the behaviours that you put a cross against. For the helping behaviours, consider how you can start to use them more when talking with young people. For those hindering behaviours that you have placed a cross against, consider how you can avoid using such behaviours in the future.

6. Monitor your behaviour when talking with young people over the next few weeks, not just when it comes to discussing drugs, but in general. See if you can boost your use of helping behaviours and stop using, or reduce your use of, hindering behaviours.

This is a good exercise to do with other people. You might try it with a friend, work colleague, your partner or another family member and compare notes and support each other to improve your communication skills. You might also ask your own child, or young people you work with, for some feedback about how they experience your ways of communicating.

The different types of questions you can ask young people to find out what has been going on for them and how they feel about it are considered in the next chapter. Confidentiality is covered in Chapter B6.

TELLING YOUNG PEOPLE ABOUT YOUR OWN DRUG USE

In some situations you may be tempted to tell a young person about your own use of drugs or they may ask you whether you have used certain drugs, especially illegal drugs. Telling them about your own drug use may be appropriate in some circumstances, especially for parents, but you may need to take care about revealing such information to young people, particularly if you are working with them in a professional capacity. Professionals who do so may be placing themselves at risk if the young person concerned passes such information on to other people.

If a young person asks you whether you have used illegal drugs, and you do not feel it is appropriate to answer them, you have a number of options. You can tell them you do not think it is appropriate to answer and explain why. You could ask them why they want to know and whether they think it would make any difference for them if they knew. You could also lie but this is probably not the best approach. If you are a professional and answer a definite 'no', be aware that this could lead to difficulties for your colleagues because young people may then feel that they can ask the same question of them and expect an honest reply.

KNOW HOW TO ASSESS YOUNG PEOPLE'S INVOLVEMENT WITH DRUGS

When first suspecting or discovering that your own child, or a young person you work with, is involved with drugs you may find yourself panicking and feel the urge to do something about it straight away. The problem with acting immediately is that you will probably not yet have much information about what has been going on, why and what underlying issues the young person concerned may be facing. In particular do be aware of the pitfalls of responding on the basis of suspicion and rumour – see Chapter C1 for more about this. As I have already emphasized earlier in Chapter B3, we need to be patient.

Try to overcome the temptation to act on the basis of insufficient information. If you feel very anxious and are thinking of trying to allay such feelings by 'doing something', try to resist making decisions and acting in ways that could turn out to be ill-advised and counterproductive and that you may later regret. Talk to someone else – your partner, a family member, friend or work colleague – who might help you to calm down and keep matters in perspective. You might also consider contacting a local specialist agency or a national helpline (see Part E) to talk matters through with them and help you maintain a sensible focus.

To find out what has been going on, you will need to talk to the young person(s) concerned. If you are going to do this in an effective way you will need to be able to put yourself in their shoes and do a good job communicating with them, as highlighted in the previous chapter. You may also need to talk to other people, including other young people, to help you get a full picture about what has been happening.

Ideally you will create sufficient time to make a thorough assessment of the situation before deciding what the best course of action may be. This may not be possible in situations where young people require immediate first aid assistance or where they have just been arrested for a drug-related offence, but even here, once you have met immediate needs, you will need time with the young person to find out what has been really happening.

IS DRUG USE A PROBLEM AND, IF SO, WHO FOR?

As I have already described in general terms in Chapter A5, and go on to describe in some detail for various drugs in Part D of this book, drug use can lead to an array of sometimes serious problems for young people. However, it is common for adults to assume that use of certain drugs by young people is a problem in itself, despite the fact that the young people concerned may be thoroughly enjoying their use and not be experiencing any, or many, difficulties with it. Indeed, there is a long history of adults, and particularly the media, governments and an array of professionals exaggerating the dangers of using drugs, to the extent that they have ended up being dishonest with young people and losing their trust and respect. Fear and ignorance are usually the drivers for such behaviours on our part.

On the other hand, young people who are clearly experiencing problems with their drug use may sometimes deny that they are having any difficulties at all. They may not trust us enough to actually tell us what they have been doing, what has happened or how they are feeling. They may fear how we might view them if we knew the truth, how we will respond and what we may do. Some young people may agree with us that they are experiencing problems but not seem at all concerned about it or what might happen to them. We may feel frustrated that they do not 'care', but it is important for us to appreciate that, right now, they are probably feeling too isolated, down on themselves and hopeless to address what they may experience as insurmountable issues.

It is important that we do not assume that all drug use brings difficulties for young people. Where they are clearly experiencing problems we need to get to know exactly what their problems are, who they are a problem for and how the young person feels about them. We also need to remember that, as I have emphasized earlier in Chapter A2, excessive drug use is nearly always symptomatic of significant underlying difficulties that young people face in their lives.

To help you think more about these issues try the exercise below. You could just think about your answers to the questions or, if you wish, you can write down your answers and then review them. However, you will probably find that the exercise is more revealing if you discuss the questions with someone else – your partner, a friend, other family member or work colleague – and compare answers. And, if appropriate, you might consider discussing the questions with your own child or a young person that you work with.

To start the exercise, imagine that your own child, or a young person you work with, became involved with drugs in a way that concerns you.

1. How might you feel? Would you feel angry, scared, anxious, relaxed, worried, concerned, disappointed, sad, disapproving, hurt or have other emotions?

2. How might your feelings affect the way you relate to the young person?

3. Do you have a tendency to exaggerate the risks of drug use when talking with young people? If so, why?

4. When do you believe drug use becomes a problem? Use of which specific drugs, and ways of using them (or supplying them), do you consider are a problem and why?

5. What underlying difficulties might a young person be experiencing in their life that might be contributing to such drug use?

6. What specific problems could such drug use lead to for a young person?

7. What specific problems could such drug use lead to for other people in the young person's life, including yourself?

8. Do you think the young person is likely to see the situation in the same way as you, and other people in their life, do? If not, how are they likely to see the situation?

ASSESSING YOUNG PEOPLE'S INVOLVEMENT WITH DRUGS

Below are some of the questions and issues you will need to explore with a young person if you are going to understand what they have been doing and why, what difficulties they are experiencing, what help they may need and how you may be able to support them. You may also need to talk to other people, including other young people, who can throw light on the situation.

- Which drug(s) is involved?

- Does it involve possession, use and/or supply?

- What amount of drug(s) is being used and/or supplied and how often?

- How does the young person take and/or supply the drug(s)?

- How long has it being going on for?

- What type of drug use is involved? Is it experimental, recreational, binge or dependent?

- Where has it been happening?

- Are they using and/or supplying on their own or are other people involved?

- Have they broken the law or the rules of an organization they are attending?

- How much do they know about drugs?

- How do they feel about themself, their life and their involvement with drugs?

- What are their concerns?

- Do they feel that they have problems with their drug use and, if so, what problems?

- Why might they be using and/or supplying? What do they get out of doing it?

- What risks or problems, if any, are they facing?

- What risks, if any, might other people who are involved or affected, face?

- Are their parents, other family members, friends and/or partner aware of what has been happening and how might they feel about it?

- What other difficulties or issues does the young person face in their life?

- What changes, if any, do they want to make and how realistic are these changes?

- What options do they have and how do they feel about each option?

- What do they expect and want to happen next and how do they feel about it?

- What help or support might they find useful?

- How might you help them?

- Do they need additional specialist help? If so, what sort of help, how do they feel about it and how can you go about supporting them to get that help?

To find out all this information, and to make a careful assessment, you will need to be sensitive about the way you talk, listen and relate to young people and use the communication skills that I have highlighted in Chapter B4.

FINDING OUT BY ASKING QUESTIONS

You will notice that there is a lot to find out. It will take time and patience on your part to begin to understand what is really going on for the young person.

You will also notice that there are a lot of questions. If you are anxious and rush the discussion with the young person, the danger is that they will feel they are being interrogated. If this happens they are unlikely to be communicative. They may respond angrily and defensively, say little and not be honest about what is really happening with them. They may give answers to your questions that are untrue because they want to please you and make you feel less anxious.

Try not to bombard young people with too many questions, too quickly. Avoid asking too many closed questions – those that only have 'yes' or 'no' answers or ask for specific pieces of information. Whenever possible, use open questions – those that invite young people to say, in their own words, what is going on for them and how they feel. In other words encourage them to tell their own story.

Avoid asking them 'why?' too often. This tends to put young people on the spot and can be a very aggressive question to ask. They may not really know why they have done certain things and either say 'I don't know' or make up an answer to please us. And also avoid rhetorical questions such as, 'I suppose you are not bothered about it?' Such questions rarely elicit useful information and tend to drive a wedge between us and young people.

PREPARING YOURSELF TO MAKE AN ASSESSMENT

To help you prepare yourself to make a careful assessment of a young person's drug use try this exercise. Think about your own child or young people you work with.

1. What type of questions – see immediately above – do you tend to ask when trying to find out information about what they have been doing and how they are feeling? Monitor yourself in general discussions you have with your own child or young people you work with over the next few weeks and see if you need to change and improve the ways that you ask them questions.

2. Look back to the list of assessment questions and issues on pages 115–116. Which, if any, of the items covered might you find difficult to discuss with your child or a young person you work with and why?

3. How might you be able to feel more comfortable discussing these matters with them?

4. What might it be important for you to do, and also avoid doing, if you are to make a careful assessment of a young person's drug use?

This is a good exercise to discuss with your partner, another family member, a friend or a work colleague so that you can share your ideas and feelings.

BE CLEAR ABOUT WHO ELSE YOU MIGHT INFORM AND INVOLVE

If your child, or a young person you work with, is involved with drugs you do not have a legal obligation to inform anyone else, including the police. However, you may feel that you need to inform the police in some circumstances and also involve other people to help the young person and to obtain advice and support for yourself.

We know that one of the reasons young people do not seek help when they experience drug-related problems is because they think that what they say will be relayed to other people who they do not want informed about what they have been doing. They may not tell their parents because they fear who else might be told. They may not talk to professionals because they worry that their parents, the police, social services, their school, college or employer could be informed.

If we are to gain the trust of young people it is important that we respect their confidentiality as far as possible. This chapter considers professional guidance about confidentiality and the issues involved for both parents and professionals when deciding who, if anyone, they should tell about young people being involved with drugs. Referring young people to helping services is dealt with in Chapter B10.

ISSUES FOR PARENTS

My work over the years with parents whose children have become involved with drugs, and my own experiences of being a father, have highlighted a number of issues regarding parents informing and involving other people about their children's involvement with drugs.

Some parents do not tell anyone and keep it to themselves. They may feel shame and guilt that their child is involved with drugs and worry that other people will look down on them if they know. They may not even tell their partner, if they have one, and try to keep it from them for fear of how their partner might respond. In some cases I have found that mothers do not tell their male partner because they are worried that he will react in an aggressive way with their child, particularly where it is their son who is using drugs. Conversely, some fathers have not told their female partner, for fear that she will be too upset.

In extreme cases, such as where young people have been using illegal drugs in very chaotic and/or dangerous ways, supplying drugs or stealing to fund drug use or been violent, some parents have been at their wit's end and reported their own children to the police. This has been the only way they have felt they could protect their child's, or their own, safety and force a change in the situation.

I am not recommending such actions to parents because it may lead to their child getting a criminal record and may result in it being even more difficult for the family to develop some trust. One problem about informing the police is having no prior knowledge about how they will respond and the implications for your child. In some instances the police may be sensitive to the issues the family faces, but in other cases may act in a heavy-handed manner. However, I can also understand why some parents report their own children to the police and, in some cases, it may have helped to stop the young person continually placing themselves at serious risk and led to them getting specialist help and making some positive changes in their life.

The difficulty for a parent who does not tell anyone else about their child being involved with drugs is that they may become isolated and have no access to support and advice for themself. If you are in this position and feel that you cannot talk to your partner, another family member or a friend, consider contacting a local specialist agency (see Part E) or a national telephone helpline (see Part E). This can enable you to talk to someone else and obtain information and advice without necessarily giving your own name, or that of your child.

Try this exercise to help you anticipate who you may want or need to talk to. Imagine that your child became involved with drugs in a way that concerned you:

1. How might you feel?

2. Who else might you talk to about the situation and why have you chosen them?

3. What would you want from talking to them?

4. Is there anyone close to you who you would be especially reluctant to talk to? Who and why?

5. How would you feel about contacting a local specialist agency or telephone helpline to talk with them?

6. Would you be likely to tell your child that you had spoken to other people?

7. How might your child feel about you talking about them to other people?

If appropriate, consider discussing these questions with your partner, another family member or a friend.

CONFIDENTIALITY GUIDANCE FOR PROFESSIONALS

While professionals do not have a legal obligation to inform anyone else about young people's involvement with drugs, they are not in a position to offer young people absolute confidentiality. As well as being subject to safeguarding obligations, especially for younger age groups, they are usually subject to the general confidentiality guidelines of the organizations they are employed by. Such guidelines may oblige you to pass on information about young people's involvement with drugs to your line manager and/or the police, and in some instances, to parents, especially where children and younger teenagers are involved. Failure to follow these guidelines is unlikely to result in legal proceedings but could lead to disciplinary action being taken against you.

There is no specific law for professionals regarding confidentiality and young people. However, people aged over the age of 16 years old are usually regarded as having a right to confidentiality in all situations where their actions do not put themselves, or other people, in immediate and serious danger.

When working with young people aged under 16 years old you should take full account of the Fraser Guidelines – sometimes also called the Gillick ruling. These were issued in 1985, by Lord Fraser and other Law Lords, to give guidance to doctors and health professionals about providing contraceptive advice and services to young people aged under 16 years of age. However, they have since come into more general use to guide professionals in work with young people around all sorts of issues, including drug use.

The Fraser Guidelines state that services and advice can be offered in confidence to young people who are aged under 16 years old provided that the following criteria are met:

- The young person understands the service and advice that is being given.

- The young person cannot be persuaded to inform or seek support from their parents.

- The young person is likely to begin, or to continue with, risky behaviours.

- The young person's physical and mental health are likely to suffer unless they receive services or advice.

- It is in the young person's best interests to receive services or advice without parental consent.

Whatever the age of the young people you work with, offering a good degree of confidentiality, and clarifying with them where the boundaries lie, are crucial to building trusting relationships. In my experience, professionals often explain confidentiality to their young clients in ways that are not easily understood by them. Giving examples of when confidentiality will be respected, and when not, often works better than using what might be termed 'counselling jargon'.

It is important to avoid gossiping about a young person to other staff members or to other young people, and to only share information with a third party on a strict need to know basis. Informed consent to pass on information should always be sought from young people, other than in exceptional circumstances, such as where their actions or behaviour presents an immediate and serious risk to their own, or other people's, safety.

Take care not to encourage young people to disclose information 'in confidence' that you may have to pass on at a later stage. Whenever possible, clearly explain the boundaries of confidentiality to young people *before* they make detailed personal disclosures to you.

In reality few young people who are experiencing significant drug-related problems, expect absolute confidentiality from professionals. Even when they initially ask for absolute confidentiality they can often be persuaded that information should be passed on to another staff member, a parent or a helping agency if they realize that doing so will clearly help them.

Key factors in deciding about whether to break confidentiality against a young person's wishes are their age, circumstances and maturity. In other words, are they competent to make their own decisions? If a young person is clearly competent to make their own decisions then breaking confidentiality against their expressed wish should only be considered where failure to do so places them, or other people, at risk of significant and immediate harm.

If you are thinking about breaking a young person's confidences consider the following questions before doing so:

- Why am I thinking of breaking confidentiality?

- How serious is the situation?

- How old and mature is the young person? How competent are they to make their own decisions?

- What immediate and significant risk does the young person, or other people, face?

- Does anyone else already know about the situation?

- Who might information be passed to and what might they be told?

- How might informing the third party reduce the risks involved to the young person or other people?

- Can the young person be persuaded to be involved in informing the third party?

- What significant harm, to the young person or other people, could result from NOT breaking their confidence?

- What implications – both positive and negative – could breaking confidentiality have?

If, after considering these questions, you are clear that someone else should be informed explain this to the young person. Wherever possible, encourage the young person to be involved in informing the third party.

If you decide that confidentiality should not be broken, make a written record of your decision and why you have made it. Also consider discussing the situation with your line manager, without necessarily naming the young person who is involved.

In some situations you may feel that you need to share information about a young person with other team members, your line manager or staff from another agency. However, in such cases do not discuss and name a young person, particularly against their expressed wishes, unless there are clear grounds for doing so. Where a young person needs to be named and discussed with other professionals or in supervision, the young person should be informed about this.

The legal obligations that you have regarding young people using or supplying drugs on your work premises are explained in Chapter A6. While there is no legal obligation to inform the police about such situations, you may feel that this is necessary especially if young people supply controlled drugs on work premises, steal to fund drug use or behave violently. However, some organizations, such as certain schools, have sometimes been too quick to call the police where young people have been involved with drugs in less extreme ways. If professionals feel that their own safety, or the safety of other staff or young people they work with, is being put at serious risk, they should have no hesitation about calling for police assistance.

PROFESSIONALS INFORMING PARENTS

Wherever appropriate, and especially with younger age groups, professionals who work with young people should be proactive in involving parents and encourage them to talk and listen to their children. However, as I have previously explained, there is no general legal duty for you to inform parents if their children are involved with drugs or experience drug-related problems. This includes cases involving young people aged under 16 years old.

In some situations you may feel that it is in the best interest of a young person that their parents are informed and involved. This may include cases involving young people aged under 16 years old and also older ones, particularly if they are immature or especially vulnerable, or it is clear that they are placing themselves, or other people, at immediate and serious risk. Even in these instances, you will need to be reasonably sure that the parents will be supportive to their child. Wherever possible, involve the young person in the decision making process and encourage them to talk with their parents. If appropriate, you can offer to be with young people, and to support them, when they speak to their parents.

In some circumstances it is definitely ill-advised to inform parents. Such situations include cases where abuse or neglect by parents is suspected or known, where they might respond by physically harming their child or throw them out of the family home. It is also not a good idea to inform parents when the home environment is significantly contributing to the young person's problems or it is clear that the parents will not be supportive to their child. Depending on the age and circumstances of the young person, you may need to consider safeguarding issues and seek additional support for them, possibly without their parent's consent. If this is decided upon, make a written record of your decision and why it was taken and involve your line manager.

If you do discuss a young person with their parents I recommend the following:

- Consider involving the young person in the discussion and, if necessary, support them to talk with their parents.

- Appreciate that parents may be alarmed about their child's involvement with drugs. Help them to remain calm and to keep matters in perspective.

- Avoid informing parents in ways that are likely to increase their anxieties or cause further problems in the family.

- Encourage parents to be positive about their child and what can be done.

- Appreciate that some parents may have different views to yours about what is acceptable behaviour for a young person.

- Listen to parents and their concerns and try to put yourself in their shoes.

- Provide information about support and relevant services that young people and parents can access.

- If appropriate, develop an action plan with parents so you can work in partnership with them to help the young person.

ISSUES FOR PROFESSIONALS

Try this exercise to help you develop a clear understanding of confidentiality and informing other people. Work through the following questions:

1. In your general work with young people:

   - what difficulties, if any, arise over confidentiality?

   - how do you go about explaining confidentiality to them?

   - do you need to change the way you manage confidentiality and, if so, how?

2. What are the confidentiality guidelines of the organization that you work for regarding informing other people about a young person's involvement with drugs?

3. How do the guidelines compare to the advice given in this chapter? Do they need changing and, if so, in what ways?

4. If they do need changing, how can you go about persuading your colleagues to make such changes?

5. What is the current policy or practice regarding informing the police about young people's involvement with drugs? Does it need changing and, if so, in what ways?

6. What is the current policy and practice about informing parents about their child's involvement with drugs? Does it need changing and, if so, in what ways?

Although you may benefit from doing this exercise by yourself, it can also be used to discuss these confidentiality issues with your work colleagues and with the young people you work with.

B7

NEGOTIATE SENSIBLE
DRUG RULES

Young people need to know what is expected of them when it comes to their drug use. Schools, colleges and universities, youth clubs and projects, housing projects, hostels, pubs and clubs and organizations that employ young people all need clear rules about drug use, supply and being intoxicated on their premises, and need to make sure that young people are aware of these rules. Parents will also benefit from conveying to their children what they consider as acceptable and unacceptable regarding their children's involvement with drugs, especially in their own homes and possibly elsewhere too.

Rules should take account of possible production, possession, use and supply of drugs, as well as young people being under the influence of drugs, on premises.

Drug rules need to be sensible and any sanctions that follow the breaking of rules need to be fair and not disproportionate. Young people are more likely to keep to drug rules if they are realistic and negotiated, rather than just imposed.

NEGOTIATING DRUG RULES WITH YOUR OWN CHILD

If you are going to negotiate drug rules with your child you will need to be realistic about what can be expected of a child of their age, development and circumstances. You will also have to be prepared to compromise, listen to what they have to say and possibly agree to differ about some matters.

Rather than just putting the spotlight on your child's drug use, it makes sense to also put your own drug use on the agenda at the same time. Your child is much more likely to discuss drug rules in an open and sensible way, and agree to rules that apply to their involvement with drugs, if you are prepared to do likewise with regard to your own use of drugs.

The exercise that follows is to help you negotiate drug rules with your child. Be aware that discussing drug rules with them may not be easy, especially if they are using drugs in ways that you disapprove of or you use certain drugs in ways that they are unhappy about. You will need to stay calm and communicate openly with them. If you have not already looked at Chapter B4 about how best to talk and listen to young people, do so before trying this exercise with them. Also bear in mind the legal obligations that you may face regarding your child's possible production, use or supply of controlled drugs in your own home – see 'Legal obligations of professionals and parents' in Chapter A6.

This exercise may work best if you have pens and paper, so that you can both write down key points that arise. Wherever possible try to reach agreement. Where you cannot agree, be prepared to negotiate and, if necessary, agree to disagree.

Discuss the following questions together:

1. Which drugs do each of you currently use and which other drugs, if any, can each of you anticipate using in the near future? This might include legal substances (alcohol, caffeine, cigarettes), illegal drugs, other drugs that are socially unacceptable, legal highs and prescribed and over-the-counter medicines.

2. What arrangements currently operate, or are assumed, for each of you when using the drugs you have identified? Focus on being in possession, using drugs and being under their influence, both at home and elsewhere. As well as which drugs you use, you might consider how much you use, how often, when and where, who with, how you take the drugs and what you do and how you behave while using.

3. How do each of you feel about the current situation for your own, and for each other's, drug use? Focus on the health, safety and welfare of each of you, how your drug use may affect each other and how it may affect other people. Be prepared to really listen to what each other has to say.

4. Which of the existing arrangements do each of you regard as sensible and why?

5. Which arrangements may need changing and what new rules may need introducing? Each of you might consider completely stopping use of certain drugs, changing how much you use, when and where you use, who with, what you do while using and so on. You may also need to consider legal issues, especially for possession and use of drugs in your own home. See Chapter A6.

6. As well as your use of drugs, do you also need to consider issues concerning producing drugs (such as growing cannabis plants), supplying other people and them supplying you? If so, discuss such scenarios in a similar way to questions 1 to 5 above.

7. Summarize the drug rules that you have agreed and any aspects that you could not agree about. If it helps, both write down what you have decided about the rules for your own drug use.

8. Discuss how you can help each other to keep to the agreed rules and what you will each do if you find you are not sticking to them. With the younger age group you may wish to consider sanctions such as being grounded, loss of privileges, paying a fine to a charity or having to carry out additional household tasks. However, don't dodge the issue of what sanctions may apply if you break the rules you have agreed for your own drug use.

9. Set a date in the future to review how well you are both doing.

What can you do if your child refuses to discuss drug rules with you or you find that they will not co-operate with this exercise? You might try another time. You could give them this book to look through and then try again. You could also consider involving another member of your family or someone else that you know your child gets on well with.

NEGOTIATING DRUG RULES AND SANCTIONS FOR ORGANIZATIONS

Production, possession, use or supply of any drugs (other than alcohol on licensed premises, caffeine and legitimate use of medicines) must not be allowed on work premises. Similarly, young people being intoxicated while attending most organizations will not be tolerated. All staff will need to be firm about this and drug rules need to be clearly communicated to young people. There cannot be much negotiation with young people about what these rules are.

However, in cases where the rules are broken any sanctions that follow should be sensible and fair and the way organizations respond is an important area to discuss and negotiate with young people.

There is a long history of some organizations, especially schools, permanently excluding young people if they are found to be involved with drugs, particularly illegal drugs. This has sometimes led to young people who have been experiencing serious underlying social and emotional difficulties being merely treated as disciplinary cases, not being offered any meaningful support and their situation becoming markedly worse. Overly punitive responses can result in already vulnerable young people becoming further labelled, isolated and alienated. Many young people who have been permanently excluded from school for involvement with drugs have ended up being passed from school to school, had their school careers ended and wandered into a life of street crime and escalating drug use. At the time, they may not even be that bothered about what has happened to them and even get a buzz from the attention they receive and the rebel image they have gained. Overly punitive responses can also mean that other young people will become reluctant to approach staff for advice and support if they, or other people they know, are experiencing difficulties with drug use.

Some organizations have operated 'set tariff' sanctions in response to drug incidents so that cases of young people supplying drugs, or using particular illegal drugs, always result in permanent exclusion. This is not good practice. It does not take account of varying circumstances and the particular issues and difficulties that young people may be experiencing. The distinction between possession, use and supply of drugs is not always as clear cut as many people assume. For example, I have been consulted about drug incidents in schools where students have supplied their friends as a favour, and at no profit, and also where they have been bullied and threatened by other students into supplying.

Permanent exclusion from any organizations that cater for young people, not just schools, should be regarded as a last resort when all other options have been exhausted and serious anti-social behaviour persists. A range of sanctions, short of permanent exclusion, are available that may help young people learn from their mistakes and still send out a warning to other young people. These include:

- a verbal or written warning

- removal of certain privileges for a specified period

- agreeing a contract of behaviour that is monitored over a set period

- additional tasks being carried out over a period of time

- detentions, in schools

- short-term exclusion, during which the matter can be properly investigated and discussed.

To develop sensible drug rules and sanctions for the organization that you work for you will need to involve your work colleagues, and especially managers, in the process, as well as the young people you work with. Young people can be consulted through informal one-to-one discussions and/or in small groups. In schools, consultation can be made part of personal, social and health education lessons.

A word of warning about discussing drug rules and sanctions with young people. In my experience they can often suggest very draconian sanctions, even if they use drugs themselves, without much regard for the implications. This may have something to do with the way so much discussion of crime and anti-social behaviour in this country, and especially in the media and from politicians, tends to very simplistic and extreme and take little account of the impact on young people or consider the issues they may be facing. It is important to take time when consulting young people about these matters and to help them appreciate the complexities involved.

To develop sensible drug rules and sanctions for your organization consider the following questions:

1. What are the rules and procedures of your organization regarding young people:

   - being in possession of drugs on the premises?

   - using drugs on the premises?

   - being intoxicated and under the influence of drugs, while on the premises?

   - supplying drugs on the premises?

   - disclosing to staff that they are involved with drugs off the premises?

   - disclosing that other young people are involved with drugs?

   You will need to consider various drugs: illegal/controlled drugs, legal drugs (such as alcohol, caffeine and cigarettes), drugs that are not illegal but socially unacceptable (such as legal highs, poppers and solvents) and possibly medicines.

2. What sanctions are currently used if the drug rules of your organization are broken by young people?

3. How do these rules and sanctions compare to the rules and sanctions used by your organization for other, non-drug, matters?

4. Do any of the drug rules or sanctions need changing or updating? If so, which and in what ways?

5. Have all staff and young people been made sufficiently aware of the rules and procedures? If not, how can you make them more aware?

Educational establishments, such as schools, colleges and youth clubs, should have an up-to-date drug policy that deals not only with rules and sanctions regarding drug incidents but also the provision of drug education programmes and access to drug information, advice and support for those who are experiencing drug problems and/or are concerned about drug use.

Chapter C4 includes advice about deciding whether or not to use sanctions in specific situations where young people use or supply drugs at home or on the premises of organizations they attend.

B8

BE PROACTIVE ABOUT
EDUCATING YOUNG PEOPLE

Whether or not your own child, or the young people you work with, are currently using specific drugs, you can help them to keep safe by making sure that they have a good education about drug use. This will not only help to protect them from future harm but also enable them to be in a position to understand, inform and support other people who use drugs, especially their peers. It will also mean they can participate in an informed manner to influence drug policies and services in the UK and elsewhere in the future. And we sorely need to develop a more creative and effective approach about how we handle drugs than we have managed to do so far.

WHAT DO WE MEAN BY DRUG EDUCATION?

There is a long history of drug education targeted at young people in the UK and other developed countries. This has included drug education programmes in schools, colleges and in more informal education settings such as youth clubs, as well as films, leaflets, poster and TV campaigns, TV programmes, information websites and newspaper coverage.

Most of these initiatives have focussed on information about drugs, rather than being more rounded educational programmes that also help young people to explore their attitudes towards drug use and develop the confidence and skills that they may need to make decisions in situations involving their own, and other people's, drug use.

Unfortunately, the drug information provided has rarely been balanced and has often been inaccurate. Commonly, risks and dangers have been exaggerated in an attempt to present drugs in a bad light and try to deter young people from using. The possibility that taking a drug might kill you, or lead to serious impairment, has often been over emphasized, despite the fact that the probability of these things happening is usually highly unlikely, and statistically a lot less likely than the dangers arising from many normal, everyday activities such as driving a car, playing sports or outdoor pursuits. I have discussed drug risks and harms in detail in Chapter A5.

Extreme cases have often been presented as almost normal and to be expected. There have been many attempts to shock and scare young people away from taking drugs. This is called 'fear arousal' and has included use of slogans like 'say no to drugs' and 'one pill kills' and ex-drug addicts talking about the terrible experiences they have had. Emotive films and theatre productions about young people dying after using drugs and garish poster campaigns have also been common. A lot of young people, and especially those who are more involved with drugs and at greatest risk, see through such misinformation, feel they are not being told the truth and start mistrusting the information about drugs that they are given.

Certain information has been censored because it might put drug use in a more favourable light. The benefits and pleasures of using drugs, other than alcohol, have often been ignored or, if they are addressed at all, portrayed as being short-lived as users inevitably begin to have problems and become hooked. This has left the issue of seeking a proper understanding about why we use mind-altering substances in the ways that we do unaddressed.

Nearly all drug use is portrayed as very dangerous, which means that strategies for using drugs, and especially illegal drugs, in safer and less damaging ways are rarely discussed with young people, other than in the case of alcohol. The fact that many people use drugs in relatively moderate and controlled ways over long periods of their lives, with few if any problems, has been seen as something that either cannot happen or, if it does occur, should not be acknowledged with young people. Many drug educators have become caught in a circle of 'if you don't condemn drug use, you condone it', despite the fact that we nearly all, including drug educators themselves, have a lifetime career of using mind-altering substances, be they currently legal or illegal drugs.

There are also often omissions of other uncomfortable facts. These commonly include not giving a full picture of current drug laws within the UK, little or no information about young people's legal rights and playing down statistics concerning the extent of drug use. A lot of drug education has also failed to make comparisons with other countries that deal with drugs in different ways to the UK, airbrushed the often contradictory history of drug use and controls in this and other countries and ignored religious uses of drugs and cross-cultural differences in drug use and production.

Such approaches see young people as ignorant about drugs and/or having the wrong ideas about drugs. The fact that even young children already have information, feelings, views and experiences concerning drugs, is often ignored. Instead they are to be given, what is deemed, the 'correct' information. In this sense a lot of drug education is something that is done to, rather than with, young people and they are not encouraged to question the information they receive about drugs from various sources. By their teenage years many young people have tired of being talked at. They begin to feel patronized and that they have heard it all before, are only being told part of the picture and know more about drugs than the people who are informing them.

Not many drug education programmes have gone beyond information provision to also address attitudes to drug use. They have rarely encouraged young people to think about and debate the many different views that there are about drug use in our society. More often they have told young people what they should think. Similarly, many programmes have told young people what they should do about the possibility of using drugs – 'Just Say No' – rather than helping them to make their own, informed decisions about drugs.

I have worked in the drug education field for many years all over the UK and have also been to America, Australia, Canada, France, Ireland, the Netherlands, Romania and Spain to witness the drug *education* in these countries. I have been struck by how little actual drug education there has been for young people. Unfortunately, much of what has been called drug education has not really been educational at all. It has had much more in common with propaganda.

DRUG EDUCATION AND DRUG PROPAGANDA

What is the difference between education and propaganda? In a broad sense education has a formative effect on the mind, character and abilities of a person, teaches them how to think and act for themselves and encourages them to develop their own, informed opinions and to make their own decisions. In contrast, propaganda tells people what they should think and how they should behave in specific ways that have been decided for them by someone else. Education is open, expansive, explorative and divergent. Propaganda is closed, narrow, predictable and convergent.

The differences between drug education (DE) and drug propaganda (DP) are summarized below.

Information

DE provides accurate and balanced information about drugs, the possible benefits and dangers of using drugs and a range of social, political and historical information about drug use. It is honest and truthful and encourages people to question sources of information.

DP carefully selects what information will, and will not, be provided. The possible benefits of drug use and other uncomfortable facts will be ignored. The risks and dangers of drug use are exaggerated, extremes may be presented as normal and an attempt may be made to shock and scare young people to try to deter them from using drugs. It will not encourage young people to question official sources of drug information.

Attitudes

DE encourages young people to become aware of and to debate a wide range of views about drug use. It challenges stereotypes and helps young people to have their own, informed opinions and to think for themselves.

DP usually involves little or no debate. It may well perpetuate stereotypes. It tries to get young people to think and feel the way they are told to.

Skills

DE helps young people to develop a range of relevant skills, so they are better placed to make informed decisions about their own drug use and how they respond to other people's drug use.

DP tells young people what decisions they should make. It often focusses on refusal skills and saying 'No' to drugs.

Overall

DE is *about* drug use and sees it as a normal human activity that has a long history. It also takes account of the fact that young people have to make decisions about other people's drug use, as well as their own. It focusses on reducing harm, promoting safety and engages with, and welcomes, young people's own ideas and views.

DP is *against* drug use and portrays it as a deviant activity. It focusses mainly on an individual's own drug use and tells young people what they should think and do. It focusses on trying to persuade young people not to use (certain) drugs.

WHAT IMPACT DOES DRUG EDUCATION ACTUALLY HAVE?

Many drug education programmes in the UK, other European countries, America, Canada and Australia have been evaluated to find out what effects they have on young people. I have closely followed what these research studies have discovered. Unfortunately, some professionals in the drug education field and government ministers and officials have suggested guidelines for drug education, and funded particular programmes, that ignore this research evidence.

Despite many people hoping, and expecting, that drug education will prevent young people from using drugs and stop those that do use, it is clear that it rarely has such an impact (Cohen 2012). Some people have also been concerned that drug education may even encourage drug use among young people, especially if it involves younger children. Again this is very rarely the case if a sensible, age appropriate approach is adopted. The only types of drug education that, when evaluated, have been found to increase drug use are American ones that adopted a shock/scare approach and were delivered as strongly anti-drug programmes by uniformed police officers.

If drug education does not stop young people using drugs is there any point in it? The good news is that sensible drug education can increase young people's knowledge and understanding of drug use, help them to clarify their feelings and attitudes about drugs and make them more discerning when making decisions about their own drug use and use by other people. In other words, drug education can help young people to have safer drug careers and reduce the harm that they, and other people they know, may experience. These are very positive outcomes, but we should still be aware that the impact of drug education on young people's drug-using behaviour is limited and that we cannot expect too much of it.

WHAT TOPICS MIGHT DRUG EDUCATION COVER?

The aims of drug *education* should, in my view, be to help young people to:

- increase their knowledge and understanding of drugs, drug use and related issues through the provision of information

- explore a range of attitudes towards drug use and drug policies and enable them to reach their own, informed views

- develop a range of skills to increase their confidence, abilities and skills to manage drug-related situations involving their own drug use and their responses to other people using.

The content of drug education needs to be tailored to the specific needs of particular young people. It needs to take account of their age, maturity and their likely current and future drug use. If we again divide drug education into information, attitudes and skills, the following topics might be considered:

Information

Drug education provides information about:

- legal and illegal drugs – appearance, possible benefits of use, effects, risks, method of use, legal status, etc.

- drug terminology, including street language

- drug types – stimulants, depressants, hallucinogens, etc.

- different forms of drug use, including dependency, and possible reasons for them

- how things about people (their physical/mental health, etc.) and the situation of drug use can influence drug effects and risks

- specific dangers and ways of avoiding them

- the law and drugs and legal rights of young people

- organizational (school, college, youth club, night club, work, etc.) rules and sanctions

- patterns and trends in drug use

- historical/cultural aspects of drug use

- support available within various agencies and on what terms

- specialist agencies and helplines – local and national

- government drug strategy – education/prevention, treatment, law and policing, etc.

- where to find out more

- drug-related first aid.

Attitudes

Drug education explores our attitudes towards:

- different drugs and different forms of use

- people who use and supply drugs – combating stereotypes

- drug laws and rules

- government drug policies.

Skills

Drug education develops skills in:

- risk assessment and anticipating consequences

- harm reduction/safer use strategies

- communicating about drugs with peers, family members, professionals, police, help agencies, etc.

- assertiveness and decision making in drug situations

- managing conflict in drug situations

- how to find out more

- how to get help if you need it

- how to help other people who experience drug problems

- first aid in drug-related situations.

HELP YOUNG PEOPLE TO GET A GOOD DRUG EDUCATION

Before considering how you can help young people to obtain a good drug education it is important to reflect on your own ideas about drug education and what, in particular, your own child, or the young people you work with, may need from it. To do this, answer the following questions. You might write down your answers or, even better, discuss the questions with your partner, a family member, a friend or work colleague. This is also a good discussion exercise to do with your own child or young people you work with to find out what they think and to compare ideas.

1. How do you feel about what I have said earlier in this chapter about the effects drug education can be expected to have and about the distinction between drug education and drug propaganda?

2. What will you need to do, and avoid doing, to make sure your approach to drug education is based on educational principles, rather than propaganda?

3. Look through the drug education topics I have listed earlier in this chapter. Which topics do you think may be particularly important for your child, or the young people you work with? What other topics may also be important to them?

Steps that you can take to help an individual young person, or a group of young people, have a good drug education include:

- Ask them which specific drugs and topics it would be useful for them to know and think more about.

- Ask them what they think it would be useful for you to know and think more about.

- Go through the learning exercises in chapters B1 and B2 of this book with them.

- Discuss with them the possibility of reading books and pamphlets and accessing websites. See the recommended books and websites in Part E. They might do this by themselves or you could do it together and discuss what you find out.

- If you know someone who is particularly knowledgeable about drug use, explore the possibility that they could discuss drug use with both/all of you and answer your questions.

- Watch and discuss together films and TV programmes that address drug use and issues.

- If they are at school or college or attend a youth project, ask them about the drug education they have received there. If necessary, advocate on their behalf with their teachers, lecturers or youth workers so they, and other young people, start to receive more and better drug education.

If you are working as a school teacher, college lecturer or youth worker you can help develop effective drug education programmes for your organization. In my experience of working with many such organizations, you will need to address the following points:

- Ensure the senior management are supportive, that someone takes overall responsibility for the programme and that there is a budget to buy any necessary resources.

- Make the drug education programme part of your organization's drug policy and try to ensure an entitlement for young people.

- Ensure the programme has sensible aims, takes account of the research evidence about the impact of drug education and that the approach is based on educational principles, rather than propaganda.

- Involve and consult young people about what they need, what will be provided for them and how.

- Make the content relevant to the young people's age, development and circumstances.

- Wherever possible, integrate drug education into your normal curriculum, such as within other personal, social and health education programmes.

- If possible have in-house staff taking the lead in delivering drug education. This will help to create an atmosphere where drug use becomes a normal thing for staff and young people to talk about and also means that you are not dependent on outside agencies for the delivery of your organization's programme.

- Build the confidence and skills of your staff to lead drug education, including by arranging relevant training for them.

- Only use outside contributors if they can add something important, that in-house staff cannot, and their approach complements the approach you are taking.

- Deliver the programme by using a range of active learning methods that encourage young people to participate, think, question and give their opinions, rather than by lecturing them or just sitting them in front of a film.

- If appropriate, involve and consult the wider community, especially parents.

- Evaluate how effective the programme is and what young people think of it. Identify any changes that can be made to improve it.

You may find that a drug agency in your locality that specializes in work with young people can support you to develop a drug education programme in the organization you work for. See Part E for information about contacting such agencies. Local health promotion agencies and local authority education departments may also be able to assist you, but recent public sector cutbacks have meant that many of the staff who used to do such work have been made redundant.

B9

LEARN BASIC FIRST AID SKILLS

What would you do if you came across your child or a young person you work with and they were really drunk, high on drugs or hallucinating? What if they became really paranoid? And what if they lost consciousness or stopped breathing? Would you know what to do to ensure their safety?

I hope you will never experience such situations, but you may, and it is important that you know some basic drug-related first aid.

What follows is not a definitive first aid manual but it will give you a good idea about what to do in a range of situations where a young person's drug use is putting their health at immediate and serious risk. For information about learning more about first aid see the end of this chapter.

Please note that in nearly all cases ambulance crews and hospitals will *not* inform the police if illegal drugs are involved.

IF SOMEONE IS HEAVILY DRUNK, HIGH, HALLUCINATING OR EMOTIONALLY DISTURBED BUT CONSCIOUS...

- Don't try to talk about what has happened in any detail, other than what they have taken and how much. For more discussion wait till they have sobered up.

- Keep a close eye on them and don't leave them alone until they have sobered up.

- Don't put them to bed. Sit them down in a quiet room.

- Open a window to let in fresh air.

- Talk quietly and calmly.

- Reassure and help calm them down, if necessary.

- Loosen their clothing at the neck, chest and waist.

- If they are cold cover them with a blanket but make sure they do not get too hot.

- Do not give them anything to eat and drink, other than sips of water.

- Do not move them unless it is essential.

- Do not try to induce vomiting.

- If you are worried about their condition, keep them awake for a time before allowing them to sleep. Some young people who have been drunk or high have died after vomiting while being left alone to sleep.

- Always err on the safe side. Call an ambulance or take them to the Accident and Emergency department at your local hospital if you are really concerned about the state the young person is in.

IF SOMEONE IS OVERHEATED AND DEHYDRATING…

This can happen especially when people take stimulant drugs like amphetamine, cocaine, ecstasy or mephedrone. Such drugs give an energy lift and raise body temperature. If users then dance for long periods in clubs where the temperature is hot and ventilation is poor they can sweat profusely and lose a lot of body fluids. If people have been drinking alcohol or coffee, together with stimulant drugs, they are likely to dehydrate even more.

Overheating and dehydration have been the cause of a few hundred drug-related deaths of young people over the last 30 years. Thankfully, in recent years, the number of such deaths has fallen as more young drug users know that they should take a break from dancing by 'chilling out' and rehydrate by drinking water. Unfortunately, drinking too much water can, in itself, be dangerous as in the tragic death of Leah Betts. Sipping a maximum of one pint of water an hour is recommended. Salt depletion can also be a problem and eating salty snacks like crisps or peanuts may help.

The warning signs that someone is overheating and dehydrating are:

- feeling very hot and thirsty

- cramps in the legs, arms and/or back

- failure to sweat

- headaches and dizziness

- vomiting

- suddenly feeling very tired

- feeling like urinating but not being able to do so

- fainting and losing consciousness.

If someone is overheating or dehydrating...

- Move the person to a cool place.

- Reassure them, if necessary.

- Splash them with cold water and fan them to cool them down.

- Give them small sips of water to drink.

- Follow the advice given at the start of this chapter about what to do if someone is heavily drunk, high or hallucinating and conscious.

- If you are really concerned about the young person call an ambulance or take them to the Accident and Emergency department at your local hospital.

IF SOMEONE HAS LOST CONSCIOUSNESS...

If someone has lost consciousness or if you are having difficulty keeping them awake, then call for an ambulance without delay. In the meantime there are a number of things you can do to keep them as safe as possible.

- Check their airway. Place one hand under their neck to support their head. Put your other hand on their forehead and gently lift their head backwards. Push their chin upwards.

- Check to see if they are breathing. See if you can hear or feel their breaths. Put your ear next to their nose and lips. Look to see if their chest or abdomen is moving.

If they are breathing...

- Loosen their clothing at the neck, chest and waist.

- Put them in the recovery position. Lie them on the floor on their side with their arms and upper leg at right angles to their body to support them. Tuck their upper hand under the side of their head.

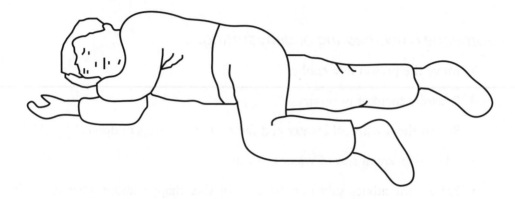

- Stay with them and keep checking their breathing. If possible, get someone else to ring for the ambulance.

- If they start to come round, reassure them.

If they are not breathing...

- Clear their mouth of any dirt or vomit.

- Tilt their head back and lift their chin.

- Pinch their nose then take a deep breath. Give them two slow, deep breaths. Their chest should rise as you blow in.

- Take your mouth away and watch their chest fall.

- Look for signs of them breathing.

- Check their pulse to see whether their heart is beating. Do this by putting two fingers in the groove at the side of their Adam's apple and press firmly. If you cannot feel a pulse within a few seconds their heart may have stopped beating.

If their heart is beating...

- Continue with mouth-to-mouth resuscitation (rescue breathing). Again give them two slow, deep breaths. If necessary, repeat a few times.

- If they start breathing again put them in the recovery position – see above – and monitor their breathing.

If their heart is not beating...

- Heart resuscitation using chest compressions and rescue breathing (together known as CPR) will be necessary. It is difficult to correctly use chest compressions effectively by just reading a book. If you want to know how to do it I suggest that you refer to a specialist first aid manual and sign up for a first aid training course.

LEARNING MORE ABOUT FIRST AID

If you are not that confident about using basic first aid please take the time to find out more. The more of us who are first aid trained the more lives we will save. This includes anyone we might come across when walking down the streets, as well as young people who may be the worse for wear from taking drugs.

It is also very important that we help to educate young people about first aid. A number of drug-related deaths among young people would not have happened if other young people around them had known what to do.

You might consider the following:

- Read a first aid manual. Dorling Kindersley publish an excellent manual in collaboration with St. John Ambulance and the British Red Cross that includes many full colour pictures.

- Look at the websites of St. John Ambulance – www.sja.org.uk – and the British Red Cross – www.redcross.org.uk – for more information about how to conduct first aid.

- Go on a first aid course or organize one in your local community or workplace. Both St. John's and the Red Cross run training courses all over the country.

- If any of your family, friends or work colleagues have been trained in first aid, ask them to teach you some of the basics.

- If you are a parent, encourage your child to go on a first aid course. If they are a student ask their school or college to put on first aid training for them and other students.

- If you are a professional who works with young people, help them to access first aid training or organize courses for them.

B10

KNOW WHERE AND
HOW TO GET HELP

There is a range of different types of help available across the country for young people who experience drug problems and/or need advice and information. However, unless your child, or a young person you are working with, is experiencing serious difficulties with their drug use, do not rush to try to send them to a specialist agency. Don't underestimate what you may be able to do to help them. Also don't overestimate what specialist agencies can do. They do not have magic wands.

It is not a good idea to try to force young people to access professional help against their wishes. In my counselling work I found that parents sometimes threatened their children and told them that if they did not come to see me they would be severely punished. Schools sometimes tried to refer young people to me on the basis that the student concerned would be expelled unless they attended. In both situations the young people were not very communicative and clearly did not want to talk with me. While I was sometimes able to get them to talk openly, it often took a long time to reach this point and in some cases it never happened. I also found that some of the young people referred to me were not experiencing serious problems with their drug use or generally in their lives. They had obviously upset their parents or professionals, especially school teachers, and often broken the assumed or explicit rules about drug use, but they were not in need of, or wanting, specialist help.

To benefit from help young people need to appreciate that they are experiencing difficulties and have some confidence that a referral to a specific, chosen agency will be beneficial to them.

Many adults, let alone young people, find it quite nerve-racking to be referred to a specialist agency where they do not know anyone. Before trying to persuade a young person that a referral to a specialist agency is a good idea my advice is to start close to home. As a first step be clear about what can you do to help them and what is beyond you, taking into account the issues involved, the time commitment needed and the nature of your relationship with them. Might you be better able to support them if you have some advice and support for yourself? This could come from a member of your family, a friend or work colleague. You could also consider contacting a specialist agency or telephone helpline to help you to support a young person in need. Details of agencies and helplines that may be able to support you are given in Part E.

It may sometimes be more appropriate that the young person concerned is directly supported by someone they already know, rather than them having to go to a specialist agency. This could be a member of their family or a teacher, college lecturer, student counsellor, youth worker or someone else they already know and get on with. Take account of what is best for the young person and discuss with them how they feel about it.

If a young person definitely needs and wants help from a specialist agency there are a number of different options.

THE DIFFERENT TYPES OF SPECIALIST HELP FOR YOUNG PEOPLE

- *GPs/family doctors*: Some GPs, especially in urban areas, are experienced in dealing with drug use and offer a range of services themselves, sometimes including prescribing of substitute drugs like methadone for heroin users. Others are not so knowledgeable about illegal drug use but most GP surgeries should have up-to-date information about other local specialist services and many will have their own counsellors.

- *Community drug and alcohol advice and counselling services*: Most areas of the country, including more rural areas, have such services which offer information and advice about drugs and alcohol (to users, professionals and parents), counselling for users and sometimes for their families, treatment (including detoxification) and sometimes syringe exchange schemes, support groups and referral to residential facilities. Some such services only see young people who are aged over 18 years old but some see under-18s and, in many areas of the country there are community drug services specifically for young people. These may see young people from 12 years old up to 18 years plus. For details of how to find out about drug services in your locality see below.

- *Generic counselling services*: Many areas have generic counselling services, and often services specifically for young people, that support people with a wide range of issues, including drug problems. Many youth services, colleges and universities also offer counselling services for young people.

- *Hospital-based services*: These are mainly for people who are dependent on drugs like heroin and crack, particularly injecting users. They may operate on a day care and/or in-patient basis.

- *Residential treatment*: This is for people who are long-term, dependent drug users and is often based in large houses, either in the countryside or the outskirts of large towns or cities. Most operate intensive detoxification programmes for between three months and one year, to help people become abstinent and stop using drugs. They tend to be for adults and few will consider young people aged under 18 years old. Some are run by charities and may be free to attend but there are not many such programmes in the UK. A growing number are run by private, profit-making companies and are very expensive for clients to attend.

- *Support groups*: There are support groups for drug users in many areas of the UK. They are mostly for people aged over 18 years old and are run by community drug services, drug user support groups or by organizations such as Narcotics Anonymous and Alcoholics Anonymous.

- *Telephone helplines*: There are a number of national telephone helplines that offer information, advice and sometimes telephone counselling for young people. Some focus on particular drugs, such as alcohol and stopping smoking, but a number also address issues with any drugs or any general issue faced by young people. Many of these helplines can also offer support for parents and professionals who are concerned about a young person's drug use and a few are specifically focussed on supporting parents, rather than young people directly. See the list of helplines in Part E of this book.

FIND OUT ABOUT HELPING AGENCIES IN YOUR AREA

To find out what specialist help and advice are available in your locality for young people, and for you, try the following:

- Ask at your local GP surgery, youth club or project, or college or university student support service. Staff there should know about local services for young people.

- Go on the Frank website – www.talktofrank.com – and from the 'Get help' menu access the 'Find support near you' page. Type in your postcode. This should bring up the contact details of a range of specialist support services in your area.

- Go to the NHS Choices website – www.nhs.uk – and access the 'All directories' tab in the 'Services near you' box. Click on 'D' and then 'Drug treatment services' to get a list of services near to you.

- Also see the other websites listed at the end of the book.

Some of the things you may need to ask about local services for young people include:

- What ages of young people do they work with?

- What services do they offer for young people?

- Are they an abstinence-based service, or will they also do harm-reduction work with young people who are continuing to use drugs?

- Do they work with young people who have difficulties with any drugs or do they specialize in particular drugs, and, if so, which?

- What support can they offer to you – professionals and/or parents?

- Where are they based and what are the opening hours?

- Can young people refer themselves to the service or do they have to go through another agency, and, if so, which agency?

- Is it a drop-in service or appointment based and, if the latter, is there a waiting list and how long is it?

- Do they see people only at their office or will they also do home visits?

- Will they work with young people and their parents together, if needed?

- What are their policies regarding confidentiality, recording information and sharing it with other agencies?

- If the young person wishes can you go along to the agency with them?

If, as a parent, you are becoming concerned or anxious about your child's drug use, or if you are a professional who works with young people, don't wait for an absolute crisis to occur before finding out about helping agencies in your locality. Be prepared.

REFERRING YOUNG PEOPLE TO HELPING AGENCIES
Before deciding that a young person may benefit from being referred to a helping agency it is important to ask yourself the following questions:

- Why are you thinking of a referral to a helping agency?

- What particular issues and difficulties is the young person experiencing?

- What might an agency be able to do for the young person that you, or other people that the young person already knows, cannot?

- How do you think the young person may feel about being referred to a specialist agency?

- How does the young person actually feel about being referred? Talk with them about it.

- What sort of agency might best help them?

- Which of your local agencies might be appropriate?

- How does the agency operate? See the questions above.

If the young person agrees to being referred you might support them in the following ways:

- Involve them as much as possible in the decision making process.

- Make sure they understand what is on offer and on what terms.

- Discuss with them how they feel about working with the agency, what they need from the agency and any concerns they have.

- If necessary, support them to make their first contact with the agency.

- If appropriate, offer to go along to the agency with them, especially for the first session.

- Discuss with them how you can best support them to work with the agency.

If the young person wants you to be present with them while they see a specialist worker this should be respected by the agency concerned. However, in most cases it will be more appropriate for the young person to see the worker by themselves. This will be the norm in most cases and will always be the case where the young person does not want you to be present. In such situations don't later nag the young person to tell you what happened at each session and how well they are doing. Feel free to enquire what it was like for them and how they are doing, but don't push them too far if they don't want to tell you much.

Similarly, don't expect specialist workers to tell you what they have talked about with young people or how young people are doing. Most agencies have strict client confidentiality rules and these often apply to even young people who are aged under 16 years old – see 'Confidentiality guidance' in Chapter B6 for more details.

Last, and not least, if your child, or a young person you work with, is working through their difficulties with a specialist worker don't expect miracles or rapid changes. You will need to be patient.

SUPPORT FOR PARENTS AND PROFESSIONALS

There are a range of organizations that can support you if you are concerned about a young person's involvement with drugs.

Many of the agencies that work with young drug users also offer information and advice for parents and professionals. There are also national telephone helplines that you can use and, in some localities, there are support groups for parents who have children who are experiencing problems with drug use. See Part E of this book for details.

This means you are not alone and there is information and advice available to help you to support young people.

DEALING WITH SPECIFIC SITUATIONS

INTRODUCTION

This part of the book provides information and advice about dealing with some of the particular scenarios you could be faced with when young people are involved with drugs. It will be especially useful if you are faced with a situation that causes you anxiety and that you find difficult to manage.

The chapters are short and to the point and signpost you to information and advice elsewhere in the book that are relevant to the specific situations and issues being faced. The fact that some of the situations discussed share similarities means there is a bit of repetition, but I have tried to keep it to a minimum.

Please also note that you may be faced with a situation where a young person is involved with drugs when more than one of the chapters in this part of the book is relevant.

GENERAL ADVICE

If you are faced with *any* situation where a young person is involved with drugs I can recommend the following general advice to you.

- Don't panic. Try to remain calm.

- Don't fear the worst.

- Don't ignore what has, or may have, happened.

- Don't blame yourself.

- Don't overreact or get angry with the young person.

- Don't rush to act. If possible, create time to think carefully and find out more first.

- Don't exaggerate risks and dangers or assume that all drug use is problematic – see Chapters A5 and B5.

- Inform yourself – see Chapter B1 and for information about the drug, or drugs, the young person is involved with, see Part D.

- Be aware of your own feelings and attitudes towards drugs and how they may influence your response – see Chapter B2.

- Be patient and realistic about what can happen. Don't expect rapid changes – see Chapter B3.

- Understand their motivations for being involved with drugs and any underlying difficulties and issues they may be facing – see Chapter A2.

- Do your best to listen to and talk with them – see Chapter B4.

- Clarify the legal situation for them and for you – see Chapter A6.

- Carefully assess their involvement with drugs and any problems they may be experiencing – see Chapter B5.

- Be clear about who else, if anyone, you may want to inform and involve – see Chapter B6.

- Help the young person to access specialist services, if they need to – see Chapter B10.

- Help to educate them about drugs – see Chapter B8.

- If necessary, negotiate clear and sensible drug rules with them for the future – see Chapter B7.

ESTABLISH CLEAR BOUNDARIES FOR YOURSELF

Many of the scenarios that are addressed in this part of the book may be challenging for parents and professionals to manage and cope with. Although it may sometimes be difficult for you to do so, it will help if you can establish clear and sensible boundaries about what you are prepared to do, and not do, for the young person concerned and what you will accept, and not accept, regarding their behaviour.

It is important that we encourage young people to take as much responsibility for themselves as they can and do not end up doing too much, or too little, for them. It will not help young people if we continually make excuses for them not doing what they could do, or say they will do.

In my experience it is mothers, rather than fathers, who mainly offer on-going understanding and support when their child is involved with drugs but this may change as gender roles in parenting become more balanced. It is also true that support groups for parents whose children are experiencing drug problems seemed mostly attended by mothers, with few fathers involved.

It is great that mothers have often provided on-going support for their children in difficult circumstances. However, I have found that, in some instances, parents (this can more often be mothers in my experience) have become too involved, run around doing almost everything for their child and have found it difficult to draw clear boundaries. In my experience, this has especially happened with their sons when they have treated them like a young child, even sometimes when the son has been aged well over 20 years old. At the other extreme, some parents (more commonly fathers in my experience) have quickly given up on their child or just responded angrily.

Such different responses have sometimes led to a lot of conflict between a child's parents and meant that the child can easily play one parent off against the other, if they want to. By no means all parents take on such extreme roles, but it is important that we are aware of ourselves as parents and the nature of the relationships we have developed with our children and our partners. If both parents are involved, it will help the young person if there is consistency about boundaries.

When at the end of their tether with a child who is dependent on drugs, some parents have placed themselves at serious risk by going out to get illegal drugs for them or confronted drug dealers. Parents have also sometimes repeatedly given their child money to fund their drug habit. I can understand why some parents have done these things but I do not recommend such actions to you.

In my experience some professionals have also lacked boundaries with young people who have been involved with drugs. This has included making promises about confidentiality which they have not been able to keep, failing to refer young people for specialist help when they probably would have benefited from it and giving a young person their personal phone number so that they can be contacted at any time. At the other extreme of involvement, some professionals have treated young people only as disciplinary cases when they have been experiencing many difficulties and have needed specialist help.

To help you to establish boundaries with a young person who is involved with drugs be as clear as you can be about your answers to the following questions:

- Which behaviours, both drug-related and general behaviours, on the part of the young person, are acceptable and unacceptable to you? This will be especially important for parents regarding young people's behaviours in their own home, and for professionals at their workplace.

- What will you do if the young person behaves in ways that you find unacceptable?

- What are you capable of doing for them and what may be beyond you?

- What are you prepared to do for them and what you are not prepared to do?

- Who else, if anyone, will you inform and involve? See Chapter B6.

Also see Chapter B7 which focusses on negotiating and establishing drug rules with young people.

When faced with a specific situation it will be important for you to try to communicate your boundaries to the young person concerned so that they know where they stand. Ideally you will be able to discuss and negotiate boundaries with them, but if they will not co-operate in doing so, you can still be clear in your own mind what your boundaries are and tell the young person about where you stand.

Boundaries will be pretty meaningless unless you stick by them. This may be difficult for you to do in some situations but try to adhere to boundaries, as far as you can, rather than immediately going back on them. If necessary, renegotiate boundaries as the situation unfolds and changes.

SUPPORT FOR YOU

It is all very well me giving you advice about managing situations in which young people are involved with drugs. It may be difficult actually doing what I have recommended, especially in a situation that you find distressing. Try your best and do not berate yourself if you don't manage to do everything perfectly. I have not been the perfect father to my daughter or the perfect support worker and counsellor for young people or their families. We are only human.

As well as doing your best to understand and help young people, make sure that you get support and advice for yourself if the situation you are dealing with is very stressful and difficult for you. Talk to your partner, another family member, a trusted friend or work colleague. If you are professional, I hope you will have access to supervision and have a supportive line manager. Both professionals and parents can also access support and advice for themselves from local drug services and from telephone helplines (see Part E).

IF YOU SUSPECT THEY ARE USING OR SUPPLYING DRUGS

There could be a number of reasons that you might suspect, but not be sure, that your child or a young person you work with is involved with drugs.

You might notice changes in their behaviour, where they are going, who they are spending time with or changes in their appearance that make you think they could be involved with drugs. However, as I have explained in Chapter A7, we need to take care before deciding that possible signs and symptoms actually indicate drug use or supply because they may occur for reasons that have nothing to do with involvement with drugs.

You might find what you think are drugs or drug paraphernalia that suggest a young person could be using or supplying drugs. However, don't be too hasty to jump to conclusions. Are you sure that what you have found are actually drugs or drug paraphernalia? Again look at Chapter A7 to help you to make an informed decision about this. Also refer to the information about the drug(s) you suspect they may be involved with in Part D.

If someone else has told you that your child, or a young person you work with, is involved with drugs decide whether you think they, and what they have said, is reliable. Don't assume that everything they tell you is definitely true. They may have got it wrong. They could even be exercising a grudge or trying to divert attention away from themselves and attempting to put the blame on someone else.

While my advice is to always question what you have found or heard before you act, I also recommend that you do not completely ignore any suspicions that you have.

In such situations there are a number of ways that you might respond.

You could decide to wait before doing anything other than just monitoring the situation by keeping an eye on the young person, how they are behaving and how they are feeling in general.

You could try to find out more by asking other people if they know what has been going on. If you decide to do this, take care about whom you ask and the possible implications this could have for them and for your relationship with the young person you are trying to find out about. Some parents and professionals have also tried to follow young people to see where they are going, who they are meeting and what they are up to. I do not recommend such actions but I can understand why some people have done this. Take care not to become an amateur detective who is anxiously 'investigating' a young person.

You may also find yourself questioning whether or not you should search a young person, their bedroom, locker, clothing or bags to see if they have drugs or paraphernalia in their possession.

In some cases, such as if they are particularly young, or you strongly suspect they have controlled drugs or paraphernalia on them at home or on work premises, it may be reasonable for parents or professionals to ask a young person to voluntarily turn out their pockets or bag. If you decide to do so, try to ask in a relaxed manner, rather than aggressively. If they refuse, back down. Be aware that forced searches of a young person can amount to assault and should be avoided.

Searching a young person's clothing or bag, or for parents their bedroom and for professionals their locker, without them knowing and consenting should, whenever possible, be avoided because such actions may result in a serious loss of trust with the young person.

Searching a young person, or their property, without their consent or knowledge is likely to have a detrimental effect on your relationship with them and make it much more difficult to have open communication and for you to find out what is really going on. In extreme cases, such as suspected possession or supply of controlled drugs on the premises of organizations (such as schools, colleges, youth clubs, pubs, clubs, workplaces or hostels), professionals might contact the police to conduct any body searches of a young person. Both professionals and parents should also be aware that it can be deemed unlawful to restrict the liberty of a young person by locking them in a room or part of a building.

Sooner or later you will probably decide that you want to talk to the young person concerned about your suspicions. Rather than confronting them directly, you could start by telling them that you are concerned about them and ask them whether everything has been alright for them, without necessarily mentioning drugs. If you are going to ask them directly whether they are involved with drugs try not to be too confrontational and do not threaten them. If you are aggressive with them they are less likely to tell you the truth. Stress that you are concerned about them and what they may have been doing. If you want them to be honest about what they have been up to you need to gain their trust.

If you ask a young person about whether they have become involved with drugs, follow the guidance I have given in Chapter B4 about how to listen and talk to them. If it becomes clear that they have become involved, follow the advice on establishing clear boundaries I have given on pages 155–157.

IF THEY DISCLOSE INVOLVEMENT
WITH DRUGS TO YOU

This is the shortest chapter in this book and I did consider omitting it completely, However, I want to emphasize that it can be very difficult for a young person to tell their parents, or professionals who work with them, that they are using or supplying drugs, especially if they fear, rightly or wrongly, that the response they will get may be disapproval, anger or simply over-the-top.

If a young person discloses involvement with drugs to you be pleased that they trust you enough to be able to do so. The fact that they have told you is a positive thing. Your role is to support them as best as you can.

In such a situation I recommend that you follow the advice I have given on boundaries on pages 155–157.

C3

IF THEY ARE DRUNK OR HIGH
OR LOSE CONSCIOUSNESS

If you are seriously concerned about the state a young person is in you need to act immediately to protect their safety as far as you can.

If they are emotionally disturbed or paranoid do your best to calm them down by following the advice on pages 141–142 of Chapter B9, especially the start of the chapter. If they are physically the worse for wear similar advice is recommended. In either situation, try to find out which drugs, or drugs, they have taken and how much they have had. Refer to Part D to find out more about the drugs involved.

Be attentive to what they say they want and need, but do not put them to bed to 'sleep it off'. There have been many cases of people being very drunk, or intoxicated on other drugs, who have choked on their vomit after falling asleep and some have died. Keep them awake for a time until they have sobered up.

For advice about what to do if a young person loses consciousness see Chapter B9, pages 143–145.

If you are seriously concerned about a young person's physical health do not hesitate in calling an ambulance. In nearly all cases where illegal drugs are involved the ambulance crew and hospital will *not* inform the police. It will help ambulance and hospital staff if you can tell them what the young person has taken and how much.

Do not try to talk with young people about what has happened, and the rights and wrong of what they have done, in any detail until they are feeling better, possibly the next day. Follow the advice I have given on pages 154–157.

If a young person is drunk or high on drugs while attending school, college, work or an agency they are working with, professionals should first address any first aid needs, as described above. Do not send the young person home if they are not in a fit state. Either keep them with you till they have sobered up or contact their partner, a friend or family member to pick them up.

If they have clearly broken the rules of your establishment by attending while drunk or high, consider what sanctions, if any, you may need to follow – see page 128–131 in Chapter B7. If they have been using or supplying drugs on the premises see the advice in Chapter C4.

C4

IF THEY HAVE BEEN USING OR SUPPLYING DRUGS AT HOME OR ON THE PREMISES OF ORGANIZATIONS THEY ATTEND

Parents have legal obligations if they know that their child uses, produces or supplies controlled (illegal) drugs in their own home and similar responsibilities apply for professionals if they know young people are doing likewise on their work premises. Read the sections on your legal obligations and young people's legal rights in Chapter A6, pages 78–82, for more detailed information about this, especially as the law is not completely clear.

It is not a legal offence for parents or professionals to allow the use or supply of drugs which are not controlled under the Misuse of Drugs Act. This includes alcohol, cigarettes, legal highs, poppers and solvents. However, the policy and practice of most organizations that work with young people bans most, if not all, of these drugs being allowed on their premises.

If you become aware of the use, supply or production of controlled drugs by other people on premises you have responsibilities for or own, the law requires you to take reasonable action to prevent these activities continuing. For both professionals and parents 'reasonable action' does not necessarily mean informing the police and there is no legal obligation to do so.

For professionals, reasonable action may include young people being requested to leave the premises and/or being asked to voluntarily hand over drugs. Where young people refuse to comply with such requests the police may have to be called. In such situations it is advisable to inform your line manager as soon as possible and to make a written report of what has happened and what actions have been taken.

Parents also have to take reasonable action to stop their children's involvement with controlled drugs at home if they want to avoid breaking the law themselves.

For example, some parents have been prosecuted for allowing their children to smoke cannabis at home or to grow cannabis plants. What the law regards as reasonable action for parents is not clear in such situations but, at minimum, it will be requesting their child not to engage in such activities in their home.

This has been a contentious part of the Misuse of Drugs Act and aspects of it are still unclear, both in terms of whether it covers the use of all controlled drugs and what constitutes reasonable action in the eyes of the law. Again see Chapter A6 for more details.

How should we respond to situations where young people have been using or supplying drugs at home or on the premises of organizations they attend?

If you find yourself in possession of controlled drugs follow the advice I have given in Chapter C5.

For parents it will be important to negotiate clear drug rules for the future – see Chapter B7.

Professionals will also have to decide which sanctions, if any, should be used when a young person breaks the rules of the organization they work with. As I have emphasized in Chapter B7, permanent exclusion should be regarded as a last resort when all other options have been exhausted and serious anti-social behaviour still persists. A range of sanctions, short of permanent exclusion, are available that may help young people learn from their mistakes and still send out a warning to other young people. These include:

- a verbal or written warning

- removal of certain privileges for a specified period

- agreeing a contract of behaviour that is monitored over a set period

- additional tasks being carried out for a period of time

- detentions, in schools

- short-term exclusion during which the matter can be properly investigated and discussed.

To help professionals to decide whether or not to use sanctions and, if so, which sanctions, I recommend that they consider the following questions:

- Are you clear about what has happened? Have you got your facts right?

- Which drug, or drugs, is involved and in what quantity?

- Does it involve possession, use, supply and/or production?

- Has the young person broken the law? See Chapter A6.

- What form of drug use is involved – experimental, recreational, binge or dependent? See Chapter A2.

- Does the young person admit to or deny being involved and breaking the rules?

- What is their attitude towards what they have done? Are they co-operative and apologetic or not?

- Is it the first time they have broken the drug rules or have they done so before?

- Have they previously been involved in other disruptive behaviours?

- Is there are any evidence of bullying or coercion? This could include them bullying other young people and also them being a victim of bullying.

- What are the circumstances of the young person, especially their physical and mental health and their situation at home? Are they experiencing particular difficulties in their life and, if so, what difficulties and what support might they need? See Chapters B5 and B10.

- What, if any, sanctions might it be appropriate to use? See above for possible sanctions.

- What are the likely consequences of using sanctions for the young person, their family and for other young people you work with?

Parents can also address some of these questions when deciding how to respond to similar situations involving their own children.

Following such an incident both parents and professionals will want to explore with the young person what has been going on with their drug use and/ or supplying and to carefully assess the situation. See the section 'Assessing young people's involvement with drugs' in Chapter B5 for guidance about how to do this.

In some situations young people have been subject to very harsh responses when they have used or supplied drugs on the premises of organizations they attend, particularly schools. Both parents and professionals may wish to act as advocates for young people in such situations to help ensure that they have been dealt with fairly and not unnecessarily excluded or banned.

IF YOU FIND A DRUG
OR PARAPHERNALIA

The first thing to do in such a situation is to be as sure as you can be that what you have found is actually a drug, or paraphernalia used to take drugs, and not something else. Read Chapters A7 and C1 and be aware that what we at first think may be drugs or paraphernalia may not always be so.

Your being in possession of drug paraphernalia does not place you at any legal risk but you need to be aware that you do have legal obligations if you are in possession of controlled (illegal) drugs. If you think that what you have found may be an illegal drug, clarify where you stand legally by looking at Chapter A6, particularly the sections on your legal obligations and young people's rights.

If you find, or are voluntarily given, what you believe to be a controlled drug there are two possible, legally permissible, courses of action open to you. One option is to call the police and hand the drug over to them. Be aware that the police may ask you who you think the drug belongs to. Alternatively, it is legally acceptable to dispose of the drug without informing the police. This might be done by flushing the substance down the toilet or disposing of it in a bin. Whichever action is chosen it should be done soon. It is not a good idea to have a controlled drug in your possession for too long because the police could surmise that the drug was for your own use. For professionals, wherever possible, a colleague should be present to witness what has been done so there can be no insinuation that the drug was kept for personal use by staff. A written report should also be made of what has been done and a line manager should be informed about the situation.

You should also be aware that you have legal obligations if you knowingly allow a young person to produce, use or supply controlled drugs, on premises you own or have responsibility for. For parents this includes their own homes and for professionals this includes their work premises. Details of where you stand in such situations, and what you must do to stay within the law, are given in Chapter A6 and in Chapter C4.

You will probably also want to find out who the drugs or paraphernalia you have found belong to. For a parent who finds drugs or paraphernalia in their own home it may be obvious who it is. However, in cases where there are a few children it may not be clear straight away which child is involved and whether it is more than one. In some cases, one of your children could be minding drugs or paraphernalia for a friend of theirs, though be aware that some young people have tried to use this as an excuse to attempt to conceal their own use.

Professionals may know who owns drugs or paraphernalia they have found but in some cases may have little idea who is involved. They may wish to ask certain young people about whether drugs or paraphernalia belong to them, or to other young people they know.

When talking to young people in such situations parents and professionals should take care not to be heavy-handed and should follow the guidance I have given in Chapter B4. If it becomes clear that they are involved with drugs follow the general advice and advice on boundaries on pages 154–157.

C6

IF THEY ARE ARRESTED FOR A DRUG OFFENCE

Many people have little idea about how the criminal justice system operates or about legal rights. This is true for professionals, parents and young people themselves.

As I have emphasized in Chapter A6, getting a criminal record can have a seriously detrimental effect on a young person's future job prospects and the possibility of international travel. Inappropriate, and especially custodial, sentences can result in a 'criminal apprenticeship' rather than having a deterrent outcome. This can impact negatively on individual young people but also reduce safety for the whole community in the long run.

It is important that young people know their legal rights and that if they are arrested for a drug offence they are dealt with fairly.

You can support a young person who has been arrested for a drug-related offence in a number of ways including:

- Talk with the young person about what happened, how they feel about it and any underlying issues that may have contributed to it. See Chapters B4 and B5.

- Clarify, as far as you can, exactly what drug offence they have been arrested for, whether or not they are guilty, what is likely to happen next and what sentence could result. See Chapter A6.

- Encourage them to take responsibility for their own actions and to be proactive in getting legal advice and support if they need it.

- Make sure they know about drug laws and their legal rights. Look at Chapter A6 and discuss it with them.

- If necessary, get some advice from Release who specialize in the legal aspects of drugs. Their website is www.release.org.uk and they have a telephone advice line on 020 7324 2989 (weekdays 11am to 1pm and 2pm to 4pm).

- If necessary, help the young person to find a good solicitor. You might do this by asking people you know if they can recommend a good solicitor, ringing local solicitors or approaching your local Citizen's Advice Bureau or Law Centre, if you have them.

- If appropriate, act as an advocate for the young person with the police, their family, school, college or employer or in court.

- If the case goes to court, if appropriate, provide a testimonial for the young person in either verbal or written form.

Once the basic legal situation has been addressed you will need to talk to the young person concerned and make a careful assessment about their situation. See Chapters B4 and B5 for advice on how to go about doing this.

IF THEY ARE USING DRUGS AND DO NOT SEE ANY HARM IN IT AND/OR WILL NOT STOP

This can be a very alarming situation for you to deal with, especially if the young person involved is using drugs in ways that are potentially harmful to them or you find very unacceptable. The danger is that we will end up repeatedly nagging them, checking up on them and feel continually anxious. If we are not careful we may become very frustrated and angry and end up in constant conflict and argue with them.

As a first step find out more about the drug, or drugs, they are using, how they may be using them and the possible harms they could be facing – see Chapters A2 and A5 and the information about the drug, or drugs, that they are using in Part D. Keep drug use in perspective and do not exaggerate the dangers, or ignore them.

Try to be patient and realistic about any changes the young person can make – see Chapter B3. Talk to them and listen to what they have to say – see Chapter B4. Make a careful assessment of their situation – see Chapter B5.

As I have emphasized in Chapter B3, all is not lost if they continue using drugs. You can build communication with them and help to ensure their safety by adopting a harm reduction approach – see the pages on harm reduction in Chapter B3 and the harm reduction advice I have given in Part D for the drug, or drugs, they are using.

If they are clearly experiencing difficulties with their drug use explore the possibility with them of help from a specialist agency – see Chapter B10. And also consider getting some support and advice for yourself as well – see page 157.

I sometimes think of this situation as being a 'holding operation' where we need to be patient and sometimes bite our tongues for a period of time, until young people decide for themselves to change their drug-using behaviours.

IF THEY ARE USING DRUGS HEAVILY AND/OR ARE DEPENDENT

This can be a very difficult situation for you to deal with, especially when it involves your own child. Professionals may also find it very taxing. It is important to remember that this is where the young person is right now but that there is hope for their future. In time they may be able to moderate their drug use or stop using the drugs they are dependent on all together. In other words, heavy drug use or dependence is not necessarily something that a young person will experience throughout their life. In the right circumstances, and with good on-going support, especially from you and possibly from specialist services, they can make positive changes.

However, supporting a young person in such a situation can be very difficult and demanding and take a lot of time, energy and patience on your part. It can be a long, and sometimes rocky, journey for both you and them. Both parents and professionals will benefit from accessing help for themselves. This can include support and advice from friends, family members and work colleagues as well as from specialist agencies and telephone helplines. In some localities there are also support groups for parents of young people who experience drug problems. See Part E for information about the help you can access.

Dependent drug users usually have underlying social and/or emotional difficulties which their drug use represents an attempt to escape from. Heavy drug use can also produce its own problems and a very chaotic lifestyle. What is happening to the young person can be very difficult to unravel. As a first step try to gain some understanding of the possible underlying reasons that they may be using drugs heavily or have become dependent. Read Chapter A2, especially those parts that discuss dependent drug use and risk and protective factors. Also read about the drug, or drugs, that they are using in Part D.

Do your best to make a careful assessment of the way the young person is using drugs and the underlying difficulties they face, as outlined in Chapter B5.

You will need to talk with and listen carefully to them using the communication skills that I have highlighted in Chapter B4.

At the same time you need to be patient with them and be realistic about what changes they can make and how quickly, as discussed in Chapter B3. Try to help them set some realistic targets for change, even if they may at first be small steps. Decide who else, if anyone, you might need to inform of the situation – see Chapter B6.

If they will not stop using or moderate their use, see the advice I have given in Chapters B3 and C7 and consider what harm reduction measures you can encourage them to follow to keep themselves as safe as possible in the meantime.

Where possible, encourage and support them to seek specialist help for themselves – see Chapter B10.

Parents should try to establish clear boundaries when their child is using drugs heavily or is dependent, even though this may be difficult – see the general advice on pages 154–155 and also the advice I have given in the next Chapter, C9, about dealing with situations in which young people are violent or steal.

Where young people have been using heavily or dependent on drugs for a time, some parents have ended up actually going out to buy illegal drugs for their child and placed themselves at risk of prosecution. Some have also given their child money to buy drugs or pay their debts to dealers or gone out to confront drug dealers and placed themselves at risk of violence. I can understand why some parents have done such things when they are desperate but the results of such actions are usually unpredictable, often counterproductive in the longer term and may place parents at serious risk themselves.

Some parents have also decided to report their child to the police in an attempt to break what they feel is a stalemate. The difficulty with doing this is that you will probably not be able to anticipate how the police will respond. In some instances they may be sensitive to your family situation but in other cases act in a heavy-handed way. While parents reporting their children to the police has sometimes resulted in the young person accessing treatment and helping services, in other cases it has not and has led to them having a criminal record and sometimes even going to prison.

Try to establish some clear rules – see Chapter B7 – about how the young person can minimize the negative impact their drug use has on themselves and on other family members, including yourself. This might include rules about when and where they use, how much and how often, not leaving drugs or paraphernalia lying around the home, especially if there are young children around, and how they behave in general.

Professionals may need to establish similar boundaries when working with young people who are using drugs heavily or are dependent. They should also, wherever possible, support young people to continue attending school, college, work or youth projects, rather than becoming even more isolated.

IF THEY ARE VIOLENT OR STEAL MONEY OR POSSESSIONS TO BUY DRUGS

Violence and stealing on a young person's part are unacceptable behaviours and drug use, including dependent use, is not a justification for such behaviours. While some people say that 'addicts' are not responsible for their actions I do not hold this view. Drug use is no excuse for abusive or anti-social behaviour.

These are especially difficult issues for parents to deal with. Many are caught between their love and concern for their child and their horror and anger about how they are being treated. It can be similarly disturbing for professionals and seem like the ultimate betrayal.

In such situations you will need to stand firm to protect yourself and other people who may be affected. This is easier said than done. I do not have clear answers but what follows are some ideas that may help.

My first advice is to seek support for yourself. This might include help from friends, family members and work colleagues as well as from specialist agencies and telephone helplines. In some localities there are also support groups for parents of young people who experience drug problems. See Part E for information about the help you can access for yourself.

Try to be clear about what your boundaries are, what behaviours are acceptable and unacceptable to you on the young person's part and what the consequences will be for them for behaving in unacceptable ways – see pages 154–155.

If a young person is violent and will not calm down call on other family members, friends or work colleagues to help you manage such behaviour. If their behaviour threatens your safety, or that of other people who are present, call the police.

Once they have calmed down, try to set clear boundaries with the young person. While I have previously emphasized in Chapter B7 that it is best that drug rules are negotiated with young people, if they have been violent or stealing, boundaries may need to be imposed, even if the young person does not agree or stick to them.

You can still use the communication skills I have highlighted in Chapter B4 to discuss boundaries with them and to listen to what they have to say, but there can be no fudging when it comes to violent behaviour or stealing. Where there has not been initial co-operation, some parents and professionals have found it useful to write a simple letter to the young person, explaining what the problem is, how it affects them and other people and what they want the young person to do and why. Some people have extended this approach to agree a written contract of behaviour for the young person to adhere to.

It is important for you to keep to the boundaries by noticing whether or not the young person is sticking to them. Acknowledge whether they keep to or break the boundaries. If they do break the boundaries again don't ignore what they have done or make excuses for them. Take time to choose your response, rather than reacting from feelings of frustration and anger. State clearly how you feel, restate what you want and need of them and, if necessary, implement the consequences that you have said will follow. It may take time for the young person to stick to boundaries and it is important that you are consistent.

In such situations some parents have reached the end of their tether and taken drastic action. Where their child is living with them, this has included throwing them out of the family home, sometimes by having to change the locks. Some parents have also reported their own child to the police as a last resort and as a way of breaking a pattern they have been unable to change through other means. I am not recommending such tough love actions to you but I do understand why some parents have done these things when nothing else seems to have worked and the situation has become unbearable.

Making a young person homeless may lead to their problems escalating even further. The implications of reporting them to the police are usually difficult to anticipate because the response from police can vary greatly. If the police successfully prosecute the young person they will have a criminal record and that will usually go against the young person's employment and travel prospects. However, I am also aware of some cases where a parent reporting their child to the police has led to the young person accessing treatment and help and doing something positive about their chaotic drug use and associated problems.

Young people have commonly been excluded from schools, colleges, workplaces, clubs, pubs and from rented accommodation and hostels for violent or abusive behaviour and stealing associated with drug use. In some instances exclusion has been permanent and professionals have understandably had little hesitation in informing the police. However, as I have emphasized in Chapters B7 and C4, our responses to young people breaking rules should not be disproportionate and ideally we can work to reintegrate them in the future so that they do not become even more isolated. You will need to be clear with them about their future behaviour if they are to be allowed to return.

Young people who behave in such ways are likely to have serious underlying difficulties. Once matters have calmed down, it is important that both parents and professionals go beyond treating them as disciplinary cases and try to support them through their problems. See the general advice I have given on pages 154–157 on how you might go about doing this, as well as the advice I have given in Chapter C8 about supporting young people who are using drugs heavily or dependent. Wherever possible, help them to seek support for themselves – see Chapter B10.

If a young person is violent or steals we will probably begin to lose faith in them. It will take time but it is important that we work to rebuild our sense of trust and the relationship we have with them.

IF THEY ARE SUPPLYING DRUGS

Our attitudes and responses to young people supplying drugs will vary depending on which drug, or drugs, are involved and the type of supplying involved. We also need to be aware of the various ways that young people can become involved in supplying drugs and their motivations for doing so. Many adults are subject to the myths that surround drug dealing and it is important that we avoid such traps and deal with the real world. Have a look at Chapter A3 which discusses drug dealing and the myths about it that people often fall for.

The first step is to establish which drug, or drugs, are involved and whether, or not, supply involves the young person breaking the law and being at risk of prosecution. Look at Chapter A6 and the information about the specific drug or drugs involved, in Part D, to establish whether or not they are involved in an illegal act.

The next step is to find out what type of drug supply has been going on. For example:

- Does it involve small or large quantities?

- Is it a one-off situation or has it been a regular occurrence?

- Who have they been supplying to and where?

- Where are they accessing the drugs from?

- Are they making a profit from supplying drugs, selling at cost or supplying for free?

- Have they become involved with people who are also committing other offences?

- Is there any evidence of bullying or coercion on their part or anyone else's?

The third step is to understand the young person's possible motivations for supplying drugs. Some young people may see it as a way to make a living, or at least a good sum of money quickly, in much the same way that, these days, young people are encouraged to be entrepreneurial and start up their own businesses with legal products. Some students have become drug dealers as a way of paying their college or university fees and expenses. For some people small-scale dealing is a way of supplying themselves with drugs for free. For others it may also be a way of becoming popular among their peers.

Some young people are pressurized or harassed by their friends or acquaintances to obtain drugs for them. Drug incidents in schools have sometimes involved students who supplied drugs being bullied by other students into doing so. Professional dealers may sometimes threaten young people to supply drugs for them, especially if they are owed money.

If the young person has been supplying drugs at home or on work premises there can be legal obligations for their parents or professionals who work with them – see Chapter C4 for further details.

To find out all this information you will need to develop a good relationship with the young person concerned and make a careful assessment of the situation. See Chapters B4 and B5 to help you do this. You will also need to decide who else, if anyone, you will inform about the situation – see Chapter B6.

Make sure that the young person understands the legal position they have put themselves in – see Chapter A6.

Last, but not least, if necessary, get some advice and support for yourself – see the organizations listed in Part E.

C11

IF THEY ARE EXPERIENCING DIFFICULTIES OR CONCERNS BECAUSE OF OTHER PEOPLE'S DRUG USE

When we think of the ways that drug use can result in difficulties for young people we tend to consider harms that result from their own use of drugs. However, as I have emphasized previously in this book, nearly everyone is a drug user and has a lifetime drug career and we can all be affected by the use of drugs by other people who we have contact with. Young people may experience a range of difficulties or concerns resulting from the drug use of their parents, other family members, friends, partners, fellow students at school or college, work colleagues and even their neighbours.

If a young person is worried about someone else's drug use you can support them to understand and help the person they are concerned about. This might include listening to them, offering them advice, showing them relevant chapters of this book and directing them to agencies and helplines that may be able to support and advise them or the person they are concerned about – see Part E.

There has been a lot of concern about problematic drug use among parents and the impact this can have on their children, especially younger children. It has been estimated that, in the UK, between 250,000 and 350,000 children aged under 16 years old have at least one parent with a serious drug problem and that three in ten children in the UK live with at least one binge drinking or alcoholic parent (Manning *et al.* 2009).

In some instances such drug use has contributed to children experiencing a very disorganized and chaotic life, broken promises, emotional inconsistency, neglectful or very authoritarian parenting and the implications of debt and financial problems. However, we should not assume that all of these parents are inadequate or that their difficulties are being caused by drug use and not by deeper, underlying issues. Even those who experience problems with drug use may be adequately fulfilling a parental role and their children may be cared for by other family members, particularly their other parent, grandparents and/or older siblings.

Professionals should offer support to young people who are known to be adversely affected by, or concerned about, their parent's drug use. Some parents may also find themselves supporting such young people, most commonly friends of their own children. Where necessary and appropriate, you can refer young people to specialist support agencies – see Part E. In some instances you may also be able to support parents directly and refer them for help.

In some cases the drug use of parents will be of particular concern and have a very negative impact on children. This may be to the extent that there are clear signs of neglect or abuse. Where children and young people are aged under 16 years old, normal safeguarding procedures apply and should be followed. Social services should be able to offer support, in such situations, to young people and their families, and also give advice to professionals.

Last, but not least, if necessary, get some advice and support for yourself – see Part E.

THE DRUGS

ALCOHOL

WHAT IT IS

Alcohol is made by the fermentation of fruits, vegetables or grains and mainly consists of flavoured water and ethyl alcohol (ethanol). Beer, lager and cider are usually about one part alcohol to twenty parts water. Wine is about two to four times as strong and distilled spirits such as whisky, rum and gin are about half water and half alcohol.

Half a pint of normal pub strength beer, cider or lager is regarded as roughly one unit of alcohol. This is the alcohol equivalent of about one small glass of wine or one single pub measure of spirits. Some beers, lagers and ciders are made to be especially strong and may contain up to twice as much alcohol as the same volume of normal brands.

STREET NAMES

Street names for alcohol include bevvy, booze, drink, jar and plonk.

BRIEF HISTORY

Making and drinking alcohol dates back to at least 6000 BC and has been an integral part of many societies ever since. While the fermentation processes needed to make wines and beers were discovered in prehistoric times, the distillation of spirits is thought to be a mere 1000 years old.

Alcohol has been central to many religious ceremonies and social events ranging from the crowning of monarchs, war-making, births, marriages, anniversaries, commemorations and funerals. It has a long history of being consumed with meals and also, especially in the form of beer, may predate bread as a basic food product that is rich in carbohydrates. In earlier times brewing was mainly left to women and many young children would have consumed beer on a daily basis. In the Middle Ages beer was also popular because it had to be boiled, contained bug-killing yeast and alcohol, and was less likely to give you cholera than local water sources. It could also be stored for longer than grain or bread without fear of pest infestation or rotting.

British people have drunk nut-brown ales for centuries. Between 1720 and 1750 there was an epidemic of gin drinking, resulting in an Act of Parliament which put a high tax on gin and curbed its retail sale. In London the response was riotous protests. In the 18th and 19th centuries excessive alcohol consumption was common in the UK, to an extent that far exceeds current levels of drinking. The year 1848 saw new laws introduced to close public houses between midnight on Saturday and noon on Sunday and in 1872 there was a ban on weekday drinking between midnight and 6am. Modern licensing controls were first introduced during the First World War in an attempt to limit drinking by soldiers. By the latter 19th century temperance movements were set up by doctors, clergy and other upholders of 'morality' to try to persuade the public of the evils of alcohol use and the need to acquire better habits.

In America the temperance movements were strong enough to persuade the then government to introduce prohibition from 1919. This attempted to outlaw the manufacture, sale and transportation of alcohol. Although overall alcohol consumption did decline, there was a rise in alcohol consumption in many cities along with significant increases in organized crime related to its production and distribution. Pressure mounted to repeal prohibition laws and by 1933 the US Government acted. Although prohibition was dead nationwide it survived in a few southern and border states.

In the UK drinking increased significantly in the 1990s, especially among young people, and saw the introduction of new high strength lagers and beers and alcopops, alcoholic drinks that do not taste so much of alcohol. In England and Wales the 2003 Licensing Act introduced more flexible licensing hours but also strengthened powers to regulate at the point of sale and deal with licensed premises.

With recent concern about increased drinking in the UK, and not only among young people, there have been fierce debates between the drinks industry and those concerned about the health impact of excessive drinking with regard to restricting alcohol advertising and promotions and introducing minimum pricing for alcoholic drinks. As yet, the UK government has prevaricated about such matters.

LEGAL STATUS

It is not illegal for a child over 5 years old to consume alcohol away from licensed premises. Strictly speaking it is illegal for an adult, including a parent, to give alcohol to children aged under 5 years old.

It is an offence for a vendor to knowingly sell alcohol to an under-18-year-old. Doing so can result in a fine and loss of licence to sell alcohol. A 14-year-old can go into a pub alone but not consume alcohol. A 16-year-old can buy and consume beer, port, cider or perry (but not spirits) in a pub if having a meal in an area set aside for this purpose. Some cities and towns have by-laws restricting drinking of alcohol on the streets at any age. Police have powers to confiscate alcohol from under-18s who drink in public places. In addition there are laws relating to being drunk and disorderly and regarding drink-driving.

AVAILABILITY, EXTENT OF USE AND COST

As with adults, other than caffeine, alcohol is by far the most common drug of choice among young people. Young children are usually introduced to using alcohol at home under parental supervision. A recent national survey of 11–15-year-olds attending secondary schools in England found that 12 per cent of 11-year-olds claimed to have ever tried alcohol, rising to almost three quarters of 15-year-olds (Health and Social Care Information Centre 2013). Only 1 per cent of 11-year-olds said that they had drunk some alcohol in the week before the survey, rising to 25 per cent of 15-year-olds. Almost one in five 15-year-olds said they drank alcohol at least once a week, usually at the weekend. Alcohol consumption increases significantly for young people aged over 16 years old, with 16–24-year-olds being more likely to binge drink and become drunk, than any other age group (Health and Social Care Information Centre 2012b).

Overall, the level of alcohol consumption among young people in the UK doubled in quantity over a ten-year period from around 1990 (Department of Health 2009). During this period new designer drinks with high alcohol content, such as strong beers, lagers, ciders and alcopops, were introduced by alcohol manufacturers and specifically targeted at young people. Young people were drinking greater quantities of alcohol and drinking more often, and more were drinking regularly with the aim of becoming drunk. While boys tended to drink greater quantities of alcohol and more often than girls, surveys began to indicate that girls were catching up with boys in their alcohol consumption, especially with their use of alcopops and spirits, particularly vodka. Class differences in alcohol consumption among young people are not as significant as those for cigarette smoking, although social class and disposable income will influence the type of drinks consumed and where drinking takes place, and binge drinking is more likely among young people in more deprived areas.

Young people in the UK remain among the highest consumers of alcohol in the whole of Europe (ESPAD 2012) but there is evidence that their overall level of consumption has decreased over the past few years (Health and Social Care Information Centre 2013). However, this more recent trend may be more indicative of a fall in the number of young people who drink, rather than any significant decrease in the amount of alcohol consumed by the many young people who continue to drink regularly and heavily.

Most young people are given their first drink by their parents or another family member. Rather than buying it directly, most of the younger age range obtain alcohol by being given it by friends and siblings or by asking someone else to buy if for them. Once into later teens many young people are able to pass for 18 years old and buy alcohol in pubs and clubs, although they may still find it difficult to buy it from shops and supermarkets and have to rely on other people to get it for them from these places.

Regular alcohol use, or a binge session, can be expensive but alcohol consumption can be relatively cheap when it involves high strength/low cost lagers and ciders bought in large bottles or in packs containing a quantity of bottles or cans. The advent of low cost brands of spirits bought in large bottles, happy hours and other offers at pubs, bars and clubs has also made regular drinking relatively inexpensive. Alcohol is also sold at low prices on the black market and is sometimes available in this way to young people, particularly in poorer areas.

EFFECTS OF USE

Alcohol is a depressant which starts to have an effect within five to ten minutes. The effects can last for several hours, depending on the amount consumed. Effects also depend on how quickly it is drunk, whether there is food in the user's stomach and their body weight.

After four units (equivalent to two pints of ordinary strength beer or three or four small glasses of wine) most people feel less inhibited and more relaxed. After about eight units drinkers become unco-ordinated and slur their speech. More alcohol may result in staggering, loss of balance, being sick and visual distortion. Excessive amounts will lead to loss of consciousness. Since tolerance develops with regular use, the effects will also depend on how used to drinking someone is.

Some drinkers become aggressive and argumentative, especially if they are already stressed or wound up. A lot of violence on the streets and in the home (much of it directed at women and children, but also much between young males) happens after people, especially males, have been drinking. The effects also depend on how people feel before they are drinking. People who feel relaxed, and in a good mood when they drink are less likely to become aggressive.

POSSIBLE HARMS

Drinking alcohol makes accidents more likely, especially when people fall over, drive or are operating machinery. It also increases the risk of being involved in fights and criminal activity. Lowering of inhibitions can make it more likely that people will put themselves in sexual situations which they later regret. They are less likely to practise safer sex and use condoms if they do have intercourse. Drinking also leads to a lot of sexual harassment, particularly of young women. There have also been cases of alcohol being spiked with drugs such as GHB and Rohypnol tranquillizers and linked to date rape, although the extent to which this happens may have sometimes been overestimated. Drinking a large amount of alcohol may, in itself, be enough to put people in a comatose state.

Drinking too much in one go can lead to losing consciousness and even death by choking on vomit. Alcohol can also be very dangerous if taken in combination with other drugs, especially other depressant drugs such as heroin, methadone or tranquillizers. Taking these drugs with alcohol has led to many fatal overdoses. Drinking alcohol, while taking drugs like ecstasy or mephedrone, can also increase the likelihood of overheating and dehydration and has in some cases resulted in fatalities.

Long-term heavy drinking can be very damaging. Physical dependence and tolerance can develop as people drink more. Withdrawal symptoms (such as trembling, sweating, anxiety and delirium) can be experienced if dependent users try to stop. At this point such drinkers may be regarded as alcoholics. Heavy, long-term drinking can also lead to damage to the heart, liver, stomach and brain and, with beers, lagers and ciders, result in obesity. There have been concerns that in recent years more young people are experiencing such long-term problems.

Pregnant women who drink excessively on a regular basis may give birth to babies of lower birth weight who suffer withdrawal symptoms, foetal abnormalities and possibly delayed physical and mental development. However, cases of 'foetal alcohol syndrome' are rare in the UK and there is little evidence that moderate drinking during pregnancy causes harm to the mother or her baby.

Excessive drinking commonly may aggravate personal, family, work and financial problems and contribute towards family breakdown, violence and other forms of crime associated with loss of control.

Alcohol-related deaths in the UK rose significantly from 1980 until the early 2000s and have since stabilized. Direct deaths through cirrhosis of the liver, other diseases directly associated with heavy alcohol use, poisoning and overdose now stand at around 9000 a year in the UK (Office for National Statistics 2013a). These do not include deaths from alcohol-related accidents and violence, road traffic accidents involving drunk drivers and diseases where alcohol may have been a contributing factor. Other than cirrhosis of the liver and other alcohol-related diseases, a significant number of alcohol-related deaths occur among young people aged 14 to 25 years old.

The number of recorded hospital admissions for alcohol-related conditions has increased significantly in recent years, with many young people being rushed to hospital to have their stomachs pumped after binge drinking (Health and Social Care Information Centre 2012b).

Medical guidelines on safe weekly levels of alcohol intake have changed. In 1986 recommended limits were 50 units a week for men and 35 for women (one unit is about half a pint of normal strength beer). Today recommended safe levels are three to four units a day (21 units a week) for men and two to three units a day (14 units a week) for women. These are figures for adults and many people would suggest they should be less for young people. However, there is controversy about how 'scientific' these figures are and some people have suggested regular, moderate drinking may even help prevent heart attacks. Notwithstanding these debates, it is widely agreed that many young people drink excessive amounts on a regular basis and that if they continue to do so this could be very damaging to their health in future.

SAFETY/HARM REDUCTION ADVICE FOR YOUNG PEOPLE
To avoid the dangers of alcohol…

1. Don't use it. But if young people do drink alcohol the advice is…

2. Don't drink too much or too often. Don't drink every day.

3. Be aware of how much you are drinking – both the quantity of alcohol and how strong it is.

4. Avoid alcohol when you feel really down. It will probably make you feel worse.

5. Beware of drinks being spiked. Keep an eye on your own drink and friends' drinks.

6. Don't drive or operate machinery after drinking.

7. Take care to avoid sexual situations you may later regret. If you do have sex, use condoms.

8. Don't mix drink and other drugs. It can be very dangerous.

9. Avoid being around people who are really drunk where violence might explode.

10. If you are trying to cut down or stop drinking, avoid people who are drinking and places where people are drinking.

11. If you are having problems with your use, seek help and advice.

AMPHETAMINES

WHAT THEY ARE

Amphetamines are man-made stimulant drugs. They are manufactured and prescribed as medicines such as Dexedrine (dexamphetamine sulphate) and Ritalin (methylphenidate hydrochloride), usually in tablet form. Illicitly produced amphetamines (amphetamine sulphate) are commonly a white, grey, yellowish or pinkish powder, often sold in a paper wrap.

The purity rate of street powder is usually only about 7 to 10 per cent. The rest is usually made up of milder stimulants such as caffeine, other drugs such as paracetamol or substances like glucose, dried baby milk, flour or talcum powder.

The powder form can be snorted up the nose, swallowed in a 'wrap' or mixed in a drink or dabbed on the gums. Amphetamines can also be prepared for injection.

There are also two very potent forms of amphetamines which are less commonly used in the UK. Amphetamine base is a paste produced before it is crystallized into a powder and usually smoked or swallowed. Methamphetamine is usually found in crystalline or powder form that can be smoked, snorted, swallowed or injected and has become widely available in America. It is very strong and can result in intense paranoia, delusions, aggressive behaviour, a dangerous rise in blood pressure and heart rate and a very unpleasant 'comedown'. It has been compared to crack.

STREET NAMES

Street names for amphetamines include speed and whizz and also amphet, billy, billy whizz, pep pills, sulph, sulphate, uppers and wake ups. Street names for methamphetamine include Christine, crystal, crystal meth, glass, ice, krank, Tina and yaba.

BRIEF HISTORY

Amphetamines were first discovered in the 1880s but not used medically until the 1930s, often to counter low blood pressure and help asthmatics breathe more easily. They were later prescribed for a whole range of disorders including epilepsy, migraine, depression, narcolepsy (falling asleep) and hyperactivity in children.

The stimulant effect has led to widespread use by soldiers to combat 'battle fatigue'. An estimated 72 million tablets were issued to British forces during the Second World War and amphetamines were widely used by American forces in the Vietnam War. Famous users have included Adolf Hitler and also the UK Prime Minister, Anthony Eden, throughout the 1956 Suez crisis.

In the 1950s and 1960s amphetamines were widely marketed as slimming tablets. Until the late 1950s many amphetamine-based drugs could be bought over-the-counter in a chemist shop without a prescription. Use among bored housewives, people who felt they needed an energy boost ('pep pills' and 'tonics') and those who worked long hours, such as long distance lorry drivers and oil rig workers, was common. Students have often used amphetamines to stay awake for long periods to revise for exams, as have sports people, such as cyclists and mountaineers, to enhance endurance.

In recent years medical prescribing has declined, although Ritalin (methylpenidate hydrochloride), an amphetamine-like drug, has been increasingly prescribed to people who have been diagnosed with attention deficit disorder (ADHD), including many young children.

Non-medical use of amphetamines grew in the UK in the 1960s especially among teenage 'mods'. The use of 'purple hearts' (a combination of amphetamines and barbiturates) led to the first post war 'drug craze', and media drug scare, in the UK. In 1964 the government moved to make unauthorized possession of amphetamines an offence.

In the 1970s and 1980s street use of amphetamines increased again and centred on a new generation of young people in the all-night Northern Soul and punk rock scenes. Powdered amphetamines replaced tablets as the main form of use. In the 1990s amphetamines found a new clientele among young clubbers and ravers and became a common drug of choice alongside ecstasy.

LEGAL STATUS

Amphetamines are prescription-only drugs under the Medicines Act. Most are also controlled as Class B drugs under the Misuse of Drugs Act. Doctors can prescribe some of them for patients but it is an offence to be in possession of amphetamines without a prescription or to supply them. If amphetamines are prepared for injection they become Class A drugs and increased penalties apply.

Methamphetamine is a Class A drug under the Misuse of Drugs Act.

AVAILABILITY, EXTENT OF USE AND COST

The annual Crime Survey in England and Wales has found the number of 16–24-year-olds who claim to have used amphetamines at least once in the past year has fallen from around 10 per cent in the middle to late 1990s to around 5 per cent in 2000 and down to 1.3 per cent in 2012/13 (Home Office 2013).

Surveys conducted until 2000 often found that, after cannabis, amphetamines were the illegal drug that more people had used than any other. Most users do not inject amphetamines but, after heroin, it is still probably the most commonly injected street drug. Despite this, and its long history of use in the UK, amphetamines have rarely made the headlines.

In recent years the popularity of amphetamines has fallen, possibly due to the increased availability of other stimulant drugs through the fall in price of cocaine and the introduction of mephedrone.

Most of the amphetamines available in the UK are illicitly made in other European countries but there are also underground laboratories here. The price of amphetamine powder has remained at a similar level for many years. It sells for about £10 to £15 a gram and less when bought in larger quantities. It is also often sold in a small 'wrap' for about £5. This will often be enough to keep a user awake all night. A heavy user might consume anything up to several grams a day.

EFFECTS OF USE

As stimulant drugs, amphetamines increase breathing and heart rate, lessen appetite and make the pupils widen. Users tend to feel more alert, energetic, confident and cheerful and less bored or tired. With high doses people often experience intensification of these effects together with sweating, headaches, jaw clenching, teeth grinding and a racing heart. A rapid flow of ideas and feelings of increased physical and mental powers are also common. Users may be very talkative and some may become aggressive.

When taken orally the effects of a single dose last for about three to four hours. If snorted, the effects last for four to six hours. Injecting tends to produce a 'rush' feeling and more intense effects that last longer. Afterwards users often feel very tired and may take a couple of days to feel normal again.

POSSIBLE HARMS

After using, the body's energy stores may become run down and feelings of anxiety, irritability and restlessness are common. Taking a lot over a few days can sometimes produce intense mood swings, panic and paranoia. These usually go once the drug is eliminated from the body. The strong 'upper' effect can be particularly dangerous to people who have heart or blood pressure problems.

Regular use can lead to dependence. Users may become depressed, lethargic, lacking in energy and very hungry when not taking the drug. This is sometimes explained as 'what goes up must come down'. They may keep repeating use to avoid these feelings. Tolerance also develops with regular use so more is needed to get the same effect.

Heavy, regular use often leads to lack of sleep and loss of appetite and lowers resistance to disease. Eating disorders, such as anorexia nervosa, may become a problem, especially among women users. Normal work and domestic routines may be disturbed. Many heavy users become very run down and alternate between periods of feeling good and energetic then feeling depressed and low. Delusions, panic attacks, paranoia, a feeling of being 'wired' may also follow. Some users experience violent mood swings and can become very aggressive.

Injecting is particularly dangerous. A very high dose may be taken in one go and the bulking agents that are mixed with the street powder may themselves be dangerous to inject. Injecting also leaves users open to abscesses and infection, including hepatitis and HIV if injecting equipment is shared.

Some people who regularly take amphetamines also use depressant drugs such as alcohol, heroin or tranquillizers to help bring them down. They may find themselves on a chemical roller-coaster of uppers and downers which can be very dangerous and difficult to stop.

Not many people who are dependent on amphetamines go to drug agencies for help. They sometimes view drug services as only being for 'junkies' – those using heroin. Many drug services provide alternative drugs on prescription, such as methadone, for those dependent on heroin. There is no similar prescription alternative for amphetamines and this may be another reason why users do not seek out drug services.

SAFETY/HARM REDUCTION ADVICE FOR YOUNG PEOPLE
To avoid the dangers of amphetamines…

1. Don't use them. But if young people do use amphetamines the advice is…

2. Don't take too much or use too often.

3. Don't inject, but if you do, use clean injecting equipment and never share it with other people. Sharing injecting equipment can lead to hepatitis and HIV.

4. Don't drink alcohol or take other drugs at the same time. Mixing drugs can be very dangerous.

5. Remember the strength of amphetamines can vary and they can be mixed with all sorts of things that can themselves be dangerous, especially if injected.

6. Remember it is illegal and you could get in trouble with the law. You could get in very serious trouble if you supply other people, whether or not you charge or make a profit.

7. Look after yourself. Try to keep to sensible sleep patterns and eat a good diet.

8. People who are trying to cut down or stop should avoid people and places where amphetamines are being used.

9. If you are having problems with your use, seek help and advice.

CAFFEINE

WHAT IT IS

Caffeine is a stimulant drug that is found in tea, coffee and cocoa and also many soft drinks, especially colas. It is also in confectionery, sweets, breakfast cereals, biscuits, cakes and ice creams that contain chocolate or cocoa. Caffeine is also present in large quantities in energy drinks like Red Bull (advertised as 'stimulation', 'increases physical endurance' and 'gives you wings'), energy tablets such as Pro Plus (advertised as 'relieves tiredness', 'picks you up', 'fast acting' and 'helps you feel more awake' and to help students revise for exams) and some chewing gums, mints and other sweets.

Legal highs, such as 'Snow Blow', mainly consist of caffeine powder that is for snorting and are sometimes promoted as 'legal speed'.

Caffeine is also used in a wide variety of medicines, especially those for headaches and to help people urinate, and is also sometimes present in illegal drugs, such as amphetamines, cocaine and ecstasy, and legal highs that are marketed as stimulants.

Caffeine can be manufactured in a laboratory but also occurs naturally in the Arabian coffee shrub, commercial tea plants, cocoa beans and kola nuts. Coffee is grown in many areas of the world including Africa, Arabia, Central and South America, Java and Sumatra and the West Indies. Tea is mainly grown in eastern Asia and South America especially India, China, Indonesia, Sri Lanka and Japan. Most of the world's cocoa is grown in West Africa.

STREET NAMES

Street names for tea include bevvy, brew, cuppa and for coffee include shot.

BRIEF HISTORY

The earliest use of tea was probably in China before the 10th century BC. Coffee use is more recent and the first record of its cultivation was in Arabia about AD 675. Tea was first imported to Europe in about 1600 and first came to the UK in about 1660.

Coffee was first introduced to the UK as a medicinal product but became very fashionable to drink in the 1670s. Coffee houses sprang up in London and caused much controversy. The authorities saw them as recruiting places for political radicals and some women's groups protested that they damaged family life. The authorities moved to close them down. A compromise was reached where coffee houses could remain open so long as they did not allow the sale of political books and pamphlets or political speeches.

Coffee houses then became less popular and changes in commerce saw coffee consumption fall. England turned to tea drinking and remains the only country in Europe that consumes more tea than coffee. However, recent years have seen a resurgence of coffee houses and coffee drinking in the UK, including stronger varieties. Concerns about the effects of caffeine have led to the manufacture of decaffeinated coffees and teas. Alongside increased coffee consumption, recent years have seen the introduction of a range of other caffeine-based products (such as drinks, tablets, chewing gums and mints) which are advertised for their stimulant qualities.

LEGAL STATUS

There are no legal restrictions on the sale or use of coffee, tea and cocoa or soft drinks, confectionery and foods containing caffeine. Highly caffeinated energy drinks are freely available in newsagents and supermarkets and energy pills can be bought at chemists and many other shops off the shelf. Some chemists have moved energy pills to behind the counter after finding how commonly they were stolen. There have been appeals for retailers not to sell energy drinks and pills to young people aged under 18 years old but this is not subject to legislation. Certain medicines that contain caffeine may only be available on a doctor's prescription.

AVAILABILITY, EXTENT OF USE AND COST

Caffeine is the most commonly used drug in the UK. Many young children consume large quantities of caffeine for their body weight through drinking colas and other soft drinks and eating food products that contain caffeine. As they get older young people often continue this consumption but also add tea and coffee. In the last few years coffee has become particularly popular with a resurgence of coffee shops and strong brands, coffee tending to have higher caffeine content than most teas.

In recent years many adults and teenagers have also started to consume heavily caffeinated drinks like Red Bull (sometimes with alcohol) and to take energy pills such as Pro Plus, which are overtly marketed for their stimulant properties. Caffeinated drinks, like Red Bull, are also commonly used as mixers for alcohol, especially vodka. Use of energy drinks and pills, together with drinking low calorie, caffeinated soft drinks, is possibly more prevalent among young women, particularly those who want to diet and keep going on a low calorie intake.

EFFECTS OF USE

Caffeine is a stimulant drug that increases heart rate and blood pressure. It combats tiredness and drowsiness and makes people feel more alert and able to concentrate. Many people have a cup of tea or coffee every morning to 'get going'.

However, people also drink tea and coffee to help them relax, although this may often be due to combating feelings of withdrawal in regular users. Caffeine also makes people urinate more. High doses can result in users having headaches and feeling very irritable.

POSSIBLE HARMS

People who drink more than six to eight cups of normal strength tea or coffee a day usually become dependent. They may find it difficult to stop using and experience withdrawal symptoms if they try. If young children are forced to give up heavy consumption of colas, soft drinks and food products that contain caffeine they may also experience withdrawal symptoms. These can include feeling tired and anxious, irritability and headaches. However, dependence on caffeine is socially acceptable and, unlike other drugs, not usually regarded as a social problem.

Regular users may find they become more restless and anxious and may find it difficult to sleep. Research into the health effects of long-term use of caffeine is inconclusive. However, some reports have suggested that it can lead to a higher incidence of asthma, peptic ulcers, kidney, bladder and heart disease and blood pressure problems.

There have also been concerns about the amount of caffeine consumed by young children. Some commentators have suggested that children who consume a lot of caffeine may become hyperactive with the possible consequence of being diagnosed with ADHD and prescribed drugs like Ritalin. A child drinking one small can of cola may be taking the equivalent caffeine intake as an adult drinking four cups of coffee.

Teenage girls in particular may be attracted to caffeine-based products (strong black coffee, diet colas and energy boost caffeine pills) as a way of reducing appetite and keeping going on few calories. In some situations heavy caffeine consumption may facilitate excessive slimming and anorexia nervosa.

SAFETY/HARM REDUCTION ADVICE FOR YOUNG PEOPLE
To avoid the dangers of caffeine…

1. Don't use it. But if young people do take caffeinated products the advice is…

2. Be aware of the different caffeine-based products you are using and how much caffeine you may be consuming.

3. Don't take too much or too often. Limit your intake.

4. Consider using decaffeinated soft drinks, teas and coffees.

5. Be aware that caffeine may depress appetite, so make sure you eat healthily.

6. Be aware of your sleep patterns and don't use caffeine to replace sleep too often.

7. If you are using caffeine-based products as a way of keeping slim and becoming obsessive about your weight, seek help to deal with your difficulties in having a balanced diet.

CANNABIS

WHAT IT IS

Cannabis is a bushy plant that grows in many parts of the world and is also cultivated in the UK. The main active ingredient is tetrahydrocannabinol (THC).

Different forms of cannabis come from different parts of the plant. 'Hashish' or 'hash' is the resin scraped or rubbed from the dried plant and then pressed into brown/black blocks. It is mostly imported from Morocco, Pakistan, Lebanon and Afghanistan.

Herbal cannabis is made from the chopped, dried leaves of the plant. It is also known as 'grass', 'bush' and 'ganja' and in America as 'marijuana'. Traditionally it has been imported to the UK from Africa, South America, Thailand and the West Indies. In recent years particularly strong herbal forms such as sinsemilla/skunk have formed a larger share of the market. These have often been imported through, and sometimes grown in, European countries such as the Netherlands and Spain.

The last few years has also seen large-scale, commercial growing of herbal cannabis in the UK by criminal gangs, often in normal residential houses, garages, lock-ups and industrial premises that are converted into cannabis farms using special seeds, growing, light and irrigation systems.

Some people also grow homegrown herbal cannabis in their own homes, greenhouses or gardens or on allotments. This may be for their personal use, to supply friends and/or to make a profit from wider sales.

Cannabis is commonly smoked in a hand-rolled cigarette – a joint or spliff – often with tobacco. The herbal form is sometimes made into a cigarette without using tobacco. Cannabis is also often smoked using pipes, hookahs, chillums, bongs, vaporizers or various home-made smoking contraptions and between 'hot knives'. It is also sometimes eaten, brewed into a tea or cooked with, hence the names 'hash brownies' and 'space cakes'.

Cannabis oil is the least common form of cannabis found in the UK. It is made by percolating a solvent through the resin and pasted on cigarette papers to make a joint.

STREET NAMES

There are many street names for cannabis. General names include Bob Hope, blow, draw, dope, puff, smoke, spliff and wacky backy.

Names for cannabis resin include black, block, brown, cake, hash, hashish, pot, resin, shit, soap and names based on the country of origin such as Afghani, Columbian, Lebanese, Moroccan, Nepalese and Pakistani.

Names for herbal cannabis include bhang, blast, bud, bush, grass, ganga, herb, home-grown, leaf, marijuana, netherweed, northern lights, purple haze, sense(milla), skunk, weed and also some based on country or origin such as Thai sticks.

A 'joint', 'reefer' or 'spliff' is a hand-rolled cigarette containing cannabis. 'Skinning up' is the process of making one and 'toking' of smoking it. A bong is a water pipe for smoking cannabis and a chillum is a clay or wooden pipe. A 'henry' is an eighth of an ounce and a 'louis' a sixteenth, when buying or selling cannabis. Despite the UK use of the metric system, cannabis still often sells in ounces.

BRIEF HISTORY

Cannabis was first documented as a herbal remedy in a Chinese pharmacy text of the first century AD. It was widely used as a medicine in the Middle East, India and China and to manufacture a range of products (such as clothes, rope and sacks), for religious ceremonies and for pleasure.

It was first introduced into Western medicine in the 1840s by a doctor who had been working in India, for painkilling purposes, particularly in childbirth and for period pains. It is rumoured that Queen Victoria was prescribed cannabis by her doctor. In the late 19th century, and early part of this century, cannabis was widely and legally available through herbalists, grocers and chemists and used by many people as a herbal remedy for a wide range of medical conditions.

Use of cannabis for pleasure, dates back to ancient China and India. The drug was brought to Western Europe by soldiers in Napoleon's North African army at the beginning of the 19th century. Use of cannabis for pleasure did take place in the UK but it was not nearly as popular as in France.

Non-medical use of cannabis was first banned in the UK in 1928 after South African and Egyptian delegates at an international conference persuaded other countries that cannabis drove people mad. This idea that cannabis drove people mad and led to them being out of control, especially sexual control, was popularized in the 1930s and 1940s in America by the head of the Narcotics Bureau, Harry Anslinger. He organized pamphlets, stories in magazines and newspapers and even a film called *Reefer Madness* to convince people that terrible crimes were committed by people who used cannabis.

At the time, cannabis was hardly used in the UK. Up to the mid-1960s its use was confined mainly to the London jazz scene and some West Indian communities. In the 1960s its use grew rapidly, especially among young university and college students. In 1973 the government decided that cannabis had no medical uses and prohibited it being available on a doctor's prescription.

With the passing of the 1960s 'hippy' period cannabis use declined in Britain. Its popularity grew again in the 1980s and it is now by far the most commonly used illegal drug in the UK. Medical interest in cannabis has revived, particularly to relieve glaucoma (a disease of the eye), multiple sclerosis, cancers and the side effects of chemotherapy, period and muscle pains and other conditions. Currently, in the UK, doctors cannot prescribe cannabis. The only exception is Sativex, a cannabis-based nasal spray that is sometimes prescribed for people who have multiple sclerosis.

There has been much debate about legalizing, decriminalizing or depenalizing use of cannabis, often motivated by the extent of use, the number of convictions and liberalizing law changes in the Netherlands, Portugal and other European countries. In 2004 the UK government downgraded cannabis from a Class B to a Class C drug under the Misuse of Drugs Act, resulting in more lenient penalties, especially for possession offences. However, in 2009 following concerns about the increased availability of stronger forms such as sensemilla/skunk, this decision was reversed and cannabis again became a Class B drug, against the expert advice of the government's Advisory Council on the Misuse of Drugs.

LEGAL STATUS

Cannabis is controlled as a Class B drug under the Misuse of Drugs Act. It is illegal to grow, possess or supply to another person. Cannabis offences are dealt with in a special manner in the UK, compared to other controlled drugs. See Chapter A6, pages 75–76 for details.

It is not illegal to be in possession of cannabis seeds but it is illegal to grow cannabis plants from them, even if the plants are not harvested or used.

In the UK doctors cannot prescribe cannabis itself but can prescribe Sativex for cases of multiple sclerosis, as described above. They can also prescribe nabilone and dronabinol, synthetic forms of cannabis, in some cases, such as for treating nausea in cancer patients, when other drugs are not effective.

AVAILABILITY, EXTENT OF USE AND COST

Estimates suggest that over 10 million people in the UK may have tried cannabis at least once (Shapiro 2010). It is by far the most commonly, and frequently, used illegal drug.

In the past, local surveys often found that over half of young people aged over 16 claimed to have used cannabis at least once but the last few years have seen a decline in use. The annual Crime Survey in England and Wales has found that the number of 16–24-year-olds claiming to have used cannabis in the past year fell consistently from over a quarter between 1996 to 2003/4 to only 13.5 per cent in 2012/13 (Home Office 2013).

Cannabis is used by many young people on a regular basis. This is in contrast to other illegal drugs which tend mainly to be used on an occasional basis. The UK appears to have higher levels of use among young people than other European countries, including the Netherlands, where it is more freely available.

After being dominated by cannabis resin, in more recent years the UK market has seen herbal cannabis, and especially the stronger sinsemilla/skunk varieties, become the main type available. This has happened to the extent that in many areas resin became almost unavailable. At the time of writing there are signs that resin is making a comeback and again becoming more commonly available.

Most young people obtain cannabis in small quantities from friends, older siblings and acquaintances rather than professional dealers. Many will buy cannabis for friends, sometimes without any profit or to give themselves a free supply. Cannabis pipes, other paraphernalia, seeds and growing equipment can be legally purchased from headshops or over the internet.

Prices of cannabis vary over time and between localities, but the monetary price has remained at similar levels for a number of years despite inflation. Resin usually sells for about £80 to £120 per ounce. Imported standard herbal cannabis usually sells at about £100 to £120 an ounce and for £120 to £200 per ounce for stronger strains, like sensemilla/skunk.

One sixteenth of an ounce will usually be enough for three to six joints. Regular smokers might consume a quarter to half an ounce per week, often some of it shared with other people, but possibly more in some cases.

THE STRENGTH OF CANNABIS

Many people have been very concerned about the increase in strength of cannabis over the last few years with the introduction of strong herbal varieties such as sinsemilla/skunk. There has been a lot of scaremongering in the media about this and it was the main reason that the government reclassified cannabis from being a Class C to a Class B drug under the Misuse of Drugs Act in 2009, against the advice of many experts in the drugs field.

The UK Forensic Science Service (FSS) has estimated the variations in the strength of cannabis by analyzing changes in the THC content over time, based on seizures by law enforcement agencies. This may not be representative of cannabis used by consumers and accurate analysis of THC content can be difficult, but the results have been instructive.

The FSS found that there had been little change in THC content of cannabis resin and traditional herbal cannabis from 1995 to 2007 (Forensic Science Service 2008). They also found that while there had been an increase in the THC content of sinsemilla/skunk between 1995 and 2000, the THC content had remained relatively constant between 2001 and 2007.

A wide range of THC content within all three types of cannabis was discovered. The THC content varied from 1 to 23 per cent for sinsemilla/skunk, from 0.5 to 11 per cent for resin and from 0.3 to 12 per cent for standard herbal cannabis. In other words, some batches of resin and standard herbal could sometimes be a lot stronger than sinsemilla/skunk.

However, it is true that sinsemilla/skunk is often very strong, with mean THC content of around 12 to 14 per cent, possibly double the mean for resin. While it has formed an increasing share of the cannabis market in the UK and is relatively easily available to many young people, it is important to be aware of how it may be used. Some users may smoke it a lot but others may take account of its strength by smoking it less often and inhaling the cannabis smoke less deeply, compared to when they use less potent types.

The potency of the cannabis that is available today is unlikely to have changed much since 2007. There is also anecdotal evidence that more users are turning their backs on stronger strains and that the demand for, and sales of, sinsemilla/skunk may have declined. It would appear that availability and use of resin may be increasing again in response.

EFFECTS OF USE

Smoking cannabis increases pulse rate, decreases blood pressure, increases appetite and sometimes results in bloodshot eyes and occasional dizziness. Effects start within a few minutes and can last several hours depending on how much is taken. When eaten, effects take longer to begin but may last longer and are often more intense.

Cannabis has mild sedative effects but the experience of using varies depending on the amount of cannabis taken, its strength and the user's mood and what they expect to happen. Many people find the first time they use nothing much happens.

Generally cannabis makes people feel relaxed and less inhibited. They may become giggly and very talkative, or alternatively quiet and subdued and be more aware of music and colours and feel that time seems to stand still.

Short-term memory recall of what has just happened or been thought about may be impaired but this stops once the effects of cannabis wear off. Co-ordination can also be affected. When stoned, people often feel hungry and get the 'munchies'.

Some users find that cannabis makes them very anxious, panicky and paranoid and feel that everyone is out to get them. This can happen with inexperienced users, if users are already anxious, consume strong varieties or high doses of cannabis or combine their use with other drugs, including alcohol. Use by people who already have mental health difficulties may sometimes help them to feel better and more relaxed but can also lead to distressing experiences.

MENTAL HEALTH AND IQ

Some people have claimed that taking cannabis, and particularly use of stronger types of cannabis, can cause long-term mental problems, or 'cannabis psychosis', in young people who would otherwise not be suffering from such difficulties. Press scaremongering has included claims that smoking just one cannabis joint greatly increases your chances of being diagnosed with a 'mental illness'.

The government's Advisory Council on the Misuse of Drugs (ACMD), a group of experts in various aspects of drug use, have twice looked into this issue and the studies and claims related to it (ACMD 2006, 2008). Their reports make for informative reading, compared to the exaggeration and misinformation in the media.

Regarding temporary psychological distress, the reports found that cannabis use can result in anxiety, confusion, paranoia, panic attacks and agitation while people are under its influence but that these effects are usually short-lived and disappear once the effects of cannabis wear off. The ACMD also found that the most recent data was not persuasive of a causal association between cannabis use and the development of depression, bipolar disorder or on-going anxiety.

When it came to people who had already been diagnosed with schizophrenia, it was found that cannabis use can worsen the symptoms of schizophrenia and lead to relapse in some cases. However, it was also noted that there was a high prevalence of use of cannabis, and other drugs, among people diagnosed with schizophrenia, often in an attempt to lessen the symptoms of schizophrenia and the adverse effects of medication.

The ACMD reports also examined whether cannabis use actually caused psychotic symptoms and illnesses, including schizophrenia. They emphasized that studying this is difficult and that the research that had been carried out was not always that reliable. Studies often have small sample sizes, a questionable diagnosis of mental health problems and do not always take account of whether or not these problems began prior to cannabis use. Cannabis use was often self-reported and this may not give a reliable picture of the extent of people's use, especially when people are asked to recall their use from many years ago. Studies also found it difficult to take account of use of drugs other than cannabis and the many life experience and lifestyle factors that may have a bearing on mental health.

The ACMD concluded that, at worst, using cannabis increases the lifetime risk of developing schizophrenia by 1 per cent and that the evidence for the existence of a causal relationship between frequency of cannabis use and the development of psychosis is, based on the presently available evidence, weak.

Another difficulty with such studies is that psychiatrists are known to be relatively inconsistent in their diagnosis of what we call 'mental health problems'. Different psychiatrists may give the same person a different diagnosis or, in some cases, decide that they are not experiencing a mental health problem at all.

The other interesting thing about this debate about cannabis and mental health is that the vast majority of heavy cannabis users, referrals to drug services and young people deemed to have cannabis-related mental health problems are young men. Where are the young women? This would suggest that heavy and sometimes dependent cannabis use, and what we call mental health problems are not necessarily causally related and that 'mental health problems' may have more to do with the difficulties and issues that many young men are facing in our society, rather than anything intrinsic to cannabis itself.

A recent study was widely reported in the press as proving that young people who started using cannabis heavily before they were 18 years old suffered a drop in their IQ by their late 30s (Meier *et al.* 2012). However, as with most of the studies that have explored the relationship between cannabis use and mental health, the sample size was small and measures of the levels of cannabis use were based on respondents' recollections many years after they had used. The researchers highlighted the fact that they had not been able to take account of all the other variables in people's lives that may have contributed to a fall in IQ and emphasized that they had not found a causal relationship between heavy cannabis use and lower IQ. There are also issues about the measurement of IQ, and whether it is a reliable measure of intelligence, but the main point is that the researchers did not find reliable evidence that cannabis use leads to lower intelligence, despite what was claimed in the media. In fact, a reworking of their data found that social class was a better predictor of IQ change than cannabis use (Rogeberg 2013).

OTHER POSSIBLE HARMS

There is no danger of fatally overdosing on cannabis. It has been calculated that it would take at least a pound and a half of cannabis to kill a human. There is no way such an amount could be smoked or eaten.

Using cannabis can lead to people feeling very disorientated. Users may sometimes experience a 'whitey' where their face goes pale and they feel very dizzy, become very hot or cold and feel they want to be sick. They tend to stop talking, become very quiet and feel tired, but find that if they try to go to sleep their head starts spinning. Having a 'whitey' can be dangerous if users fall over and hurt themselves and can be a very unpleasant experience. It tends to happen more if people take a lot of cannabis, use strong types, use when they have not eaten much or combine their use with drinking alcohol or use of other drugs. If it happens, users need to try to relax and wait for the feelings to pass. It may take up to an hour to feel OK again, by which time they often want to sleep. Other people who are present can offer reassurance and take care of them until they feel better.

Eating cannabis may mean a large dose is taken in one go. While effects take longer to materialize they may be more intense and unpleasant, compared to smoking cannabis, where people can more easily control how much they are consuming.

Loss of inhibitions may mean users are more likely to get into sexual situations they may later regret. They may be less likely to practise safer sex and use condoms. Effects on co-ordination and reaction times may make accidents more likely, especially if people drive or operate machinery while stoned. It is dangerous to drive under the influence, but possibly not to the extent of alcohol. Research on driving simulators suggests that, unlike with alcohol, many stoned drivers compensate by driving more slowly (Sewell, Polling and Sofuoglu 2009).

There is no conclusive evidence that moderate, long-term use of cannabis causes lasting damage to physical health. However, frequent inhalation of cannabis smoke over a period of years may contribute towards bronchitis and other respiratory disorders and possibly cancers of the lung and parts of the digestive system. These risks will be greater if cannabis is smoked with tobacco. It is not clear whether cannabis or tobacco is the most damaging. While cigarette smokers tend to smoke a lot more cigarettes, compared to the numbers of joints smoked by cannabis users, smokers of cannabis tend to inhale more deeply and also hold the smoke in longer than cigarette smokers.

Strong types of cannabis are not a new phenomenon but increased availability has led to more young people using them and possibly finding the experience disorientating. This may be even more likely if other drugs are used at the same time, including alcohol and legal highs, as well as other illegal drugs. There have also been growing concerns that use of strong types of cannabis can lead to mental health problems – see above.

Regular users who stop smoking cannabis do not suffer physical withdrawal symptoms in the same way as users of drugs like heroin. However, regular users can become psychologically dependent and experience agitation, disorientation, lethargy and mood swings and have difficulties with their sleep patterns and diet if they stop using. This is possibly more likely with stronger types of cannabis. In recent years, probably more young people, and much more commonly young males than females, have used cannabis so frequently that they are almost constantly 'stoned' and come to rely on it to get them through the day. They may have exited from the 'normal' world to the extent that they find it difficult to enter back into it.

Someone who uses regularly and heavily may be apathetic, lack energy and motivation and perform poorly at their work or education.

There is some evidence that heavy cannabis use may adversely affect fertility by impacting on sperm and egg ducts. However, research findings about the effects of cannabis use on fertility are inconclusive. It has also been suggested that frequent cannabis use during pregnancy may contribute to premature birth but results are conflicting and cannabis use is likely to be one of a number of factors affecting foetal development.

It has been claimed that cannabis use leads to use of drugs like heroin and cocaine. Most heroin and cocaine users have used cannabis but the vast majority of people who have used cannabis have never used heroin or cocaine. The main market for cannabis also tends to be relatively separate from that for other illegal drugs, especially heroin. Cannabis use does not inevitably lead to use of other drugs.

SAFETY/HARM REDUCTION ADVICE FOR YOUNG PEOPLE
To avoid the dangers of cannabis…

1. Don't use it. But if young people do use cannabis the advice is…

2. Don't take too much or use too often. Don't smoke it every day.

3. Be aware that some types are very strong and could make you feel bad.

4. Remember it is still illegal and you could get in trouble with the law.

5. Don't smoke it with tobacco and do use a filter system.

6. Avoid using it when you feel really down. It will probably make you feel worse.

7. Don't drive or operate machinery while stoned.

8. Avoid sexual situations you may later regret. If you do have sex, use condoms.

9. Don't take other drugs at the same time, particularly alcohol. Mixing drugs can be dangerous.

10. If you are trying to cut down or stop, avoid people and places where cannabis is being used.

11. If you are having problems with your use, seek help and advice.

COCAINE AND CRACK

WHAT THEY ARE

Cocaine is a stimulant drug made from the leaves of the coca shrub, which grows in the mountainous regions of South America in countries such as Bolivia, Colombia and Peru. Coca is used in many different forms. South American Indians in the Andes mountains where the shrub grows, chew or suck wads of leaves. A popular South American tea called mate de coca is also made from the leaves of the coca shrub. Coca paste (also known as basuco) is a smokable form made from leaves and mainly used in countries where the plant grows.

In Britain and America the most common form of cocaine is a white crystalline powder. Most users finely chop the powder (often using a credit card, razor blade or sharp knife), arrange it in lines and snort it up the nose, often through a rolled banknote, straw or from the indentation in a Yale key. It is also occasionally made into a solution and injected, sometimes in combination with heroin.

During its production and in readiness for distribution cocaine is repeatedly mixed with other, often inert substances such as glucose powder, to bulk it out and with synthetic drugs like levamisole or benzocaine. Purity rates have been falling in recent years and by the time it reaches the streets may only be between 10 per cent and 35 per cent (Power 2013).

Crack is a smokable form of cocaine that is made into small lumps or 'rocks'. It is usually smoked in a pipe, glass tube, plastic bottle, tin can or by using tin foil. It gets its name from the cracking sound it makes when being burnt. It can also be prepared for injection. Although often reported as a new drug, crack has been made by some cocaine users for a number of years. However, large-scale manufacture and availability of crack is relatively new to the UK.

STREET NAMES

Street names for cocaine include C, charlie, coke, dust, gold dust, lady, nose candy, snow, toot and white. A 'line' means a line of powder on a flat surface ready to snort. 'Speed balling' is mixing cocaine with heroin for smoking or injecting. 'Tooting' is snorting cocaine.

Street names for crack include – base, freebase, flake, gravel, rock, stones and wash. 'Freebasing' or 'basing' means smoking crack. 'Washing' is producing crack from cocaine powder.

BRIEF HISTORY

Coca leaf chewing began among South American Indians as long ago as 2500 BC. Cocaine was first extracted from coca leaves in 1855. By the 1870s it was a popular stimulant and tonic in Europe and used in a wide range of patent medicines for all sorts of ailments. The famous psychoanalyst, Sigmund Freud, recommended its use for a range of medical and psychological problems, including alcohol and morphine addiction. Doctors also used cocaine as a local anaesthetic for eye surgery and in dentistry.

Sherlock Holmes, the fictional detective in Arthur Conan Doyle's books, was a regular cocaine user. Coca laced wines were enjoyed by popes and royalty in the 19th century. Coca-Cola was originally sold as 'a valuable brain tonic and cure for all nervous afflictions' and until 1904 contained small quantities of cocaine. At the turn of the century doctors began to warn of possible dependence and other problems. In America fears developed among white people about 'cocaine crazed' black people who were rebelling against new discriminatory laws.

In Britain concerns arose about use by troops during the First World War. Hysterical press reaction claimed that this was a German plot to destroy the British Empire. In 1916 emergency laws were rushed in to ban possession of cocaine and opium and limit medical use. At the time there was very little recreational use in Britain.

Cocaine resurfaced in the UK in the 1950s, especially around the London jazz scene among heroin users, but its use was still rare. It was not until the mid-1970s that cocaine became more commonly used. Snorting cocaine became fashionable among the 'smart and successful' middle classes and was seen as a glamorous and expensive drug. Use became very common in showbiz circles, among musicians and traders and bankers, particularly in the City of London.

In America cocaine use was much more widespread than the UK. In the mid-1980s there were a series of stories about famous sportsmen dying from the use of cocaine. This was upstaged by the emergence of a 'crack epidemic' among the poor and especially blacks and Hispanics in America's largest cities. Gang warfare, shootings and drug-related crime hit the headlines. In the 1990s crack use, and related violence and criminal activity, came to British inner cities but not anywhere near the scale of America. Crack became more commonly used, often alongside heroin, and increasing numbers of users became dependent on it.

In the late 1990s cocaine prices fell and availability and use increased among a wider range of young people, especially among those who attended all-night dance clubs. However, in more recent times the quality of cocaine that is available has often been poor and may have led to many users choosing other stimulant drugs instead, especially cheaper ones such as mephedrone or stimulant legal highs.

LEGAL STATUS

Cocaine and crack are controlled as Class A drugs under the Misuse of Drugs Act. They are illegal to be in possession of or to supply to other people. Cocaine can, under special circumstances, be prescribed by doctors but this is very rare.

AVAILABILITY, EXTENT OF USE AND COST

In the past, cocaine powder was very expensive and regarded as a middle class, 'yuppie' drug, particularly popular among film stars, pop musicians, bankers and other financial traders. In contrast crack use has mainly occurred among disenfranchised people alongside heroin use in poor, inner city areas with associated problems of dependence, drug-related crime and violence.

In recent years with falling prices cocaine has become more readily available and increasingly part of the club scene. This has meant that more young people, mostly those over 16 years old, have become involved with cocaine. While over the past 15 years most surveys have shown fewer numbers of young people using various drugs, this has not always been the case for cocaine. The annual Crime Survey in England and Wales found that cocaine use increased in the late 1990s and that over 5 per cent of 16–24-year-olds claimed to have used it in the past year for each of the surveys carried out between 2000 and 2009/10. Since then slightly lower numbers have claimed to have used in the past year – 3 per cent of 16–24-year-olds in 2012/13 (Home Office 2013). This may be because of the reduced quality of cocaine powder that has been available and the availability of cheaper alternative stimulant drugs such as mephedrone.

Prices of cocaine powder have dropped, sometimes dramatically, over the years making it available to a wider range of people. In 1990 a gram of cocaine powder may have cost over £100. Today it usually costs between £40 and £50 a gram. £10 will buy enough for a few lines. A session may involve using between a quarter of a gram and one gram but some users, who have enough money, may use more.

The last few years has seen a decline in the purity of much of the cocaine available in the UK and prices for better quality powder may still be very high.

When asked, few people claim to have ever tried crack, usually less than 1 per cent of young people (Home Office 2013). Its use is still mainly associated with deprivation and it is commonly used by heroin injectors as a 'come up' after the 'comedown'.

A single rock of crack can sell for anything from £5 to £20, partly depending on size and availability. This may be enough for between one and three short-lived 'hits'.

EFFECTS OF USE

Cocaine and crack are strong but short-acting stimulant drugs. They increase heart and pulse rate and make users feel more alert and energetic. Common physical effects include dry mouth, sweating and loss of appetite.

Many users say they feel very confident and physically strong and believe they have great mental capacities. They tend to talk a lot. At higher dose levels users may feel very anxious and panicky and may be oblivious to others and possibly aggressive.

The effects from snorting cocaine start quickly but only last for up to 40 minutes unless the dose is repeated. Effects come on even quicker when smoking crack but are more short-lived.

Cocaine has a reputation for improving sexual performance including heightened pleasure and delaying orgasm. However, high doses or repeated use may diminish sexual desire and may result in men finding it difficult to get or maintain an erection. In some situations it may contribute to sexual harassment or abuse and people having sex they may later regret.

Large doses, or quickly repeating doses over a period of hours, can lead to extreme anxiety, paranoia and even possibly hallucinations. These effects usually disappear as the drug is eliminated from the body. The after-effects of cocaine and crack use may include fatigue and depression as people come down from the high.

POSSIBLE HARMS

Neither tolerance nor heroin-like withdrawal symptoms occur with regular use of cocaine or crack. However, regular users may develop a strong dependence on the feelings of physical and mental well-being and may be tempted to keep taking cocaine to avoid feeling tired and depressed. Dependence may be more likely, and more severe, from smoking crack than from snorting cocaine. The commonly held view that crack is instantly addictive is a myth. The fact that regular use of cocaine and crack are expensive – despite recent price falls – means that people who become dependent may spend vast amounts of money.

With regular use restlessness, nausea, hyperactivity, insomnia and weight loss may develop. Some regular users become very 'wired', paranoid and aggressive. Lack of sleep and weight loss may lead to exhaustion and being very run down.

Excessive doses can cause death from respiratory or heart failure but this is rare. Injecting cocaine and heroin together in a 'speedball' is particularly dangerous. Taking cocaine or crack with hypertensive drugs and some anti-depressants can also result in raising blood pressure to dangerous levels. Regular cocaine users often combine their use with drinking alcohol, sometimes in large quantities. This combination increases the possible dangers.

Repeated snorting of cocaine damages the membranes which line the nose. Many regular users suffer from nose bleeds. Repeated smoking of crack may cause breathing problems and partial loss of voice. Long-term injecting may result in abscesses and infection with the added risk of hepatitis and HIV if injecting equipment is shared. Cocaine may be adulterated with other substances and this may make it particularly dangerous to inject.

Pregnant women who heavily use cocaine or crack may experience complications and find that their babies are adversely affected. Much has been made in the American press of so-called 'crack babies' and although some babies of crack-using mothers may be irritable, difficult to comfort and feed poorly, the extent to which this happens has probably been exaggerated.

Drug agencies have started to be approached for help by more cocaine and crack users. However, there are very few specialist services and, unlike with heroin dependence, substitute medicines are rarely prescribed.

SAFETY/HARM REDUCTION ADVICE FOR YOUNG PEOPLE
To avoid the dangers of cocaine and crack…

1. Don't use them. But if young people do use cocaine or crack the advice is…

2. Don't take too much or use too often.

3. Snorting cocaine is probably safer than smoking crack, even though both can be dangerous.

4. Don't inject cocaine, either by itself or with other drugs.

5. If people do inject they should use clean injecting equipment and never share with other people. Sharing injecting equipment can lead to hepatitis and HIV.

6. Remember that the strength of cocaine can vary and it can be mixed with other things that can themselves be dangerous to inject or snort.

7. Don't take cocaine or crack with other drugs, including alcohol. Mixing drugs can be dangerous.

8. Remember cocaine and crack are Class A drugs and you could get in trouble with the law. You could get in very serious trouble if you supply other people, whether or not you charge or make a profit.

9. Avoid sexual situations you may later regret. If you do have sex, use condoms.

10. If you are trying to cut down or stop, avoid people and places where cocaine or crack are being used.

11. If you are having problems with your use, seek help and advice.

ECSTASY

WHAT IT IS

Ecstasy is a synthetic manufactured drug that comes in tablet, capsule or powder form. Tablets or capsules (or 'pills' as users often call them) are taken orally. The powder form can snorted, swallowed in a paper wrap ('bombed') or dabbed on the gums. The chemical name of ecstasy is methylenedioxymethamphetamine or MDMA for short. It is a stimulant drug that also has mild hallucinatory properties. Some people say it is like a combination of amphetamines and a mild form of LSD.

Tablets vary in colour, but often are brown, white or pink, and may have designs or logos on. Capsules are less common and can also be various colours. The powder form is usually white but sometimes other colours and consists of small crystals.

MDMA is part of the MDA family of drugs which also includes MDEA, MMDA, MBDB and MEDA.

STREET NAMES

Street names for ecstasy include E, pills and XTC. The street names for tablets and capsules tend to vary depending on their colour and shape and the motifs and pictures on tablets. These have included adam, angel, apple, brownies, burgers, cowies, Denis the Menace, disco biscuits, dollar, dolphins, doves, Edward, essence, fantasy, love doves, lips, M and Ms, mitsubishis, New Yorkers, rhubarb and custard, rolex, shamrocks, star, white doves, X and many other names.

Street names for ecstasy powder include crystal, mandy and molly.

BRIEF HISTORY

An ecstasy type drug, MDA, was first made by two German chemists in 1910. Ecstasy itself was first made in 1914 in Germany as an appetite suppressant. Little interest was shown in the new drug until the late 1930s and early 1940s when it was tested on animals and unsuccessfully trialled for relief from Parkinson's disease.

In the 1950s an American researcher experimented with ecstasy and reported heightened perception and distortion of the senses. The American military experimented with a whole range of drugs, including ecstasy, for use in chemical warfare, to extract information from prisoners and to immobilize armies. In the 1970s some American doctors and therapists prescribed ecstasy, especially when dealing with their patient's relationship problems. It was seen as encouraging empathy between partners and dissipating anger and hostility. Ecstasy is still used by doctors and therapists in Switzerland for this purpose.

It was not until the early 1980s that ecstasy became a street drug in America and its use was made illegal in 1985. It first came to the UK in 1987/88 via the Acid House music scene which had developed in America and Ibiza, even though it had already been declared illegal to use here in 1977. Since then ecstasy, a stimulant drug which promotes empathy and communication between people quickly became an important part of the dance and rave scene.

In more recent years the price of ecstasy tablets and capsules has decreased significantly – see below – and the quality has often fallen. The amount of other drugs and adulterants in tablets and capsules has increased. It has become notoriously difficult to find good quality tablets and capsules and it has become difficult for users to know exactly what they are taking. The last few years have seen more ecstasy powder available, with more users snorting the drug and some swallowing it in a paper wrap or dabbing it on their gums.

LEGAL STATUS

Ecstasy is controlled as a Class A drug under the Misuse of Drugs Act. It is illegal to be in possession of or to supply it. It cannot be prescribed by doctors in the UK.

AVAILABILITY, EXTENT OF USE AND COST

In the 1990s commentators suggested that there were over 500,000 regular ecstasy users in the UK. However, the number of young people who have used ecstasy seems to have fallen over recent years. The annual Crime Survey in England and Wales has found that the number of 16–24-year-olds who had claimed to have used ecstasy in the past year has fallen steadily from around 5 per cent to 7 per cent in the late 1990s and early 2000s, down to between 3 per cent and 4 per cent in more recent years (Home Office 2013).

There have been some signs that ecstasy has lost some of its popularity due to the decline in quality of tablets, the number of ecstasy-related deaths and concerns about health implications of long-term use. However, the more recent advent of ecstasy powder for snorting, rather than use of tablets, may be leading to ecstasy becoming more popular again.

Ecstasy is particularly used by young people who frequent late night clubs, raves and festivals. Most of them probably use occasionally although a minority may use nearly every weekend for a period.

In the late 1980s, when ecstasy first hit UK raves and clubs, a single tablet would cost £20 to £25 and it would probably be MDMA. By the late 1990s the price of a single tablet had fallen to £6 to £10, with cheaper prices for bulk purchases. Today, tablets may cost as little as £3 each, and perhaps £10 for a really good one. Many users will take more than one tablet in a session. Two to three tablets is possibly most common but some users will take more. There is no guarantee what a tablet or capsule actually contains, even whether it has any MDMA in. Ecstasy powder usually costs £30 to £40 a gram. Users typically take between a quarter and a half gram per session but sometimes more.

EFFECTS OF USE

Ecstasy is a stimulant drug which also has mild hallucinogenic effects. The effects of taking a moderate dose in pill or capsule form start after 20 to 60 minutes and can last for up to several hours. Snorting it in the powder usually means effects happen quicker but do not last as long.

Effects often include the pupils dilating, the jaw tightening, brief nausea, sweating and a dry mouth and throat. Users often grind their teeth. Blood pressure and heart rate increases and loss of appetite is common.

Many users experience an initial rushing feeling followed by a combination of feeling energetic and yet calm. Loss of anger, empathy with other people and an enhanced sense of communication are commonly reported. Some users also report a heightened sense of their surroundings, greater appreciation of music and increased sensual experience. In this sense ecstasy is psychedelic or 'mind expanding' without being truly hallucinogenic like LSD.

Some users have unpleasant experiences. These may include feeling anxious and panicky, confusion and distressing distortion of the senses. These are more likely to occur if users take high doses or are already feeling anxious or unstable.

POSSIBLE HARMS

After taking ecstasy users may feel very tired and low and may need a long period of sleep to recover, much like taking amphetamines. Regular use may lead to sleep problems, lack of energy, dietary problems (including anorexia nervosa) and feeling depressed. Increased susceptibility to colds, flu and a sore throat may follow. Tolerance develops with regular use so more is needed to get the desired effects. While physical dependence does not seem to be a problem, psychological dependence on the feelings of euphoria and calmness and the whole scene around ecstasy use can develop, especially if the comedown is experienced as a lack of energy and depression. Some regular users may be tempted to use depressant drugs, like heroin or tranquillizers, to smooth the comedown.

Snorting ecstasy powder on a regular basis may lead to nose bleeds and damage to the nasal passages.

There is debate about whether or not ecstasy use promotes unsafe sexual activity. It may be more likely to promote sensuality rather than sex. The disorientating effect may make accidents more likely.

There have been over 300 deaths associated with ecstasy use in the UK since the mid-1980s (ACMD 2009). Few would appear to be solely connected to the direct effects of the drug. Many have been connected with non-stop dancing in hot, crowded clubs leading to overheating and dehydration. Taking a break from dancing, cooling down and drinking water regularly (to replace that lost by sweating) can prevent this happening. Drinking too much water can, in itself, be dangerous and has been associated with some deaths. Many clubs and raves now operate 'safer dancing' campaigns with chill-out areas, staff trained in first aid and free access to water for ecstasy users.

There have also been other cases of users going into a coma, and sometimes dying, after taking ecstasy. This may sometimes be due to people already having health problems such as heart problems or high blood pressure or mixing ecstasy with use of other drugs. It may also be related to the fact that the strength of different batches can vary greatly and that some pills and powders combine ecstasy with other drugs or are other drugs and do not contain any ecstasy at all. In the last few years a drug called PMA has been associated with some young people dying after they thought they were taking ecstasy, especially when they have taken large amounts. Tests have shown the quality of the ecstasy that is sold varies greatly. It is impossible to know what is in a tablet or powder just by looking at it.

Ecstasy is often taken in combination with other drugs with possibly dangerous outcomes. Taken with amphetamines, cocaine, mephedrone or stimulant legal highs it may increase the risk of overheating. Combining use with drinking alcohol also increases the risk of dehydration. Taken with ketamine, LSD, magic mushrooms or nitrous oxide it may result in unpleasant hallucinations.

Little is yet known about the effects of heavy, long-term use of ecstasy but there are increasing concerns about the possibility of mental health problems, especially for people who may already be mentally unstable. There are also concerns that regular, long-term use can result in liver damage and, for women, irregular periods.

SAFETY/HARM REDUCTION ADVICE FOR YOUNG PEOPLE

To avoid the dangers of ecstasy…

1. Don't use it. But if young people do use ecstasy the advice is…

2. Don't take too much or use too often. Take regular breaks from using.

3. Be aware that it is impossible to know what is in a tablet or powder just by looking at it.

4. Remember it is a Class A drug like heroin, cocaine and crack and you could get in trouble with the law. You could get in very serious trouble if you supply other people, whether or not you charge or make a profit.

5. Take breaks from dancing and make sure you stay cool and do not overheat.

6. Drink water or fruit juice regularly but not too much. Half to one pint per hour is advised but no more because drinking a lot of water can in itself be dangerous.

7. Avoid using it together with other drugs, particularly alcohol.

8. Don't drive or operate machinery while on ecstasy.

9. Avoid sexual situations you may later regret. If you do have sex, use condoms.

10. If you are trying to cut down or stop, avoid people and places where ecstasy is being used.

11. If you are having problems with your use, seek help and advice.

GHB/GBL

WHAT THEY ARE

The full name for GHB is Gamma hydroxybutyrate (sodium oxybate). It is a man-made depressant drug and usually comes as a colourless, odourless liquid, with a slightly salty taste, which is drunk. It is often sold in small glass or plastic bottles which may have warnings on about not mixing it with alcohol. It is also available in powder form which is then dissolved in water, fruit juice or milk and sometimes comes in capsule form. While GHB is usually swallowed, often with water or a soft drink, there have been occasional reports of it being injected.

GBL (Gamma butyrolactone) is similar to GHB, but faster acting and stronger. It usually comes as a clear, colourless liquid. GBL is converted to GHB shortly after entering the body.

STREET NAMES

Street names include fantasy, G, Geeb, g-juice, gamma-0, GBH, liquid E, liquid ecstasy and liquid X.

BRIEF HISTORY

GHB was first made in the early 1960s by a French researcher into brain chemistry. It was originally used medically as a pre-med drug to promote sleep before surgery. It has also been used medically to treat insomnia, narcolepsy (falling asleep), as an aid to childbirth and to treat alcoholism and heroin addiction.

In the 1980s GHB became widely available in health-food shops and became popular among body-builders to promote 'slow wave sleep' during which growth hormone is released. In the 1990s it became available on the dance and club scene and its use has grown since, followed by the introduction of GBL.

LEGAL STATUS

GHB and GBL are controlled as Class C drugs under the Misuse of Drugs Act. They are illegal to be in possession of or to supply.

AVAILABILITY, EXTENT OF USE AND COST

Little research has been conducted into how widely GHB and GBL are used and national surveys have rarely asked respondents about whether they have used them. However, informal surveys, especially among clubbers, have shown increased use in recent years. Across the general population of young people prevalence levels are probably low. Users are likely to be over 16 years of age. Most will probably be occasional, rather than regular, users, and many use it in combination with other drugs.

Until it was made illegal in 2003 under the Misuse of Drugs Act, GHB was available in small bottles costing £5 to £10 from sex shops and headshops, by mail order and in some clubs and pubs. A small bottle is usually enough for two or three doses. Since becoming illegal GHB and GBL are no longer available from shops, and purchasing over the internet or by mail order is more difficult. They are now mainly available from dealers, especially at clubs, often at a cost of £10 to £15 for a bottle and a few pounds for a capful of liquid.

EFFECTS OF USE

GHB and GBL are depressant drugs which slow down body actions. Effects usually begin within ten minutes up to one hour and can last one and a half hours for a low to medium dose but longer for a large dose.

Small doses (possibly one capful) may feel like having a few drinks of alcohol. Inhibitions are lowered, users often feel more confident and relaxed, talk a lot and libido is often increased. At higher doses (possibly a whole bottle) the sedative effects take over, often causing lack of co-ordination, sleepiness and muscle stiffness and possibly confusion, nausea and vomiting.

POSSIBLE HARMS

Badly made GHB can result in caustic soda burning the mouth. The strength of GHB can vary greatly from bottle to bottle so it may be very difficult to know how much is being taken. The effects of the same dose can also vary greatly from person to person.

As with alcohol, lack of co-ordination can result in increased likelihood of accidents. GHB can act as a disinhibitor and heighten sexual feelings and performance. This may make it more difficult to practise safer sex. GHB has also been implicated in a number of date rapes where people have had their alcohol spiked but the extent to which this happens is unclear. It is probably true that alcohol itself remains the main 'date rape' drug.

Large doses result in deep sleep from which it may be difficult to waken people. If users are sick while asleep they could choke on their own vomit. Very high doses can be especially dangerous and can lead to convulsions, coma and respiratory collapse. A number of people have been rushed to hospital after taking GHB. Most have recovered quickly but a few deaths have occurred, usually involving large doses while drinking alcohol. Combining GHB with use of other depressants such as heroin, methadone or tranquillizers is likely to be particularly dangerous. It will also be more risky for those who have heart or blood pressure problems or epilepsy to use it.

GBL, a similar drug, tends to be even more potent than GHB. Taking large doses can be particularly dangerous and has led to people falling into a coma and some deaths, especially when they have taken other drugs at the same time.

Not a lot is known about the effects of long-term use of GHB or GBL. Few young people seem to use it on a regular basis. However, it has been suggested that tolerance, withdrawal symptoms, physical and psychological dependence can result from regular use.

SAFETY/HARM REDUCTION ADVICE FOR YOUNG PEOPLE
To avoid the dangers of GHB/GBL…

1. Don't use them. But if young people do use GHB/GBL the advice is…

2. Don't take too much or use too often. Take regular breaks from using.

3. Be aware that it is impossible to know for sure what is in the liquid or powder or how strong it is just by looking at it.

4. Remember they are now illegal and you could get in trouble with the law. You could get in serious trouble if you supply other people, whether or not you charge or make a profit.

5. Avoid using them together with other drugs, particularly alcohol or other downer drugs. People can easily lose consciousness if they combine GHB/GBL and alcohol use.

6. GHB/GBL have sometimes been used to spike drinks and as a date rape drug. Do not put them in anyone else's drink and take care with your own drinks.

7. Avoid sexual situations you may later regret. If you do have sex, use condoms.

8. GHB/GBL slows down reactions so don't drive, operate machinery or go swimming while intoxicated.

9. If you are trying to cut down or stop, avoid people and places where they are being used.

10. If you are having problems with your use, seek help and advice.

HEROIN, OTHER OPIATES AND OPIOIDS

WHAT THEY ARE

Heroin (medical name diamorphine) is one of a group of drugs called opiates that are powerful painkillers and derived from the opium poppy. Opium itself is the dried 'milk' of the opium poppy and contains morphine and codeine. Heroin is refined from morphine and, in its pure form, is a fluffy white powder.

UK street heroin mainly comes from opium grown in the Golden Crescent countries of South West Asia, mainly Afghanistan, Iran and Pakistan. Opium is also grown in the Golden Triangle (Burma, Laos and Thailand) and increasingly in South America, especially Columbia, Mexico and Peru.

Street heroin is usually an off-white or brown powder. It is often only 15 per cent to 45 per cent pure, the rest usually being powders such as lactose, glucose or mannitol but also sometimes paracetamol, caffeine, quinine, vitamin C or talcum powder, chalk dust or sand. For medical use, heroin is manufactured as tablets or as an injectable liquid.

Synthetic opiates (opioids) are manufactured for medical use and have similar effects to heroin. These include dihydrocodeine (DF 118s), pethidine (often used in childbirth), dipanone (Diconal), dextromoramide (Palfium), buprenorphine (Subutex) and methadone (Physeptone). Methadone is often prescribed as a substitute drug in the treatment of heroin dependence and Subutex is prescribed for detoxification.

Heroin can be smoked (usually on tin foil and inhaled through a tube), snorted or prepared for injection. Medical opioids are sometimes used for non-medical reasons, especially by heroin users who cannot get hold of heroin.

Methadone is usually prescribed as a green or brown syrup which is drunk, and occasionally in injectable form.

STREET NAMES

Street names for heroin include boy, brown, china white, dragon, gear, H, Harry, horse, jack, junk, scat, shit, skag and smack and for methadone include green, juice, linctus and meth.

'Cooking' is preparing heroin for injection. 'Skagging', 'chasing', 'chasing the dragon' and 'tooting' refer to smoking heroin. 'Shooting up' and 'fixing' means injecting. 'Works', 'gun', 'spike', 'pistol' and 'barrel' refer to needles and syringes. 'Backtracking' and 'flushing' means drawing blood back into a syringe before or during injecting.

BRIEF HISTORY

The first recorded use of opium was in the Middle East 6000 years ago. It was used as a medicine and recreational drug among the Ancient Greeks and by the 7th or 8th century AD was commonly used in Chinese medicine.

By the 1800s opium use in China had become widespread and caused great concern. Most was imported from India by the British East India Company, with the British government benefiting greatly from the tax revenue. The Chinese introduced harsh laws to try to stop opium use. This failed and in 1839 the Chinese authorities in Canton seized opium from British ships and flushed it into the sea. The British sent in troops to defend the opium trade and the Chinese authorities backed down. The opium trade doubled in the next decade. In 1856 a similar incident led to a second 'Opium War', with the British navy shelling Canton and opening up other ports. The opium trade increased again so that up to 15 million Chinese became addicted. The Chinese authorities made opium use legal and began to grow their own poppies. Within a few decades Chinese opium production outstripped the Indian grown supplies and British sales and influence declined. In time China became a major supplier of opium for use in Europe.

Europeans used opium in medicines from the 1550s and by the 17th century drugs like laudanum – a mixture of opium and alcohol – were used for all sorts of ailments, including to reduce pain, aid sleep and for coughs, diarrhoea, period pains, toothache and colic in babies. This trend continued with the introduction of opium-based beers. Many famous writers and poets, including Byron, Thomas de Quincey, Sir Walter Scott, Keats, Coleridge and Shelley, were heavy opium users. Even Florence Nightingale used it.

Opium was also widely used by working class people. In the latter part of the 19th century the tiny Chinese community in London was singled out as the cause of opium smoking and luring white people, and especially women, into its use. Racism against the Chinese followed and hid just how widespread the use of opium-based drugs had become.

225

Morphine was first synthesized from opium in 1805 by a German chemist. It was portrayed as a new wonder medicine that was non-addictive and could even be used for the treatment of opium dependence. About 1850 the hypodermic syringe came into use and at that time people believed that smoking, rather than injecting, opiates led to dependence. Thousands of soldiers in the American Civil War came home addicted to morphine. In 1874 heroin was first made from morphine and promoted as a strong, non-addictive substitute for morphine.

Heroin use was not restricted in the UK until after the First World War. Doctors were still allowed to prescribe it, and morphine, to people who had become dependent on opiates. Not many people used heroin and most who did so obtained it from doctors. Users tended to be middle-aged and middle class. Overprescribing by some doctors led to the number of users increasing in the 1960s, and included younger people and 'drop outs'. The government responded by banning all but a few specialist doctors from prescribing it.

The mid-1970s saw the beginnings of a significant market in imported, illegally manufactured heroin. By the mid-1980s the number of users of heroin had increased dramatically, particularly in inner city deprived areas. The government responded by developing new community-based drug services and running anti-heroin media campaigns, as well as needle exchange schemes to reduce needle sharing and the incidence of HIV.

The number of users in the UK continued to rise, with concerns in the late 1990s about a new wave of young people starting to use. However, recent years have seen a definite fall in the number of heroin users, with fewer young people taking up use.

Medical treatment for heroin dependence focusses on prescribing of methadone, usually on a reducing dose or 'detoxification' basis. Buprenorphine (marketed as Subutex) is also sometimes prescribed by doctors for users who are coming off heroin completely, particularly as withdrawal from it tends to be easier than with methadone and it has less of a sedating effect. In the UK very few doctors are now licensed to prescribe heroin to dependent users.

LEGAL STATUS

Heroin is a Class A drug under the Misuse of Drugs Act. It is illegal to possess heroin, without it being prescribed by a doctor, or to supply it to other people. Morphine, opium, methadone, pethidine and Diconal are also Class A drugs. Codeine and dihydrocodeine (DF 118s) are Class B drugs. Buprenorphine (Subutex) is a Class C drug.

Only specially licensed doctors can prescribe heroin for anything other than physical illness. Very few doctors prescribe heroin for people who are dependent. Methadone is much more commonly prescribed. Heroin, and other opiates and opioids, can be prescribed by doctors to relieve severe pain and have been found very effective with the terminally ill.

AVAILABILITY, EXTENT OF USE AND COST

Across the population as a whole only small numbers claim ever to have used heroin, often as low as under 1 per cent (Home Office 2013). Most young people are very anti-heroin, even if they use other illegal drugs. In some areas, and particularly deprived areas, heroin use is more common.

In recent years there have probably been up to 400,000 dependent heroin users in the UK (Department of Health 2011) but numbers have definitely been declining in recent years and fewer young people now use it.

In 2013 small-scale surveys and anecdotal evidence pointed to the possibility that many dependent heroin users may have switched to using medical painkillers, rather than giving up drug use (Wakeman and Seddon 2013).

There was a decrease in availability of heroin in 2010/11 in many areas of the UK, with purity rates falling from around 45 per cent to between 15 per cent and 20 per cent (Office for National Statistics 2013b). This heroin drought continued in some areas well into 2013, alongside concerns in some localities about the sudden availability of super strength heroin, leading to an increase in fatal overdoses.

In the mid-1990s heroin was costing £80 to £100 a gram. Prices then fell to under £40 a gram in the early 2000s and have since fluctuated between £35 and £60 a gram, although the price can vary depending on availability in different locations and over time.

Heroin is often sold in £5 and £10 bags meaning it is fairly cheap to afford in small amounts. A dependent user may use a quarter of a gram or more per day. The amount used can vary greatly between different users.

EFFECTS OF USE

Heroin and other opiates and opioids are sedative drugs that depress the nervous system. They slow down body functioning and combat both physical and emotional pain. The effect is usually to give a feeling of warmth, relaxation and detachment with a lessening of anxiety. Effects start quickly and can last several hours, varying with how much is taken and how the drug is taken.

Some people describe heroin use as like being wrapped up in cotton wool. It kills feelings, especially unpleasant emotions. It should be no surprise that regular heroin use is often associated with economic and emotional deprivation.

First use can result in nausea and vomiting but these unpleasant reactions are less common with regular use. At high doses the sedative effect takes over and users become drowsy and can lose consciousness.

POSSIBLE HARMS

With regular use tolerance develops. Physical dependence can develop relatively quickly from regular use over a few weeks. Withdrawal can produce unpleasant flu-like symptoms and may include aches, tremor, sweating and chills and muscular spasms. These fade seven to ten days after stopping use but feelings of weakness and feeling ill may last longer. While many people successfully give up long-term use, it can be very difficult. A commonly used phrase is 'Getting off is relatively easy, staying off is another matter'.

Large doses can produce stupor and coma and even death from respiratory failure.

Fatal overdoses can occur, especially if use follows a break during which tolerance has faded, or when use is combined with other depressant drugs such as alcohol, tranquillizers or other opiates. Many regular heroin users will use other opoids (especially methadone) or drugs such as tranquillizers when they cannot get hold of heroin.

It is often difficult to know exactly what is being taken because the purity of street heroin can vary greatly and it is often mixed with adulterants. It is quite common for injectors to die after taking too much and/or contaminated heroin. Injecting also puts users at risk of serious abscesses, a range of infections and hepatitis and HIV if injecting equipment is shared.

The physical effects of long-term heroin use are not usually serious in themselves but may include chronic constipation, irregular periods for women and possibly pneumonia and decreased resistance to infection. This can be made worse by poor nutrition, self-neglect and bad living conditions. Regular injectors may suffer more health problems including damaged veins, heart and lung disorders. However, the tiny minority of users who have regular supplies of unadulterated heroin and lead a relatively stable life may be indistinguishable from non-drug users and suffer little physical damage.

Opiate use during pregnancy tends to result in smaller babies who may suffer withdrawal symptoms after birth. These can usually be managed with good medical care. Opiate withdrawal during pregnancy has resulted in babies dying so the preferred option may be to maintain the mother on low doses until birth of the child.

There is debate in the UK about the treatment of people who are dependent on heroin. Normally they are prescribed a substitute drug, methadone, usually in a syrup form taken orally. Detoxification treatment programmes prescribe methadone in decreasing doses over a few weeks with the idea that users will be weaned off heroin and become drug-free. Subutex is sometimes prescribed, rather than methadone.

Some treatment programmes have prescribed methadone on a 'maintenance' basis where users receive the same dose level until they feel ready to give up. These programmes have sometimes given methadone in injectable form. However, methadone is itself easy to become dependent on, is implicated in many overdoses and tends to be unpopular among many heroin users. Many users quickly go back on heroin, including using it while being prescribed methadone. Some people say that more doctors should prescribe heroin, as sometimes happened in the past, but this is resisted by the government.

Many people are also concerned about heroin-related crime, especially theft, burglary and forgery, when dependent users are desperate to get money for drugs. A lot of crime is drug-related, although the extent has sometimes been exaggerated. Many dependent heroin users were involved in acquisitive crime before becoming dependent and some have other sources of income that mean they do not have to resort to crime to have money to buy drugs.

There has been debate for many years about whether heroin should be more freely available to users on prescription and whether its possession should be decriminalized to help combat drug-related crime. However, in recent years government policy has moved towards tougher laws and penalties and compulsory treatment for people who are dependent. It is clear that a lot of heroin use and related crime occurs in deprived areas. A key question is whether we can really do a lot about heroin use while there are existing levels of poverty and deprivation.

SAFETY/HARM REDUCTION ADVICE FOR YOUNG PEOPLE
To avoid the dangers of heroin...

1. Don't use it. But if young people do use heroin the advice is...

2. Don't take too much or use too often. If you start using regularly you may become dependent, even if you smoke it.

3. Don't inject, but if you do, use clean injecting equipment and never share works with other people. Sharing injecting equipment can lead to hepatitis and HIV. Use a needle exchange scheme.

4. Don't take other drugs at the same time, especially other downer drugs like alcohol or tranquillizers. The combination can lead to overdose and death.

5. Take care because the strength of heroin can vary and it can be mixed with all sorts of things that can themselves be dangerous, especially if injected.

6. It is a Class A drug and you could get in trouble with the law. You could get in very serious trouble if you supply other people, whether or not you charge or make a profit.

7. It slows down reactions, so don't drive, operate machinery or go swimming while intoxicated.

8. If you are trying to cut down or stop, avoid people and places where heroin is being used.

9. If you are having problems, seek out and use drug services.

KETAMINE

WHAT IT IS

Ketamine is a powerful man-made anaesthetic drug which can also have dissociative and hallucinogenic effects. It has a history of medical use in operations on humans and animals.

Sources of ketamine include supplies diverted from medical and veterinary use, and illicit manufacture.

It comes as a white, grainy crystalline powder that can be snorted, swallowed in a paper wrap (bombed) or with a drink or sometimes smoked. It also sometimes comes as tablets and can be purchased in liquid form that can be injected or swallowed.

STREET NAMES

Street names include donkey dust, green, K, Kit-Kat, special K, super K, tekno (on ket backwards), tekno smack and vitamin K. Hallucinating on ketamine is called 'K holing'.

BRIEF HISTORY

Ketamine was first made in 1962 as an anaesthetic by Parke-Davis, a pharmaceutical company in America. It was used for emergency surgery and in field hospitals during the Vietnam war. It is still used medically for humans under the brand name Ketalar, particularly for operations on children. It is commonly used in poorer countries like India where it is cheap. It is also widely used for animal surgery and sometimes referred to as a 'horse tranquillizer'.

Until the 1990s it was used recreationally by only small numbers of people. In the 1990s ketamine found its way on to the club/rave scene, initially when people took it by mistake, thinking they had bought ecstasy tablets. Since then its use has grown among clubbers and young people, sometimes in combination with other drugs.

LEGAL STATUS

Ketamine was first controlled as a Class C drug under the Misuse of Drugs Act in 2006, but has recently been upgraded to a Class B drug. It is illegal to be in possession of or to supply.

AVAILABILITY, EXTENT OF USE AND COST

Ketamine use has increased in recent years especially among young people who go clubbing and use drugs like ecstasy. Over the past few years drugs services have been approached for the first time by some young people who have been using ketamine excessively and have experienced problems with their use.

It is only in recent years that ketamine has been included in UK national surveys. Since 2006/7 the annual Crime Survey in England and Wales has shown between 1 and 2 per cent of 16–24-year-olds claiming to have used ketamine in the past year (Home Office 2013). Across the general population of young people prevalence levels will be low, especially among young people aged under 16 years old. Most young people who do use ketamine are unlikely to do so very often.

It is available from street and club dealers who sell drugs like ecstasy. Prices of ketamine can vary greatly but are currently usually about £20 per gram for powder, with a 'wrap' of powder or a pill costing anything between £5 and £20.

EFFECTS OF USE

Effects vary with the route of administration. Snorting the powder form brings on effects within minutes which can last up to an hour. Swallowing powder or tablets produces effects within 15 minutes that may last up to four hours without repeating the dose. Injecting gives immediate effects which may last longer.

The initial effects are usually of stimulation and feelings of energy and euphoria that have been compared to using ecstasy. However, this is followed by sedation and often slurring of speech, lack of co-ordination and numbness and possible nausea and vomiting. This can happen to the extent that users may experience temporary paralysis and find it difficult to move or speak. Users also sometimes experience stomach cramps – K cramps – especially if they have swallowed the drug. They may also urinate more frequently.

With higher, or repeat, doses hallucinations occur which are different from LSD trips. These often include a loss of sense of time, feeling disconnected from the body and floating sensations. Users have described feeling very alone and having 'out of body' and 'near death' experiences. This is called 'K holing'. Hallucinations tend to start and recede faster than with LSD but can be very powerful and disorientating.

Users also sometimes report that ketamine can make them feel very aggressive.

POSSIBLE HARMS

The anaesthetic properties of ketamine produce lack of co-ordination, numbness and reduce the experience of pain. Large doses can lead to loss of consciousness. Together with the hallucinatory effects this can increase the possibility of accidents. As with most anaesthetics, eating or drinking before using can result in vomiting. If users take a large dose and become unconscious they could choke on their vomit.

Associated hallucinations can be pleasant but can also be very disturbing and will vary, partly depending on the user's mood and expectations. Effects can be very disorientating if someone is already anxious or depressed. Periods of heavy use can also lead to loss of appetite and weight loss.

If very large doses are taken there is a risk of respiratory collapse or heart failure. A few people have died after injecting large doses. Ketamine can also be particularly dangerous if used at the same time as depressant drugs (such as alcohol, heroin or tranquillizers) and can lead to loss of consciousness and possibly fatal overdose. It can be difficult to know how strong a dose is being taken or what else might be mixed in with it.

In recent years some regular, longer-term users have experienced a range of physical health problems. These have included problems with urinating (pain, burning, leaking and blood in urine) and damage to the bladder and kidneys that can be severe and irreversible. KBS, Ketamine-induced Bladder Syndrome, has become a recognized disease.

Little is known about the psychological risks of long-term ketamine use but it has been linked to a range of mental health problems such as psychosis, delusions, panic attacks, depression, suicide and insomnia. It is not clear whether these are caused by the drug or if it exacerbates already existing conditions.

Physical dependence and withdrawal are not usually associated with ketamine but tolerance and psychological dependence can develop with regular use. In the last few years drug services have started to see clients who have serious problems with ketamine use.

SAFETY/HARM REDUCTION ADVICE FOR YOUNG PEOPLE

To avoid the dangers of ketamine…

1. Don't use it. But if young people do use ketamine the advice is…

2. Don't take too much or use too often.

3. Don't inject but if you do, use clean injecting equipment and never share works with other people.

4. Don't take other drugs at the same time, especially other downer drugs like alcohol, GHB, heroin or tranquillizers. The combination can kill.

5. The strength of ketamine can vary and it can be mixed with all sorts of things that can themselves be dangerous, especially if injected.

6. It slows down reactions, so don't drive, operate machinery or go swimming while intoxicated.

7. If you are trying to cut down or stop using, avoid people and places where ketamine is being used.

8. Remember it is now an illegal drug and you could get in trouble with the law, especially if you supply it to other people, even if you do not charge them or make a profit.

9. If you experience problems with urinating or your bladder or kidneys, stop using and seek medical advice.

10. If you are experiencing problems, use drug services. Many are becoming used to helping people who have problems with ketamine.

KHAT

WHAT IT IS

Khat is a herbal product consisting of the green leaves and shoots of the shrub Cathaedulis. It is chewed to obtain a mild stimulant effect.

Khat is cultivated throughout eastern Africa and the Arabian peninsula and has been imported into the UK. There are a number of varieties of the plant but the two main types found in the UK are Miraa, which is imported from Kenya, and Harari, from Ethiopia.

It is cut from the 10 to 20 feet tall, flowering evergreen shrub and the leaves are bundled into plastic bags to retain moisture and the freshness of the active ingredients, cathinone and cathine. The fresh plant remains potent for only a few days after it is picked.

The fresh leaves and small stems are chewed to a pulp, left in the mouth for a time and then spat out. A khat chewing session is often a social affair that has an important social function, similar to the caffeine or alcohol use of Europeans, and may last three to four hours and sometimes longer.

Khat can also be brewed into a tea and some dried preparations have been available in the UK, although their effects are likely to be milder because of reduced potency compared to fresh khat.

STREET NAMES

Street names include chat, ghat, mriaa, qaadka, qat and quat.

BRIEF HISTORY

Khat chewing has a long history as a social custom dating back thousands of years among communities in the Horn of Africa (Djibouti, Eritrea, Ethiopia, Somalia) and the Arabian peninsula. The Ancient Egyptians used the plant for more than its stimulating effects and considered it a divine food, which was capable of releasing humanity's divinity, making the user god-like.

Khat also has been used for many years as a medicine to treat depression and lack of energy, and by farmers and other manual labourers who perform physical work over long hours. It has also been used by some Muslims in the celebration of Ramadan to relieve fatigue and reduce appetite.

LEGAL STATUS

Until recently, khat was not controlled under the Misuse of Drugs Act and was not illegal to import into the UK, have in your possession, supply or sell. It has been a controlled drug for a number of years in some other countries, including the Republic of Ireland, France, Norway, Sweden, Canada, the US and, more recently, the Netherlands. There has been an on-going debate about the legal status of khat in the UK, based on whether or not it is harmful to use and concerns that the UK could become a hub for an illicit trade in khat with it being exported to other European countries where it is illegal.

In June 2013, the UK government announced, against the advice of its Advisory Council on the Misuse of Drugs, that khat would be controlled as a Class C drug under the Misuse of Drugs Act, making its importation, possession for personal use and supply an offence.

Personal possession of khat will probably be subject to an escalation framework, similar to that used for possession of cannabis – see pages 75–76 – with a warning issued for first time possession cases but arrest and prosecution for persistent offenders.

AVAILABILITY, EXTENT OF USE AND COST

Until it was recently made illegal, khat was imported into the UK on a regular basis and openly sold at greengrocers, market stalls and other shops in certain inner city areas where Kenyans, Ethiopians, Yemenis and Somalis live.

Khat use has been common among some older members of these communities, particularly men, who may use it in their family homes, at community parties or 'marfashes', cafes frequented especially by Somalis.

There have been reports of younger members of these communities, and occasionally other young people, also using khat, again mainly males. As well as being available through traditional sources, khat has also been sold in some headshops and on the internet.

While there have been increasing concerns about khat dependence and health issues among some of the communities in which it is used in the UK, there have been indications of a decrease in its importation and use in recent years.

It has usually cost between £4 and £6 to buy a bundle of the stringy green plant, often wrapped in banana leaves.

It remains to be seen what will happen to availability, extent of use and cost now that khat has become an illegal drug. Some commentators are predicting that new, illicit markets for khat will open up and that it will be sold alongside drugs such as cannabis, amphetamines and/or cocaine. There is also the possibility that some regular users may switch to use other, possibly more dangerous, drugs instead of khat.

EFFECTS OF USE

The stimulant effects of khat are sometimes described as being somewhere between using caffeine and amphetamines. First effects are felt after about an hour of chewing and users often feel more alert, energetic, talkative and sociable, often followed by feeling calm. A typical chewing session may last three to four hours, but sometimes longer.

Considerable chewing is needed to get and maintain the effects and these will only be achieved if the khat is relatively fresh. This, together with the bitter taste, limits its attractiveness. As with use of many other stimulant drugs, appetite is reduced.

POSSIBLE HARMS

The government's Advisory Council on the Misuse of Drugs in the UK has recently examined the possible harms related to khat use and concluded that there was insufficient evidence to indicate that it caused serious health problems for users or many wider problems in society (ACMD 2013).

While most people who use khat do not experience serious problems, psychological dependence can occur and regular users may feel anxious, irritable, tired and depressed after using. However, these difficulties may sometimes have as much, if not more, to do with many users experiencing poverty and racism and their frustrations at being refugees, often to escape the trauma of civil war in their home lands.

Regular khat chewing can lead to a sore mouth and put users at risk of infections, especially if the leaves have not been washed. Some commentators have suggested the pesticide residues in khat may be more dangerous than the drug itself.

Khat use can also result in constipation and stomach ulcers. There is some concern that excessive use over a long period may increase the risk of heart disease, cancer of the mouth, liver damage and result in a loss of sex drive in men but there is no clear evidence about this.

Khat sessions often involve users smoking large numbers of cigarettes, sometimes in badly ventilated rooms, and the consumption of large amounts of fizzy drinks, again making it difficult to judge the health impact of khat alone.

Anecdotal evidence, reported from communities in several UK cities, has suggested that regular khat consumption is linked with a range of social harms, such as men, including young men, not working or contributing to family life. However, research into these concerns has found no robust evidence for these claims being caused by khat itself.

Discussion of khat use has become heated in some communities, particularly among Somalis, between those who see it as an important part of their social and cultural heritage and those that feel its use is not acceptable and undermines their struggle to improve their economic situation and integrate into life in the UK.

SAFETY/HARM REDUCTION ADVICE FOR YOUNG PEOPLE
To avoid the dangers of khat…

1. Don't use it. But if young people do use khat the advice is…

2. Be aware that khat has now become a controlled drug that is illegal to import, be in possession of or supply.

3. Don't take too much or use too often.

4. Wash the leaves before chewing them to remove pesticide residues.

5. Don't smoke too many cigarettes and ventilate the room you are in.

6. Don't drink too many sugar-based drinks.

7. Be aware of the need to have a decent diet and a good sleep pattern.

8. Be careful with use if you have high blood pressure or heart problems.

9. If you are trying to cut down or stop, avoid people using and places where khat is being used.

10. If you are having problems with your use, seek help and advice.

LEGAL HIGHS

Note: Nitrous oxide is considered separately on page 259.

WHAT THEY ARE

Legal highs are substances that are marketed as mimicking the effects of illegal drugs but are not (yet) controlled under the Misuse of Drugs Act and so not illegal to be in possession of or, in most cases, to supply or sell.

Some are made from naturally occurring plants. Some are manufactured as synthetic substances. Others may be a mix of natural and synthetic substances. While many legal highs have been imported from China or Eastern Europe, some come from other countries and manufacture and preparation also takes place here in the UK.

Some drugs sold as legal highs have also been found to contain illegal substances, either drugs that have been controlled for a time or those that were, until recently, legal highs and have now been banned.

Legal highs are sold in many forms. Some are tablets or capsules ('pills'). Some are powders that may be snorted, dabbed on the gums or swallowed in a paper wrap ('bombed') or with a drink. Others come in a liquid form, usually for swallowing or inhaling. As with many illegal drugs, the same substance may be available in more than one form. There are also legal high smoking mixtures which are usually used in a similar way to smoking cannabis. A few legal highs may be prepared for injection but this is relatively rare.

Legal highs are commonly marketed as 'not for human consumption', 'not for sale to under-18s' or as 'plant food', 'fish food', 'room odorizers', 'bath salts' or 'incense' in an attempt to avoid controls on their sale and to keep them legal. Some have trade names but their packaging may give no indication of the active ingredients, while others are sold as 'research chemicals' under a specified chemical name. The contents of branded products can change markedly from batch to batch and 'research chemicals' may not always be the chemicals declared on the packaging.

Legal highs are often advertised as legal alternatives to particular illegal drugs or groups of drugs. Many are stimulants that may have similar effects to drugs like amphetamines and cocaine. Mephedrone was an example of a stimulant legal high before it was made illegal. Other legal highs are advertised as mimicking the effects of ecstasy or ketamine or of hallucinogenic drugs like LSD or magic mushrooms. Salvia is an example. There are also a variety of cannabis-like smoking mixtures, although some of these, such as Annihilation, Black Mamba and Spice, have now been made illegal. Although less common, there are also legal highs that are depressant/sedative drugs and may mimic the effects of drugs like heroin and tranquillizers.

If you want to find out more about the legal highs that are currently available, their names (see below) and how they are promoted, carry out an internet search of 'buy legal highs' or 'headshop' and see what is on offer. You are not breaking the law by doing so.

THE MANY AND CONFUSING NAMES

Legal highs are sometimes called New or Novel Psychoactive Substances (NPS) and also 'synthetic drugs', 'designer drugs', 'research chemicals', 'legal pills', 'legal party powders' and 'new age herbs'.

Specific legal highs are advertised under a huge number of often confusing names. These have included words and phrases that are designed to entice users (such as Bliss, Charge+, Cloud 9, Holy Sage, Magic Mint, Nirvana Plus, Sparkle and White Lightning) and reassure them (such as Legal Crack, Herbal Ecstasy and Legal Ecstasy). They may also be sold under their chemical name, such as ethylone, buphedrone and dimethocaine, or via a baffling array of letters and numbers, such as AKB48, 5-MeO-DIPT, DMC and MPA.

The same chemical substance may be sold under a number of different names. If you are confused by all these names you are not alone. And, of course, this often makes it very difficult for users, and particularly young novice users, to know exactly what they are taking.

BRIEF HISTORY

Humans have tried new substances for their mood-altering qualities throughout history. This has included use of naturally occurring substances and plants, concocting special mixes and 'psycho-chemists' synthesizing and manufacturing a range of substances to develop new drugs for wider circulation.

The last few years has seen a huge increase in the variety of legal highs available with many chemists – 'psychonauts' – around the world carrying out experiments to find the next new intoxicant. The rise of the internet has led to chat rooms where chemists and consumers share information and experiences and has also made it much easier to purchase legal highs. The advent of legal highs has also seen more headshops opening in many of our cities and larger towns.

It has been estimated that in recent times about 40 to 70 new legal highs have come on to the market every year. Currently there are probably well over 300 different legal highs available in the UK.

LEGAL STATUS
Legal highs are, by definition, not controlled under the Misuse of Drugs Act and are not illegal to be in possession of or, in most cases, to supply and sell. However, over the last few years the UK government has increasingly acted to make some legal highs illegal.

In 2009 Spice, a synthetic cannabis-like smoking mixture, became a Class B drug, then BZP and GBL were made Class C drugs. This was followed by the widely publicized criminalization of mephedrone as a Class B drug in April 2010. Since then, methoxetamine (Mexxy, MXE), naphyrone (NRG1), 2-DPMP (Ivory Wave), phenazepam (Bonsia, Supersleep), and more cannabis-like smoking mixtures, such as Annihilation and Black Mamba, have also been made illegal.

In 2011 the government introduced Temporary Class Drug Orders (TCDOs) to make it easier to ban legal highs that were causing concern. Under these orders drugs are banned for one year while the health risks are considered. During this period a drug that is subject to an order is illegal to supply, with maximum penalties being 14 years' imprisonment and an unlimited fine, as with Class B drugs that are controlled under the Misuse of Drugs Act. However, the drug is not illegal for individuals to be in possession of, if small quantities are involved. Despite this, the police are allowed to seize the drug from individuals and dispose of it. If an individual has a large quantity of a legal high in their possession, the police may consider that they are supplying and arrest them.

So far the government has issued TCDOs for methoxetamine (Mezzy, MXE), 5 and 6-APB (Benzo Fury) and NBOMe (N Bomb), probably with more legal highs to follow. These three drugs have all now become controlled drugs under the Misuse of Drugs Act.

There is now an on-going game of cat and mouse where chemists synthesize new legal highs and governments race to ban them. In cases where the UK government decides to ban a legal high, it often takes only a slight alteration to the chemical structure of the drug for it to fall outside the remit of the Misuse of Drugs Act and become a new legal high.

There have also been changes to the Medicines Act, making some legal highs illegal to sell, but not to be in possession of. The government is currently considering further changes to the Medicines Act in an attempt to restrict legal highs.

The UK government is continually making more legal highs illegal and bringing them under the control of the Misuse of Drugs Act. By the time you read this, more legal highs may have been made illegal. The government is also currently exploring ways of banning, or at least more stringently controlling, sales of legal highs from headshops and other retail outlets, but this is a complex matter and, as yet, no new legislation has been forthcoming. For the latest information go to the Release website (www.release.co.uk) or Frank website (www.talktofrank.com), although do be aware that neither of these websites are necessarily completely up to date.

If the police find a young person in possession of a powder, tablets or a smoking mixture, they may not know whether it is a legal high or an illegal drug. They may arrest the young person, confiscate the drug and have it tested to see what it is. If it turns out to be a legal high, the young person will not be prosecuted. However, some legal highs may, often unbeknown to the people using them, contain illegal drugs mixed in with them, and in such cases, young people are likely to be prosecuted.

AVAILABILITY, EXTENT OF USE AND COST

Legal highs are sometimes available through local drug dealing networks alongside illegal substances, such as from local neighbourhood dealers and those who sell at clubs, pubs and music gigs and festivals. However, the main source of supply is through headshops and the internet.

A headshop is a retail outlet specializing in selling legal highs, drug paraphernalia used for consumption of cannabis and other recreational drugs, as well as counterculture art, magazines, music, clothing and home décor. There has been an increase in the number of headshops in the UK and they now exist in every large city and in many larger towns. Most say they only cater for people aged over 18 years old but under-18s who do not look too young should have few problems purchasing from headshops and, even if they do, may have older (looking) friends who can buy for them. Some legal highs are also now being sold from other retail outlets, including petrol stations, tattoo parlours, take-aways, newsagents, sex shops, market stalls and even at car boot sales.

The other way to access legal highs is through the internet and online mail order businesses. There are a small number of major importers and retailers and a much larger number of small traders who deal in small purchases, often sourced from the majors. Many headshops also sell legal highs over the internet. The best way to see what is available and how it works is to do a bit of research yourself. If you carry out an internet search of 'buy legal highs' or 'headshops' you will have the choice of hundreds of sites to explore. A wide range of legal highs are now available on the internet to young people. All they need is a credit card and their purchase will be delivered by post to their door very soon, possibly the next day.

As governments have made particular legal highs illegal, most headshops and internet businesses remove them from sale. However, there is a constant supply of new legal highs to take their place.

There are internet forums dedicated to buying and discussing legal highs. These, together with other social networking media, mean young people can share information about different legal highs, new ones as they become available, advice about their effects and dangers and where and how to purchase them. While some of this information may be useful to young people, some is not, especially when it may be provided by heavy users and people trying to promote and sell legal highs.

There has clearly been a large increase in availability and use of legal highs over the last few years but the extent of use is difficult to judge because few large-scale surveys have yet asked people whether they have used them. Recent studies of clubbers and those replying to online surveys have found that growing numbers of young people have been using legal highs but small samples have been involved and the findings are not representative of the population as a whole.

In June 2013, a United Nations report suggested that the UK had the largest market for legal highs in the whole of Europe (United Nations 2013). It estimated that almost 700,000 of our 15–24-year-olds had used them at least once, although this figure was disputed because it may include mephedrone use, mephedrone having been made an illegal drug in 2010. The 2012/13 Crime Survey in England and Wales found that just over 1 per cent of 16–24-year-olds claimed to have used Salvia, a short-acting hallucinogenic legal high, in the previous year (Home Office 2013). However, the survey did not ask respondents about their use of other legal highs.

There may be a number of reasons for the surge in use of legal highs in the UK, apart from our young people tending to have a greater appetite for drugs than their European counterparts. The poor quality of illegal drugs such as ecstasy and cocaine over recent years may have something to do with it. Legal highs tend to be cheaper than illegal drugs, especially cocaine. These were some of the reasons given for the sudden explosion of mephedrone use in 2009 and 2010. Young people who use legal highs may not think they are putting themselves at risk of being arrested and getting a criminal record. Of most concern is that they may also, wrongly, think that the word 'legal' means that legal highs are safe to use.

A few pounds will buy pills, powders or smoking mixtures that will give at least one, and possibly more, drug use sessions of a good few hours' duration.

EFFECTS OF USE AND POSSIBLE HARMS

The effects and risks of legal highs will depend on the specific type of legal high used and the drug factors, set and setting involved – see pages 67–70.

Stimulant legal highs may have similar effects and harms to drugs like cocaine, amphetamines and mephedrone while some, particularly those marketed as being akin to ecstasy, may have also some hallucinogenic properties. As with ecstasy and mephedrone, heatstroke has been associated with the use of some stimulant legal highs.

Hallucinogenic legal highs may bring effects and dangers similar to those experienced with high doses of ketamine and with use of LSD and magic mushrooms. Depressant legal highs are less common but may have effects and dangers similar to drugs such as alcohol, GHB, heroin, ketamine and tranquillizers.

Cannabis-like smoking mixtures will, if they work as advertised, share some similarity with the effects and risks of using cannabis, but some expert commentators say they tend to be potentially more harmful than cannabis itself. For example, some people have found that using smoking mixtures has led to breathing difficulties, a racing heartbeat, severe rashes and vomiting.

This all sounds a bit too straightforward. As with illegal drugs, but possibly even more so, it is often difficult to know exactly what is in a specific legal high and how strong the dose is. The effects and dangers of using legal highs are often unpredictable.

It is clear that some of the deaths reported in the media as being due to young people taking legal highs have been grossly inaccurate. Some have occurred from people taking illegal drugs and/or alcohol, and not legal highs, or from other causes. However, there have been deaths, both in the UK and in other countries, when young people have taken legal highs, particularly when they have, through ignorance or mistake, consumed far too much or combined use of a legal high with other drugs, including alcohol.

Some commentators suggest that many legal highs can be more dangerous to take than the illegal drugs they supposedly mimic and replace. There is little doubt that many young people are using legal highs without much, if any, idea about exactly what they are taking, the effects the drugs may have and the level of dose that it is safe to use.

Some legal highs that are purchased from dealers, rather than headshops or over the internet, have been found to also contain illegal drugs. The interaction between different drugs can have unpredictable and sometimes dangerous results.

Taking a legal high also will be more risky if users drink alcohol or take other drugs, including medicines, at the same time.

Some young people have also become dependent on particular legal highs and found that once they are taking them on a regular basis it is difficult to stop.

Young people will sometimes not regard legal highs as 'proper' drugs and take other drugs at the same time or take especially large doses. The very word 'legal' may wrongly convince inexperienced young users that they are safe.

SAFETY/HARM REDUCTION ADVICE FOR YOUNG PEOPLE
To avoid the dangers of legal highs…

1. Don't use them. But if young people do use legal highs the advice is…

2. Find out as much as you can about the particular legal high, before you take it but don't believe everything you read or hear. A lot of the information available on the internet is inaccurate and posted by people who are 'out of their head' or selling legal highs.

3. Be aware that using legal highs may be more dangerous if you have physical health problems (such as with blood pressure, your heart or asthma), you feel unwell or you are very stressed or unhappy.

4. Anticipate what the effects could be and what could go wrong.

5. If you are new to using, or unsure about what you are taking or how strong it is, start with a small amount and wait for at least an hour before deciding whether to take more. Start low and go slow.

6. Don't take too much or use too often.

7. Be aware that some products sold as legal highs also contain illegal drugs and you could be breaking the law without knowing it.

8. Don't drink alcohol or take other drugs, including medicines, at the same time. The mix may have unpleasant and possibly dangerous effects.

9. Don't use by yourself. Use in a safe environment with other people and look after each other.

10. Don't drive, operate machinery, go swimming or take a bath while high. If you think you may have sex, use condoms.

11. Know how to do first aid. If someone becomes disturbed calm them down. If they overheat help cool them down and give them sips of water, but not too much. If they collapse put them in the recovery position. And if they are in a bad way call an ambulance straight away.

12. If you start having difficulties with your use, seek help and advice. These days more drug agencies know about legal highs and how to help people who have problems using them.

LSD

WHAT IT IS

Lysergic acid diethylamide (LSD) is a hallucinogenic drug that is made from ergot, a fungus found growing wild on rye and other grasses. It is a white powder but comes in a variety of forms as a street drug. The main form is made by a solution of LSD being dropped onto paper or gelatine sheets. The sheets are cut into small squares like postage stamps or transfers and often have pictures or designs on.

LSD is also sometimes dropped onto sugar cubes or formed into tablets or small capsules. Only tiny amounts are needed to get an effect and the strength of LSD can vary greatly. It is usually taken orally.

STREET NAMES

Street names for LSD include acid, tabs and trips but also sometimes A, blotter, cheer, dots, drop, flash, hawk, L, lightning flash, lucy (Lucy in the Sky with Diamonds), micro dot, paper mushrooms, rainbows, smilies, stars, sugar, tripper, window and many other names, some of which describe the pictures on the squares, such as strawberries.

'Dropping' mean using LSD. An 'acid head' is an LSD user. 'Tripping' means the experience of using LSD.

BRIEF HISTORY

LSD was first discovered in 1938 by a research chemist, Albert Hofmann, while working to produce new medicines. In 1943 he underwent the first ever LSD trip by mistake when carrying out an experiment in his laboratory. In the 1950s and 1960s doctors in America and the UK used LSD to help long-term, mentally ill patients recall repressed thoughts and feelings. It was also used by the military in experiments to find a 'truth drug' for interrogating enemy troops.

In the early 1960s people began to experiment with LSD use for pleasure. Among fringe and hippy groups LSD use was seen as an almost religious/spiritual experience and a way of getting in touch with the self, other people and the wider environment. The authorities moved against LSD and in 1966 its use was made illegal in the UK, followed in 1968 with a ban on doctors being able to prescribe it.

Availability and use declined in the 1970s and early 1980s but its popularity grew again in the late 1980s and early 1990s among young people. It tended to be less strong than in the 1960s but was very cheap. Stories regularly circulated in local areas about young children being innocently given LSD 'Blue Star' transfers which seeped through the skin and made them 'hooked'. This was completely untrue and another example of a lurid drug myth.

Since the late 1990s availability and use has declined again. It is now rare to find that it is used in the UK, although this situation could change in the future.

LEGAL STATUS

LSD is a Class A drug under the Misuse of Drugs Act. It is not available for medical use and is illegal to possess or supply.

AVAILABILITY, EXTENT OF USE AND COST

Some mid-1990s local surveys in the UK found between 10 per cent and 24 per cent of 16-year-olds claiming to have used LSD at least once. Late 1990s surveys recorded lower figures – commonly around 5 per cent for 15–16-year-olds and 10 to 14 per cent for 16–24-year-olds. The 1996 Crime Survey in England and Wales found 5 per cent of 16–24-year-olds claimed to have used LSD in the past year, but the figure for each survey carried out since 2002/3 has been under 1 per cent (Home Office 2013). There has been a sharp decrease in availability and use in recent years.

When it is available LSD tends to be cheap, possibly £2 to £5 for one 'tab', which may be enough for a trip lasting many hours. Regular use is very rare, partly because it becomes ineffective if used too often. It tends to be used on an occasional basis.

EFFECTS OF USE

LSD is usually described as a hallucinogenic drug. Strength can vary but one dose will usually result in a mild 'trip' and two or three doses in a full blown hallucinogenic experience. A trip usually begins about 30 minutes after taking

LSD, peaks after two to six hours and fades within eight to 12 hours. The effects vary greatly depending on dose level, how the user feels and the situation they are in. Users often report visual effects such as intensified colours, distorted shapes and sizes and movement in stationary objects. Distortion of sound and changes in the user's sense of time and place are also common. Users are usually aware of the fact that these effects are unreal.

POSSIBLE HARMS

Emotional reactions vary greatly. Some people claim they become more aware of themselves and other people and describe LSD trips as being similar to a religious or spiritual experience. Feelings of being separated from the body are also common. Unpleasant or frightening experiences are more likely if the user is already anxious or depressed. This may include feelings of panic, paranoia ('everyone is out to get me') and becoming very afraid and scared by people and objects.

The fact that once LSD is taken there is no going back until it wears off – possibly up to 12 hours – means a bad trip can be very disturbing. The same person may have good and bad trips on different occasions and even varying experiences within the same trip. Strengths vary and it can be difficult to know how strong a dose is being taken. If users become anxious they can usually be calmed down and reassured by others.

It may be difficult to concentrate while on a trip and dangerous to drive or operate machinery. There is no evidence of LSD use leading to physical dependence or fatal overdose. People tend to not use LSD daily partly because further doses are usually ineffective without a few days' break. However, some people use it so often that they can become out of touch with the real world. There have been a few well-publicized deaths after people have taken LSD. These have been rare and tend to be suicides among people who are already experiencing mental health problems.

There are no clear physical health dangers from long-term use of LSD. There is no reliable evidence that LSD causes damage to the brain or to future children.

Some LSD users experience flashbacks. This is when a trip is re-experienced some time afterwards. Flashbacks tend to be short-lived but can be disturbing, especially if the user does not know that they can happen.

SAFETY/HARM REDUCTION ADVICE FOR YOUNG PEOPLE

To avoid the dangers of LSD...

  1. Don't use it. But if young people do use LSD the advice is...

2. Be careful what you buy and who from. You may not know what it is or how strong it is.

3. Don't take too much or use too often.

4. Don't use alone. Make sure someone else is with you.

5. Carefully prepare and make sure the situation is as safe and relaxed as possible and you will not be disturbed.

6. Avoid using if you are depressed or anxious. Using will probably make you feel worse.

7. Be aware that LSD is a Class A drug under the Misuse of Drugs Act, the same as heroin, crack and cocaine.

8. If someone has a bad trip, reassure them and calm them down.

9. Don't drive or operate machinery while under the influence.

MAGIC MUSHROOMS

WHAT THEY ARE

These are hallucinogenic mushrooms that grow wild in many parts of the UK in autumn. The main type used is the liberty cap (psilocybe), a small light brown mushroom with a pointed bell head.

Liberty caps are usually eaten raw but are also dried out and stored for later use. They can also be cooked and then eaten and made into a tea or infusion to drink. Twenty to thirty liberty cap mushrooms are usually regarded as a full dose but the degree of active ingredient may vary between different mushrooms.

Fly agaric mushrooms (amanita muscaria) are also occasionally used. They are a larger mushroom with white warts on a red/orange cap and a thick white stem. Fly agaric can be eaten raw but are often cooked in a low oven or hung up to dry. One mushroom is regarded as a full dose and three an upper limit.

STREET NAMES

Street names include liberties, liberty caps, magics, mushies and shrooms. A 'trip' is the experience people sometimes have using magic mushrooms.

BRIEF HISTORY

Many different hallucinogenic plants and fungi were used by ancient tribes and civilizations as a means of entering the spiritual world. Fly agaric mushrooms were used by medicine men or 'shaman' of north-east Asia and Siberia. Liberty caps were seen as sacred intoxicants by the Aztecs of Mexico at the time of the Spanish invasion in the 1500s.

Magic mushrooms do not feature so much in European history, although pagan witches used hallucinogenic plants from the potato family, especially deadly nightshade and henbane. Reports of witches 'flying' may have their origins in reports of hallucinations experienced by those using such plants.

There is a possibility that in 1865 Lewis Carroll (Reverend Charles Lutwidge Dodgson) wrote his most famous book, *Alice's Adventures in Wonderland*, drawing on his experiences of using mushrooms.

Use of magic mushrooms for pleasure in the UK developed in the late 1970s, partly as a legal and more natural alternative to LSD, and has continued since.

LEGAL STATUS

Magic mushrooms containing psilocybin or psilocin are Class A drugs under the Misuse of Drugs Act and are illegal to be in possession of or to supply. Until 2005 it was not illegal to be in possession of fresh mushrooms and it was only illegal to make them into a preparation by drying them out or preparing them for use. Fly agaric mushrooms do not contain psilocybin or psilocin and so are not illegal.

AVAILABILITY, EXTENT OF USE AND COST

National surveys in the UK have usually found less than 5 per cent of young people claiming to have used magic mushrooms in the past year. In recent years there may have even have been a fall in the number of users with the 2012/13 Crime Survey in England and Wales finding under 2 per cent of 16–24-year-olds claiming to have used magic mushrooms in the past year (Home Office 2013).

Use of magic mushrooms tends to be on an occasional, rather than regular, basis and particularly in autumn.

Most users pick their own mushrooms or obtain them from friends and acquaintances, although they may also be sold by dealers. Some mushrooms that are not illegal to be in possession of, or to sell, can be purchased from headshops and via the internet.

Fly agaric use is very rare but use of liberty caps has become commonplace, especially in autumn, and tends to be mainly seasonal.

EFFECTS OF USE

The effects of magic mushroom use are similar to those of LSD and can vary greatly depending on the mood, situation and expectation of the user.

Effects from taking liberty caps come on after about half an hour and can last up to nine hours, depending on how many are taken. Twenty to thirty liberty caps is usually regarded as a full dose. Users often laugh a lot and feel more confident. Some users feel sick, develop a stomach ache and vomit. These effects tend to be even more common with fly agaric. Fly agaric use also often results in a drunken feeling, stiffness in the joints and lack of co-ordination and possibly an initial light sleep.

High doses of liberty caps result in a trip, with visual and sound distortions similar to those experienced with LSD.

POSSIBLE HARMS

A bad trip can be very frightening and may include feelings of fear, anxiety and paranoia. This is more likely with high doses and where the user already feels anxious. Reassurance from other people can usually calm them down. As with LSD, flashbacks can be experienced. This is when people re-experience part of a trip at a later time. It can be very frightening, especially if they do not know it can happen.

Another risk is picking the wrong type of mushroom and being poisoned. Some mushrooms, and particularly some that resemble the fly agaric, are poisonous and can kill. In contrast, it would take huge amounts of liberty caps to overdose fatally. There have, however, been occasional fatalities associated with an overdose of fly agaric.

Like LSD, tolerance to mushrooms develops very quickly so that the next day it might take twice as many liberty caps to repeat the experience. There is thus an in-built discouragement to daily use and most people only use occasionally. Physical dependence and withdrawal symptoms do not result from regular use though some people may become psychologically dependent and feel a desire to use on a regular basis. At present there is no evidence of serious health damage from long-term use.

Use of fly agaric gives strong hallucinatory effects but also often results in feelings of increased physical and mental energy and sometimes, in high doses, derangement and convulsions.

SAFETY/HARM REDUCTION ADVICE FOR YOUNG PEOPLE

To avoid the dangers of magic mushrooms...

1. Don't use them. But if young people do use magic mushrooms the advice is...

2. Be careful if you buy mushrooms or are given them. You may not know what they are or how strong they are.

3. Make sure that you pick the right mushrooms and not poisonous ones.

4. Don't take too many or use them too often.

5. Avoid fly agaric mushrooms. They are more dangerous.

6. Don't use alone. Use with other people and look after each other.

7. Carefully prepare and make sure the situation is as safe and relaxed as possible and you will not be disturbed.

8. Avoid using them if you feel depressed or anxious. Using will probably make you feel worse.

9. Be aware that they are Class A drugs under the Misuse of Drugs Act, the same as heroin, crack and cocaine. A lot of people do not realize they are illegal to be in possession of, even if you have just picked them.

10. If someone has a bad trip, reassure them and calm them down.

11. Don't drive or operate machinery while under the influence.

MEPHEDRONE

WHAT IT IS

Mephedrone (4-methylmethcathinone) is a man-made stimulant drug with effects similar to amphetamines, cocaine and ecstasy. It is part of a group of drugs derived from cathinone, the same chemical found in the khat plant.

It usually comes as a white or off-white powder that is either snorted, swallowed after being wrapped in paper (bombing) or dabbed on the gums. The powder often has a distinctive smell, a bit like a cat's litter tray. Occasionally it is found in pill or capsule form. It is sometimes prepared for injection but this is rarer.

Methylone and methedrone are similar but even more ecstasy-like in their effects.

STREET NAMES

Street names include bounce, bubble, charge, drone, fert, magic, MC, M-cat, meow, meph, miaow, plant feeder, plant food, white magic and 4MMC.

BRIEF HISTORY

Mephedrone was first synthesized in 1929 but remained obscure until 2003 when it was re-discovered and publicized on the internet by an underground chemist who experimented with it and compared the effects to ecstasy.

Use was reported in Israel, France and Australia before it became widely available in the UK in 2009 as a legal high through internet sales, headshops and local dealers. Supplies were mostly imported from China. The popularity of mephedrone was associated with the poor quality of amphetamines, ecstasy and cocaine that was often sold and the fact that it was a lot cheaper than cocaine.

Media scare stories about young people dying after using mephedrone, some of which were later shown to be untrue, led to the government making it illegal in the UK in 2010.

LEGAL STATUS

Mephedrone is controlled as a Class B under the Misuse of Drugs Act and is illegal to be in possession of or to supply.

AVAILABILITY, EXTENT OF USE AND COST

Mephedrone burst into the headlines in 2009 as a 'legal high' and use among young people was recorded all over the UK. The extent of use is difficult to judge and mephedrone has only recently been included as one of the drugs in annual surveys of drug use in the UK. The Crime Survey in England and Wales has found that, in the last three years, between 1.6 per cent and 4.4 per cent of 16–24-year-olds claimed to have used mephedrone in the past year (Home Office 2013).

Since being made illegal in 2010 expert commentators have suggested that the price of mephedrone has doubled. It is also more likely to be adulterated and of lower quality. Despite this, the number of young people using it does not seem to have decreased. In fact some people say use has increased since mephedrone was made illegal.

In 2012 some drug services reported an increasing number of injectors of mephedrone. Some of these injectors were existing heroin and/or crack users but others were people injecting drugs for the first time, after first snorting or swallowing mephedrone.

Prior to being made illegal in 2010 mephedrone was available as a legal high through the internet, headshops and local dealers. Since being banned, availability is mainly through local dealers.

Mephedrone sells for anything between £10 and £20 a gram. Prices have generally increased since it became illegal.

EFFECTS OF USE

Users report feelings of 'coming up' and a rushing feeling where they are excited and euphoric and more alert, energetic, confident and chatty. They may feel a closeness and empathy with other people, similar to the effects of ecstasy.

Experience of a dry mouth, grinding the teeth and clenching the jaw are common and users may sometimes experience chest pain, headache and difficulty urinating. They also often feel a loss of appetite.

When snorted, effects come on very quickly and tend to peak within half an hour. When swallowed, effects may take over 45 minutes to appear, partly depending on how much food is in the stomach, and last for one to two hours. Effects from injecting mephedrone are more intense but do not last as long.

POSSIBLE HARMS

Mephedrone use increases heart rate and may lead to palpitations or irregular heartbeat. Users can experience blurred vision, hot flushes and muscle tension. They may also feel anxious and paranoid. Some users may become aggressive, especially if they drink alcohol at the same time. As with ecstasy, there is a danger of overheating, especially if users have been dancing in hot clubs or are involved in other vigorous physical activity.

If users snort the drug they may get a sore, bloody nose. The comedown from the stimulant effects can make users feel miserable, tired and drained but not able to sleep. These feelings may last a few days after heavy use.

Regular users may find that diet and sleeping may become erratic. They may be tempted to use depressant drugs like tranquillizers, or even heroin, in an attempt to smooth out the comedown.

As use is relatively new, we are still learning about the long-term risks but it is clear that some young people find it very 'more-ish', have become dependent on mephedrone and experience a powerful need to keep taking it. Some users have gone on binges that can last a week or more.

There have been a number of deaths in the UK attributed to mephedrone use, though not as many as reported in the media. In the most publicized case two young men were found to have methadone and alcohol in their bloodstream, but no mephedrone. Most mephedrone-related deaths have been associated with very high doses, using together with other drugs (including alcohol and prescription drugs) or users having pre-existing heart or liver conditions. There have also been cases reported of young people committing suicide while on mephedrone.

Injecting mephedrone carries the same risks as injecting other drugs, such as increased risk of overdose, abscesses and of catching hepatitis and HIV if equipment is shared.

In the last couple of years drug services have started to see clients, often young people, who have serious problems with mephedrone use, including dependency.

SAFETY/HARM REDUCTION ADVICE FOR YOUNG PEOPLE

To avoid the dangers of mephedrone…

1. Don't use it. But if young people do use mephedrone the advice is…

2. Don't take too much or use too often. Start with a small amount and wait for an hour before deciding whether to take more.

3. Set limits. The more you take, the greater the risks of having a bad reaction.

4. Don't drink alcohol or take other drugs, including medicines, at the same time as using mephedrone.

5. Do not use if you have heart or blood pressure problems or are feeling really down about yourself.

6. Swallow, don't snort it. Snorting may damage your nose and skin. If you do snort, chop the powder finely.

7. Stay hydrated, especially if you are dancing or involved in physical activity. Sip water regularly rather than drinking a lot in one go.

8. If dancing, or involved in physical activity, take regular breaks to cool down and avoid overheating.

9. Don't use on your own. Use with friends and look after each other.

10. If someone starts overheating take them to a cool, relaxing place and give them sips of water, but not too much. If they get worse call an ambulance and tell the medics what they have taken.

11. If you start having problems with use, seek help and advice.

NITROUS OXIDE

WHAT IT IS

Nitrous oxide (N_2O) is a colourless gas that is slightly sweet smelling and tasting. It can be classed as a 'volatile substance' and is similar to some solvents – see the 'Solvents' section later in this part of the book. Nitrous oxide is a depressant drug with anaesthetic effects.

It is used medically for anaesthetics and relieving pain, such as in dentistry work and for women in childbirth, and for increasing the power output of petrol engines. Nitrous oxide is also used as whipping agent in whipped cream canisters.

Current use for intoxicating purposes commonly involves whipped cream chargers ('whippets'). These are small, single-use cartridges containing highly pressured nitrous oxide. The gas is discharged with a dispenser or a small widget called a 'cracker'. Users may then inhale the gas, usually through the mouth. In many cases a balloon is filled with nitrous oxide and it is then inhaled.

Some people also inhale nitrous oxide from cans of whipped cream, although this is more difficult to do. The other source of nitrous oxide is full-sized gas cylinders intended for medical use.

STREET NAMES

Nitrous oxide is sometimes called charger, cream charger, hippy crack, happy gas, laughing gas, N20 and whippet.

BRIEF HISTORY

Nitrous oxide was first synthesized before 1800 and experimented with by the physician Thomas Beddoes and the chemist and inventor, Humphrey Davy, from as early as 1799. Their reports of using it for intoxicating purposes earned nitrous oxide its enduring nickname of laughing gas.

In America and England in the late 19th century there were crazes for nitrous oxide and ether inhalation, especially at parties and balls for the upper classes and medical students. Nitrous oxide has a long history as a medical anaesthetic and of being taken for pleasure by some medical professionals.

The last few years has seen a resurgence of the inhalation of nitrous oxide among young people, often in combination with other drugs.

LEGAL STATUS

As with solvents, nitrous oxide is not controlled under the Misuse of Drugs Act and it is not illegal to be in possession of or to buy at any age. Under the 1985 Intoxicating Substances Supply Act it is an offence to supply, or offer to supply, a person aged under 18 years old with any solvent, if the trader knows that the young person will use it for intoxicating purposes. In theory, this law could be applied to nitrous oxide.

AVAILABILITY, EXTENT OF USE AND COST

Whipped cream canisters can be purchased easily and cheaply at supermarkets. Nitrous oxide chargers and dispensers can be bought over the internet from online suppliers and also from some of the headshops that exist in many cities and larger towns. Balloons filled with nitrous oxide are commonly sold at music festivals and events for as little as £1.50 to £3 each.

Over the last few years nitrous oxide has become more commonly used by some young people, particularly in combination with other drugs such as alcohol, cannabis, ecstasy, ketamine, magic mushrooms and mephedrone. The 2012/13 Crime Survey in England and Wales asked respondents, for the first time, whether or not they had used nitrous oxide. Six per cent of 16–24-year-olds claimed to have used it in the previous year (Home Office 2013). This figure was higher than that for any other controlled drug, except cannabis.

EFFECTS OF USE

When people inhale nitrous oxide the effects start almost immediately. They often feel a rush of euphoria, burst out laughing and feel dizzy but at the same time may experience a relaxed state. Sound is usually distorted and voices and music are often heard as a throbbing roar. There may also be some hallucinatory effects, ranging from moving bright dots to more detailed dreamscapes.

Nitrous oxide is an anaesthetic, meaning that co-ordination is strongly affected. People using it may fall over if they are not already sitting or lying down. It is also regarded as a dissociative drug and users may feel a sense of detachment from themselves and other people.

Using reduces the amount of oxygen in the bloodstream, meaning heartbeat increases and the limbs can feel heavy and tingle. Using may also result in a headache.

These effects peak very quickly and then die away almost as fast. The whole experience may only last a couple of minutes, without repeating the dose.

POSSIBLE HARMS

Lack of co-ordination may mean people fall over if they are standing up and makes accidents more likely. They may also pass out, often momentarily. It will be particularly dangerous to use nitrous oxide while driving or operating machinery.

As with solvents, particular ways of using nitrous oxide can be very dangerous. Placing a bag filled with nitrous oxide over the head can lead to death though suffocation. Attempting to fill a car or room with nitrous oxide can be similarly fatal. Some people have also inhaled from a gas mask strapped to medical cylinders of nitrous oxide and died through suffocation.

Gases at pressure can be dangerous. As well as sometimes exploding, they can be very cold. Inhaling nitrous oxide directly from a 'cracker', or from the nozzle of a gas cylinder, can result in frostbite of the lips and mouth and could freeze the airways, leading to suffocation. Dispensing several gas canisters, one after the other, from one cracker can cause cold burns to the hands.

The safest way of taking nitrous oxide is by inhaling from a balloon. If users do lose consciousness they are likely to drop the balloon and, unlike some of the other methods of using, not keep inhaling the gas.

Nitrous oxide is often used by people who are already under the influence of other drugs. The effects of mixing drugs can often be unpredictable and may be dangerous. Used in combination with potentially hallucinogenic drugs (such as stronger forms of cannabis and also ecstasy, ketamine, magic mushrooms and certain legal highs) the effects can be very intense and sometimes disturbing. Use together with depressant drugs, including alcohol, may increase the risk of losing consciousness and can be particularly dangerous.

Risks will be increased if users have existing physical health problems, such as with their heart or blood pressure. If users are already feeling emotionally insecure or unstable they may find the sensory distorting effects particularly disturbing.

As the effects of using are so short-lived, users may often repeat the dose a number of times. While not regarded as a drug that leads to physical dependence, it is possible that some people could develop a psychological need to take nitrous oxide every day. However, most people only use occasionally.

Although few people take nitrous oxide regularly over a long period, such use can lead to vitamin B12 deficiency and possibly limb numbness and spasms and tinnitus.

SAFETY/HARM REDUCTION ADVICE FOR YOUNG PEOPLE
To avoid the dangers of nitrous oxide…

1. Don't use it. But if young people do use nitrous oxide the advice is…

2. Don't take too much or use too often.

3. Don't use alone or use in dangerous or out of the way places.

4. Don't inhale from within a large bag placed over your head or from a face mask. Don't try to fill a room or car with nitrous oxide. You could suffocate.

5. Don't inhale directly from a cracker. Inhale from a balloon and make sure you are sitting or lying down.

6. Take special care if you are using other drugs at the same time. Mixing drugs can have unpredictable, disturbing and dangerous effects.

7. Using slows down reactions, so driving, operating machinery or going swimming while under their influence will increase the risks of accidents.

8. If you are trying to cut down or stop using, avoid people using and places where nitrous oxide is being used.

9. If someone collapses know your first aid. Put them in the recovery position and, if they do not quickly come round, call an ambulance.

10. If you are having problems with your use, seek help and advice.

POPPERS

WHAT THEY ARE

Poppers are amyl, butyl or isobutyl nitrites, collectively known as alkyl nitrites. In the UK poppers are usually sold as a gold-coloured liquid in a small bottle. They are usually inhaled, either straight from the bottle or from a cloth.

Amyl nitrite originally came as small glass capsules that were popped open. This led to them being given the name 'poppers' but this form is rarely found in the UK.

Poppers tend to have a sweet odour when fresh and are sometimes marketed as room 'deodorizers', but this tends to turn to a dirty socks smell when stale.

STREET NAMES

Street names include amyl, butyl, buzz, climax, hardware, liquid gold, locker room, ram, rock hard, rush, snapper, stag, stud, thrust, tribal juice and TNT, many reflecting the reputation of poppers as sex enhancers, particularly among gay men.

BRIEF HISTORY

Amyl nitrite was discovered in 1857 and used medically to ease chest pains (angina). In recent years it has been replaced by other medicines and its only remaining medical use is as an antidote for cyanide poisoning. Poppers became popular in show-biz circles in the 1950s and as a street drug in America in the 1960s, especially among gay men who had anal intercourse. This is because it relaxes muscles making anal intercourse easier.

Butyl nitrite has no medical uses and was originally sold in America as a room deodorizer and aphrodisiac. Since the late 1980s, poppers have become more widely used among young people in general in the UK, rather than just in the gay community.

LEGAL STATUS

Poppers are not covered under the Misuse of Drugs Act but some types are covered under the Medicines Act. Most are not illegal to manufacture, supply or be in possession of. However, it is illegal to supply amyl nitrite, under the Medicines Act. Most of the nitrites available in this country are butyl nitrite so this does not have much effect on their use.

The fact that poppers are volatile liquids means that they could be classed as solvents. This has led to some police forces considering prosecution of people who sell poppers to young people aged under 18 years old under the 1986 Intoxicating Substances Supply Act. To date there do not seem to have been any such prosecutions.

AVAILABILITY, EXTENT OF USE AND COST

Recent national surveys have found that under 3 per cent of 15-year-olds and 2 to 4 per cent of 16–24-year-olds said they had used poppers in the previous year (Home Office 2013). These figures are likely to be underestimates of the true picture, although one would not expect popper use, especially regular use, to be that common among young people.

In the UK it is mainly butyl nitrite imported from America which is sold in sex shops, some clubs, tobacconists and clothes shops targeted at young people and by mail order and over the internet, retailing at £4 to £6 for a 10ml bottle. They are often used in clubs, either by themselves or in combination with other drugs and tend to be used on an occasional, rather than regular, basis.

The use of poppers to aid anal intercourse may be going beyond gay men to encompass use among more women because of an increase in anal intercourse among young heterosexual couples in recent years.

EFFECTS OF USE

The effects start soon after inhalation but only last for a few minutes without repeating the dose. Users experience a rush as heartbeat quickens and blood pressure falls. Feelings of light-headedness, a slowed down sense of time and a flushed face and neck are commonly reported sometimes alongside dizziness, a pounding headache and nausea.

Users also often report sexual enhancements including a prolonged sensation of orgasm and prevention of premature ejaculation, although some men have also reported problems achieving an erection. Poppers also relax the anal muscles making anal intercourse easier.

POSSIBLE HARMS

Users can lose consciousness, especially if they are engaged in vigorous physical activity such as dancing or running. Accidents from falling over are also possible. Poppers use has led to heart attacks when people already have heart or blood pressure problems. Drinking poppers, as opposed to inhaling the vapours, is very dangerous and has resulted in some deaths.

Poppers increase pressure on the eye ball and are dangerous for people to use if they have the eye disease glaucoma. Regular use can result in people experiencing skin problems around the nose and lips from inhaling them. The fact that some people use nitrites to enhance sexual pleasure may make it more difficult to practise safer sex and use condoms, while high.

Poppers are often used in combination with other drugs. Some people say they help boost drug effects but any combination of drugs can be dangerous and lead to unpredictable effects. There have been concerns about some clubbers combining poppers with use of Viagra, which in combination could lead to a dangerous drop in blood pressure or even a stroke.

Regular users may find tolerance develops so they need increasing amounts to get an effect. Long-term use may lead to psychological dependence but there are no reports of physical dependence or withdrawal symptoms.

In the 1980s, especially in America, some people linked the use of poppers to the development of a rare cancer called Kaposi's sarcoma in gay men who had AIDS. Kaposi's sarcoma is one of the earliest symptoms of AIDS in those gay men who are HIV positive. However, the evidence for a link between poppers use and Kaposi's sarcoma has not been established.

SAFETY/HARM REDUCTION ADVICE FOR YOUNG PEOPLE

To avoid the dangers of poppers…

1. Don't use them. But if young people do use poppers the advice is…

2. Don't take too much or use too often.

3. Don't drink them.

4. Be aware that the strength of liquid in a bottle, and what is in it, may vary.

5. Take care if you dance or run while under the influence. You could collapse.

6. Don't drink alcohol or take other drugs at the same time. Mixing drugs with poppers can be very dangerous.

7. Don't get into sexual situations you will later regret. If you do have sex make sure you use condoms.

8. Co-ordination is affected so avoid driving, operating machinery or swimming while under the influence.

9. If you are trying to cut down or stop using, avoid people using and places where poppers are used.

10. Know how to do first aid in case someone else around you collapses after taking poppers.

SOLVENTS

WHAT THEY ARE

Some organic – carbon based – compounds can produce effects similar to alcohol or anaesthetics when their vapours are inhaled. A number are used as solvents in glues, paints, nail varnish removers, dry cleaning fluids and de-greasing compounds. Others are used as propellant gases in aerosols and fire extinguishers or as fuels, such as petrol or cigarette lighter gas (butane).

These products give off vapours or are gases at normal temperatures and can be inhaled through the mouth and/or nose to give an intoxicating effect. This is sometimes called 'glue sniffing', 'solvent abuse' or 'volatile substance abuse' (VSA).

Nitrous oxide is a volatile gas that has been increasingly used, mainly by young people, over the last few years and is discussed in detail on page 259.

Solvents can be directly inhaled but are also sometimes inhaled from inside a large plastic or paper bag, put on a rag or in a small bag first or squirted up a clothing sleeve before being drawn in.

STREET NAMES

Street names for solvents include aero, butane, glue and sniffers. Street names for solvent use include cogging, glue sniffing, huffing, sniffing and sucking. 'Bagging' means inhaling solvents from a bag and 'space-helmeting' means placing a large bag over the head.

BRIEF HISTORY

In America and England in the late 19th century there were crazes for nitrous oxide (laughing gas) and ether inhalation, especially at parties for the upper classes and medical students. Use of anaesthetic gases for pleasure by the medical profession and of petrol among soldiers also has a long history.

The modern phenomenon of solvent use by young people was first reported in America in the 1950s. The first cases of solvent inhalation among young people in the UK were reported in 1962, but there was not much concern about it until the 1970s. Use grew significantly in the 1980s economic recession. The 1980s and early 1990s witnessed many solvent-related deaths in the UK, with up to 150 users, many of them young people, dying each year.

In the 1970s and 1980s concerns focussed on the use of glue but since then glue sniffing has declined and inhalation of aerosols and other products has become more common. Some commentators suggested that this trend from glue to gas was one of the effects of the campaign with shopkeepers and manufacturers to stop young people having access to glues. In recent years solvent use, and associated deaths, have fallen among young people, with some people speculating that this has partly been due to the younger age range having easier access to alcohol and cannabis.

LEGAL STATUS

Solvents are not controlled under the Misuse of Drugs Act and it is not illegal for young people to be in possession of them or buy them at any age. Under the 1985 Intoxicating Substances Supply Act it is an offence to supply, or offer to supply, a person aged under 18 years old with a solvent, if the supplier knows the young person will use the solvent for intoxicating purposes. Under 1999 regulations, it is also illegal to sell lighter fuel (butane) to under-18s, whether or not it will be used for intoxicating purposes.

There have only been a few prosecutions of shopkeepers under this law. Proof is difficult to establish and most prosecutions have been when shopkeepers have made up 'glue bags' or 'sniffing kits' to sell to youngsters. The government has published guidelines for retailers advising them to keep solvent-based products out of the reach of children and to refuse the sale of solvents to any youngsters they believe may inhale them.

Some young people who have used solvents in public have offended against a variety of laws and local by-laws concerned with unruly, offensive, intoxicated behaviour or breach of the peace.

AVAILABILITY, EXTENT OF USE AND COST

Use of most solvents has tended to be concentrated in poorer areas among the younger age range, especially 12–16-year-olds. It often goes in phases, coming and going quickly, sometimes on a seasonal basis with less use in winter.

Most households and workplaces use a range of solvents that can be inhaled and many solvents are cheap to buy and sold in a wide range of shops. Most youngsters who use try solvents a few times and then leave it at that, but a small minority get into a habit of regular use.

Some surveys in the past found between 7 and 10 per cent of secondary school students said they had used solvents at least once. More recent national surveys of school students in England have found between 4 per cent and 5 per cent of 11–15-year-olds claiming to have used solvents in the past year and around 8 per cent claiming to have ever used them (Health and Social Care Information Centre 2013).

In recent years there has been a definite decline in solvent use and in the number of solvent-related deaths. This is possibly because of easier availability of cheap alcohol and cannabis to younger age ranges. There has also been a move away from glue sniffing to more use of gas and aerosols, despite commentators still often talking about glue sniffing.

EFFECTS OF USE

Inhaled solvent vapours are absorbed through the lungs and rapidly reach the brain. Oxygen intake is reduced, breathing and heart rate slow and repeated or deeper inhalation leads to a drunk-like feeling with loss of co-ordination and disorientation. In some cases users momentarily lose consciousness but usually come round quickly with no lasting damage.

Solvent inhalation is a bit like rapidly becoming drunk on alcohol. Users often quickly feel euphoric and merry but also calm and relaxed. Feelings of dizziness are common and some users may feel sick and drowsy. Lowering of inhibitions may result in unusually loud behaviour. Some users claim to see or hear things that are not there.

The effects are short-lived and usually last less than 45 minutes without a repeat dose. As the effects wear off users often feel tired and drowsy and may experience a hangover.

POSSIBLE HARMS

Accidental death or injury can result from intoxication and lack of co-ordination, especially if people use in an unsafe environment such as a canal or river bank, on a roof or near a busy road or train line. Driving, operating machinery or swimming while under the influence of solvents will increase the possibility of serious accidents.

Inhaling to the point of becoming unconscious can mean users risk dying through choking on their own vomit. If the method of use obstructs breathing, such as inhaling from within a bag over the head, death from suffocation can result.

Some solvents, such as aerosols and cleaning fluids, sensitize the heart to the effects of exertion and can lead to heart failure, especially if the user is running around and exerting themselves. If the gases in aerosols and lighter fuel refills are squirted directly into the mouth the airways can freeze, leading to death through suffocation.

The highest number of solvent-related deaths recorded in one year in the UK was over 150 in 1990. The number of deaths has fallen in recent years to under 50 a year (Ghodse 2012). A large number of these deaths have been of young people aged under 16 years old but some have been older, even a few over 30 years old. In the last few years the average age of people dying through solvent inhalation has been rising and involved more young adults, rather than teenagers. While most deaths are still of males, in recent years growing numbers have been females.

Taking solvents in combination with other drugs can have unpredictable effects and increase the likelihood of losing consciousness and having disturbing experiences. Using with alcohol can be particularly dangerous because both drugs are depressants and slow down body functions.

Very long-term heavy use or exposure to solvents can damage the brain, kidneys and liver but this is very rare and most likely in industrial settings where people work every day in environments where solvents are used. The research literature has not found that young people who inhale solvents experience long-term health problems, despite fears about brain damage.

Tolerance can develop with regular use so that more is needed to get the same effect. While physical dependence is not a problem, psychological dependence on the effects of solvents occurs with a small minority of users. They may come to rely on solvents to deal with unhappiness and underlying personal, family or social problems. They often use alone rather than in a group with friends.

Long-term regular use may also lead to people becoming very tired and forgetful and not being able to concentrate. Weight loss, depression and interference with kidney and liver functions can occur but these tend to clear up once use stops.

SAFETY/HARM REDUCTION ADVICE FOR YOUNG PEOPLE
To avoid the dangers of solvents...

1. Don't use them. But if young people do use solvents the advice is...

2. Don't take too much or use too often.

3. Don't use alone or use in dangerous or out of the way places.

4. Don't squirt aerosols or gases straight down the throat. It could freeze your airways.

5. Don't inhale from within a large bag put over your head. You could suffocate.

6. Don't use near a naked flame such as a lighter or lit cigarette. Many solvents can easily catch fire.

7. Don't drink alcohol or take other drugs (especially other downer drugs like tranquillizers or heroin) at the same time. The combination could kill.

8. Solvents slow down reactions so driving, operating machinery or going swimming while under their influence will increase the risks of accidents.

9. If you are trying to cut down or stop using, avoid people using and places where solvents are being used.

10. If someone collapses, know your first aid. Put them in the recovery position and call an ambulance.

11. If you are having problems with your use, seek help and advice.

STEROIDS

WHAT THEY ARE

Anabolic steroids are synthetically produced drugs that mimic the male hormones which occur naturally in the body and are responsible for growth, physical development and functioning of reproductive organs. They are similar to the male hormone testosterone, which is also the basis for masculine features such as growth of body hair and a deeper voice.

Anabolic steroids have an 'anabolic' building effect on the body and increase muscle tissue. Most people take them to help build their muscles and strength, to try to look more 'manly' and muscular or to improve how they perform at sports.

They usually come as tablets that are swallowed or in liquid form and prepared for injection.

There are many different types and brands of steroids. Some are diverted medical products, some are illicitly manufactured, usually abroad, and others may be promoted as for veterinary use only.

Anabolic steroids are sometimes prescribed by doctors for men to promote the development of male sexual characteristics, to help people recover from serious illness or major surgery and to treat anaemia and jaundice. They have also been prescribed for women to treat cancer of the breast and uterus. Most medically prescribed steroids are not anabolic but corticosteroids, which are widely used to treat inflammation.

STREET NAMES

Steroids are sometimes called 'roids' or 'juice' and also known by their generic and brand names such as anadrol, anavar, dianabol, durabolin, equipose, finajet, maxibolin, nadrolone, oxandrolone, oxandrin, primobolin, stanozolol, testosterone, testovis and winstrol.

'Roid rage' refers to aggressive and/or violent behaviour by steroid users. 'Stacking' refers to users combining use of fast and slow acting steroids over a specific timescale.

BRIEF HISTORY

The use of performance enhancing drugs in sport has been going on ever since the Olympic Games of ancient Greece. Anabolic steroids were probably first used by athletes in the 1940s and by the 1960s their use was widespread.

In the 1980s doping became a big issue at the Olympic Games and other sporting events. Drug testing came into many sports and a number of famous athletes failed tests, often for steroids, and were banned from competing.

Anabolic steroid use has since become common among athletes, other sports people, body builders and what might be termed certain fitness fanatics in many countries, and drug testing in sport has become a huge, on-going issue and concern.

LEGAL STATUS

Anabolic steroids are controlled under the Misuse of Drugs Act as Class C drugs. They are illegal to supply or sell but the possession offence is usually waived so that, in most cases, they are not illegal to possess for personal use without a prescription. However, if an individual has a large quantity of steroids they could be charged with possession with intent to supply under the Misuse of Drugs Act.

Most steroids used in the UK are manufactured abroad. While it is still legal to go abroad and bring back steroids to the UK for personal use, the importation law was changed in 2012. It is now illegal to buy steroids through internet or mail order suppliers that are based in other countries. In other words, it is now illegal to import steroids in these ways for personal use.

Anabolic steroids are also prescription-only medicines under the Medicines Act meaning, as with their status under the Misuse of Drugs Act, it is an offence to sell or supply them unless it involves a pharmacist processing a doctor's prescription. This will include friends supplying to each other as a gift or at no profit.

AVAILABILITY, EXTENT OF USE AND COST

In recent years a huge trade in anabolic steroids has developed among body builders, gym users, various athletes and other sportspeople. These people often think of themselves as self-improvers – healthy, fit and getting ahead in the world, rather than drug users.

Use has also been common among men who want to be and look strong and tough, such as construction works, security guards and police officers. There has also been an increase in use among young men, and some young women, who take steroids in the belief that they enhance not only physical performance but also sexual performance, physical appearance and desirability.

While use has increased in recent years, steroids are not used by many of the UK population. For every Crime Survey conducted in England and Wales from 1996 to 2012/13, under 1 per cent of 16–24-year-olds claimed to have used steroids in the past year (Home Office 2013). However, some surveys have shown that larger numbers of people using particular gyms take steroids.

Injecting has become a popular method of use and in recent years some UK needle exchange schemes have reported that they have more steroid injectors than heroin injectors on their books.

Steroids can be very expensive to use on a regular basis and many users also pay a lot of money for high protein foods, special vitamin supplements and other drugs that form an integral part of their fitness programme. Many use a number of steroids in combination over cycles of six to eight weeks. The cost of one cycle may be between £70 and £140, with an annual cost of buying steroids possibly between £500 and £2500 a year.

With supply being an offence in the UK, most steroids have been imported from abroad through mail order magazines and via the internet. They are also sold illegally at some gyms. Regular users have sometimes purchased steroids while abroad and brought them back to the UK, without breaking the law.

The 2012 law change has criminalized the purchasing of steroids by mail order and internet suppliers that are based abroad. This may have resulted in a lack of supplies in the UK, an increase in steroid production by illicit underground laboratories in this country and the possibility that poorer quality products have become a greater part of the market.

EFFECTS OF USE

Taking anabolic steroids, combined with training and exercise regimes, builds body weight and increases the size of muscles. This often makes users feel more competitive and better able to perform strenuous physical activity for longer. Many users become very 'wired' and focussed on their body and fitness. Steroid use can also lead to some users feeling paranoid, irritable, aggressive or even violent. Intense mood swings are common. Violence is more likely to happen if users already have aggressive tendencies in the first place. 'Macho' men could become even more 'macho' and there have been reports of male users acting in sexually aggressive and threatening ways towards women.

POSSIBLE HARMS

Users often take steroids in multiple combinations and at much higher doses than would be prescribed medically. Regular use can lead to a wide range of health problems. These include hypertension – steroids encourage the body to retain water and raise blood pressure – and liver abnormalities. Hepatitis, HIV and other infections are a risk if users inject and share equipment.

Use by young people can lead to stunted growth. Regular use, at any age, changes the male reproductive system whereby sperm output and quality is reduced and can take six months to return to normal. Sex drive may at first increase but then be lowered leading to erectile problems and shrinking of the testicles. Some men have also experienced over-development of their breasts and find acne becomes a problem. Increased aggression, including sexual aggression, may result from regular use.

Women who regularly use steroids may experience increased sex drive, menstrual problems, an enlarged clitoris and acne. They also run the risk of developing 'male' features such as growth of facial and body hair, deepening of the voice and decreased breast size. Once these things happen they are usually irreversible, even when steroid use stops. If a pregnant woman uses steroids she can, in some cases, pass on some 'male' characteristics to a female foetus.

Sleep disorders, confusion, depression and paranoia have been reported among regular users although these tend to lessen once steroid use is stopped.

There are concerns about the quality and safety of steroids that are sold on the black market, with falsified, substandard and counterfeit products often being used. Some of these counterfeit steroids may not have the effect that the buyer expected or wanted. Some may have no active ingredient at all. Potency of similarly named steroids may also vary. This means users may find it difficult to anticipate the effects of the steroids they take and thus put themselves at risk.

While steroids are not regarded as drugs of physical dependence, regular steroid use can lead to psychological dependence when the user is convinced they cannot perform well or look good without being on drugs. Some users say they feel lacking in energy and depressed after stopping use and continue to use them rather than face these symptoms.

SAFETY/HARM REDUCTION ADVICE FOR YOUNG PEOPLE

To avoid the dangers of anabolic steroids...

1. Don't use them. But if young people do use steroids the advice is...

2. Don't use counterfeit products which may not be what they appear to be.

3. Be aware that the potency of what are advertised as particular steroids may vary. Take care about how much you take.

4. Only use for short periods in a strictly controlled way, then take a break from use.

5. Be aware that they are now illegal to purchase from mail order and internet businesses based abroad.

6. Be aware of any adverse changes to your body or appearance and, if necessary, stop using and seek medical assistance.

7. Be aware of any changes to your mood, particularly any increase in aggression, and problems with diet and sleep patterns and, if necessary, stop use and seek assistance.

8. Take tablets, rather than inject steroid solution.

9. If you do inject, take care about how you inject, avoid sharing injecting equipment with other people and use a needle exchange scheme.

10. If you are having problems with your use, seek help and advice. Many drug services that work with heroin users have now become experienced in helping steroid users.

TOBACCO

WHAT IT IS

Tobacco is made from the dried leaves of the tobacco plant that grows in many parts of the world. The main active ingredient is nicotine, a mild stimulant drug. Most tobacco used in the UK comes from America and is sold as cigarettes. Cigars and pipe tobacco are made from stronger, darker tobacco. Snuff is powdered tobacco that is sniffed up the nose.

STREET NAMES

Street names include backy, cigs, fags and snout.

BRIEF HISTORY

The first recorded examples of tobacco smoking were from the Mexican Mayan civilization in about 500 AD. Tobacco was first brought to England in the second part of the 16th century by Sir Walter Raleigh. This was mainly in the form of pipe smoking.

By the early 1600s tobacco was sold in specialist tobacconist shops and from grocers and drapers. Extravagant claims were made about the use of tobacco to cure a variety of diseases and ailments. Smoking tobacco for pleasure was first confined to the wealthy classes but its use gradually spread. In the early 1600s King James and the puritans came out strongly against smoking tobacco and regarded it as a moral and health risk. Duty was increased on its importation.

From the late 17th century to early 19th century snuff replaced pipe smoking in England. Cigar smoking also became more common. Cigarettes were first introduced to England by troops returning from the Crimean War (1854–86) who had seen French and Turkish soldiers smoking them. They were of the roll-your-own variety.

By the 1870s English companies started making ready rolled cigarettes. In the 1880s, with the development of automatic machinery, cigarettes as we know them today, became more widely available. Filter tip cigarettes were first introduced in the 1950s.

It was not until the 1960s that tobacco smoking was associated with health problems. Until that time tobacco products were often seen as health enhancing and a good way of relaxing. Smoking was even advertised by famous sportsmen.

Health warnings led to a fall in tobacco consumption in developed countries, increased tax on tobacco products, controls and bans on advertising, low tar varieties and bans on smoking in public places. It has also led to new products and schemes to help people stop smoking, including smoking cessation groups and a wide range of nicotine replacement products.

As sales of tobacco products have recently fallen in the developed world, the large multi-national companies which dominate the industry have searched for new markets with developing countries and Eastern European countries being targeted.

LEGAL STATUS

It is not illegal to buy, possess or use tobacco products. However, selling tobacco products to young people aged under 18 years old is an offence. Local authority Trading Standards officers monitor retail outlets which sell tobacco products. Smoking is now banned in most public spaces.

AVAILABILITY, EXTENT OF USE AND COST

In recent years cigarette smoking has been declining in the adult population, particularly among the middle classes, and also young people. Some primary school aged children will have tried a cigarette but surveys show less than 1 per cent of 11-year-olds can be classed as regular smokers – at least one cigarette a week. A large-scale, long-term national survey of school students in England found that the percentage of people who were regular smokers by age 15 years old was 10 per cent in 2012, a decline from figures of between 24 per cent and 28 per cent in the 1990s (Health and Social Care Information Centre 2013). Current smoking rates for 16–19-year-olds have fallen to below 20 per cent from over 30 per cent in 1998, and for 20–24-year-olds have fallen to below 25 per cent from 40 per cent in 1998 (ASH 2013; Health and Social Care Information Centre 2012a).

From the mid-1980s until relatively recently, surveys usually showed a greater percentage of young girls than boys as being regular smokers. However, more recent surveys have shown less difference in young female and male smoking rates. There is still a strong link between cigarette smoking and socio-economic class among both adults and young people. People from lower social classes are more likely to smoke.

Sales of cigarettes are still a major source of government revenue in the UK despite the fall in the number of smokers. Prices have risen markedly in an attempt to deter people from smoking. Young people who are regular smokers may be more inclined to smoke cheaper brands. Some, and particularly those who live in poorer areas, may also have access to cigarettes from illicit sources that cost between a quarter and a half of the full retail price.

EFFECTS OF USE

Tobacco smoking involves the inhalation of tar, nicotine, carbon monoxide and other gases. Nicotine is a stimulant drug which increases pulse rate and blood pressure. Regular smokers often find that smoking combats anxiety and stress, helps them to concentrate and alleviates boredom, although this may be mainly about the fact that they have become dependent on nicotine and feel relief at smoking another cigarette to combat the withdrawal symptoms. Some smokers also find it suppresses appetite. First-time users often feel sick, dizzy and experience a headache.

POSSIBLE HARMS

Smoking tends to yellow the hands, make people and their clothes smell of tobacco, result in breathing and respiratory problems and make asthma worse. Tolerance develops quickly to the effects of nicotine so more is needed to get an effect. Many younger children manage to be occasional smokers but most young people aged over 14 years old who smoke become dependent and feel restless and anxious if they try to stop. Very few people find they can just have the occasional cigarette.

Regular, long-term smoking greatly increases the risk of a number of serious diseases including lung and other cancers, heart diseases, bronchitis, bad circulation and ulcers. It has been estimated that over 80,000 people die prematurely in the UK each year through smoking-related diseases (Health and Social Care Information Centre 2012a).

Women who smoke cigarettes during pregnancy tend to give birth to babies of smaller birth weight. Smoking while taking oral contraceptives (the pill) increases the risk of heart and circulatory problems.

Research has also shown that smoking can damage non-smokers who inhale tobacco fumes. Passive smoking has been claimed to cause several hundred deaths in the UK each year and to greatly increase the risk of asthma among children whose parents smoke.

ADVICE FOR YOUNG PEOPLE ABOUT GIVING UP

Of all drug use, smoking cigarettes probably least lends itself to harm reduction. Most people are either regular smokers or do not smoke at all. Very few people manage to just have the occasional cigarette without starting to increase their use. Using lighter brands and filters may help a bit but for most people they either smoke cigarettes or do not. Some people may use nicotine replacement therapy (NRT) products such as patches, chewing gums and E-cigarettes, in an attempt to give up smoking cigarettes, but many remain dependent on nicotine and still find it difficult to actually quit. In contrast to the other drugs covered in this book, the advice below is more about ways of stopping than cutting down.

To avoid the dangers of smoking cigarettes...

1. Don't use them at all. But if young people are hooked on cigarettes the advice is...

2. Make a date to stop smoking and stick to it.

3. Stop. Don't just cut down. Most people successfully quit by stopping altogether rather than trying to cut down.

4. Try nicotine replacement products and electronic cigarettes but beware of becoming dependent on them.

5. Drink plenty of water and/or fruit juice, become more active and take more exercise.

6. Improve your diet. If you need to snack eat fruit, raw vegetables or sugar free gums rather than sugary and fatty foods.

7. If you find it unpleasant and hard to stop, remember that these feelings will pass in time. If you manage to really get into giving up, withdrawal symptoms can be mild and last for less than a week.

8. Avoid people who smoke and places where smoking takes place.

9. Treat yourself. If you can, use the money you save to buy yourself something nice.

10. Consider seeking specialist support and joining a local stop-smoking group.

TRANQUILLIZERS

WHAT THEY ARE

Minor tranquillizers are synthetic, depressant drugs that are manufactured as medicines to treat anxiety, epilepsy and other conditions and as sleeping tablets. (Other drugs called major tranquillizers are used for the treatment of long-term mental health problems.)

They are also known as benzodiazepines and include anti-anxiety drugs such as alprazolam (Xanax), chlorodiazepoxide (Librium) and diazepam (Valium), sleeping tablets such as flurazepam (Dalmane), nitrazepam (Mogadon) and temazepam (Normison or Restoril) and also lorazepam (Ativan) which is prescribed both as an anti-anxiety medicine and as sleeping pills. Flunitrazepam (Rohypnol) is no longer available on general prescription in the UK but can be obtained on private prescription and purchased over the internet.

A new generation of what are called 'Z drugs', such as zopiclone, have been developed that act in a similar way to tranquillizers.

For medical use, tranquillizers are usually swallowed as pills or capsules and occasionally in liquid form. They are also used in the same way as street drugs but some, such as temazepam, have sometimes been prepared for injection.

STREET NAMES

Street names include benzos, BZDs, downers and tranx. Mogadon pills are sometimes called moggies. Rohypnol are sometimes called ropies, ruffies, roofies or rope. Temazepam have been called green eggs, jellies, jelly babies, rugby balls, tems and yellow eggs.

BRIEF HISTORY

Minor tranquillizers were first manufactured in the 1960s and seen as safe, non-addictive medicines to treat anxiety and as sleeping pills. They were originally promoted as a hazard-free alternative to the prescribing of barbiturates.

Although many people, particularly women, suffered serious side effects and dependence, prescribing of tranquillizers continued to grow. It was not until the late 1970s that these problems were acknowledged. Despite this, today they are still one of the most commonly prescribed mood-altering medicines in the UK, alongside anti-depressants.

LEGAL STATUS

All minor tranquillizers are prescription-only medicines under the Medicines Act. This means they can only be legally supplied by a pharmacist in accordance with a doctor's prescription.

They are also controlled as Class C drugs under the Misuse of Drugs Act. Until recently, possession was not an arrestable offence if you did not have a prescription, except for Rohypnol and temazepam tranquillizers. The law has been changed so that police can arrest people who are in possession of any minor tranquillizer and cannot show a legitimate prescription for them. Tranquillizers are also illegal to supply to other people, whether or not money changes hands. If someone obtains tranquillizers on a doctor's prescription and gives them to someone else they are committing an offence.

AVAILABILITY, EXTENT OF USE AND COST

Although exact figures are difficult to ascertain, it has been suggested that as many as one in seven British adults are prescribed tranquillizers at some time each year and that one in 40 take them throughout the year (Shapiro 2010). Many people are on long-term repeat prescriptions that may be given without them seeing their doctor. Twice as many women as men are prescribed tranquillizers. In recent years estimates for the number of people who are dependent on them in the UK have varied from 200,000 to over one million people (Lane 2012). This prescribing will include some young people, particularly young women.

Relatively small numbers of young people will have experience of non-medical use of tranquillizers. For many years, the annual Crime Survey for England and Wales has found that under 2 per cent of 16–24-year-olds claim to have taken them, non-medically, in the year prior to being asked, the figure for 2012/13 being only 0.4 per cent (Home Office 2013).

Temazepam tranquillizers have a history of being prepared for injection either as a cheap drug of first choice or when drugs such as heroin are unavailable.

Manufacturers have changed them from being capsules, containing gel, to solid tablets in an attempt to stop this happening, although they are still sometimes available in liquid form on prescription. Rohypnol tranquillizers have been implicated in cases of date rape but the extent to which this has happened is unclear.

Some young people may try tranquillizers as a one off-experiment, possibly obtaining them from parents. Some regular users of stimulant drugs like amphetamines, cocaine, crack, ecstasy and mephedrone may take them to smooth the comedown. Some dependent heroin users may use tranquillizers when heroin is scarce. The extent to which these things happen is unclear but regular use probably only involves small numbers.

There is not much illegal manufacture of tranquillizers. Some prescribed or stolen tablets find their way on to the street selling for as little as 25p each. Tranquillizers are also available for illegal purchase over the internet.

EFFECTS OF USE

Tranquillizers are sedative drugs which slow down reactions. They relieve anxiety and tension and can make users feel more calm and relaxed and also, especially with higher doses, make them feel drowsy, lethargic and forgetful. Effects usually begin ten to 15 minutes after taking them and can last up to six hours without repeating the dose.

POSSIBLE HARMS

The effect of slowing reactions and making users drowsy can make accidents more likely. It can be dangerous to drive or operate machinery while on tranquillizers. With regular use tolerance can develop quickly so increasing amounts are needed to get the same effect. Dependence can also quickly develop with regular use so that withdrawal can lead to intense feelings of anxiety, nausea and irritability and headaches and insomnia. Dependent users may feel they cannot face the world and cope without them. Sudden withdrawal from very high doses can be very dangerous and result in confusion and convulsions. Many long-term users find it very difficult to give up and they may need to gradually reduce the dose to do so.

Regular users often find that, after a time, tranquillizers become ineffective in giving the desired effect. They may become ineffective as sleeping pills after two weeks and ineffective to combat anxiety after four months. The temptation is to then increase the dosage. Tranquillizers are only really effective as short-term medicines but many people become dependent on them and use them for years on a repeat prescription from their doctor. Regular, high dose use in the later stages of pregnancy can result in withdrawal effects in a newborn baby.

A lot of tranquillizers have to be taken to fatally overdose but there have been many cases where people have died, especially when they have also taken other depressant drugs, such as alcohol, heroin or methadone, at the same time. The number of people recorded on death certificates as dying each year, over the past five years, from using tranquillizers has been between 230 and 284 in England and Wales (Office for National Statistics 2013b).

Injecting tranquillizers, such as temazepam, can be particularly dangerous and in the past resulted in a number of fatal overdoses, especially in Scotland, when combined with use of other depressant drugs. Rohypnol tranquillizers have been implicated in a number of cases of date rape, when they have been slipped into people's alcoholic drinks. However, it is unclear to what extent this has happened and it is probably the case that alcohol itself remains the most common date rape drug.

SAFETY/HARM REDUCTION ADVICE FOR YOUNG PEOPLE
To avoid the dangers of tranquillizers...

1. Don't use them. But if young people do use tranquillizers the advice is...

2. Don't take too much or use too often. It is easy to become dependent with regular use.

3. Injecting them can be very dangerous, so don't inject.

4. If you do inject, use clean injecting equipment and never share with other people. Sharing injecting equipment can lead to hepatitis and HIV.

5. Don't take other drugs at the same time, especially other downer drugs like alcohol or heroin. The combination can result in fatal overdose.

6. If you have been prescribed tranquillizers by your doctor do not use them long term. Ask for help to come off them.

7. They slow down reactions, so don't drive or operate machinery while too intoxicated.

8. If you are having problems with your use, seek help and advice.

E

WHERE TO FIND OUT MORE

Helping Organizations and Websites

INFORMATION ABOUT DRUGS AND DRUG USE

Alcohol Concern

www.alcoholconcern.org.uk

Information about alcohol and related health and policy issues.

Ash (Action on Smoking and Health)

www.ash.org.uk

Information about smoking cigarettes and health and policy issues.

Drinkaware

www.drinkaware.co.uk

Information and advice about personal alcohol use.

DrugScope

www.drugscope.org.uk

Information about a wide range of legal and illegal drugs and drug policies.

Drugs-forum

www.drugs-forum.com

International information and message site that educates about responsible drug use from a harm reduction perspective. Users have to register to participate fully, including in the discussion forums.

Erowid

www.erowid.org

Detailed information about a wide range of mood-altering drugs.

Frank
www.talktofrank.com
Government funded website providing information and advice for young people. The information provided is not always that balanced and can sometimes exaggerate dangers.

HIT
www.hit.org.uk
Health information agency that publish a range of publications about drugs for young people, professionals and parents, including many written by Julian Cohen, the author of this book.

Independent Scientific Committee on Drugs
www.drugscience.org.uk
Information about drugs provided by Professor David Nutt.

NHS Choices
www.nhs.uk
Information about medicines.

Release
www.release.org.uk
Information about illegal drugs, drug laws and legal rights.

Re-solv
www.re-solv.org
Information about solvent use.

The Site
www.thesite.org
Information about drugs and alcohol and also about the law.

UK Government
www.gov.uk
Information about drugs and the law, and drug policy in the UK.

Urban 75
www.urban75.com/Drugs
Detailed information about a wide range of drugs.

Why not find out?
www.whynotfindout.org
Information for young people about a wide range of drugs.

WEBSITES THAT CAN DIRECT YOU TO LOCAL HELPING SERVICES

You can find local services by typing in your postcode in the websites below.

Adfam
www.adfam.org.uk
Support services and groups for parents and other family members, who have a child or relative that is experiencing problems with drugs.

Frank
www.talktofrank.com
Support services for young people who experience problems with drugs and for their families.

NHS Choices
www.nhs.uk
Services for people who have problems with their drug use, alcohol use or want to stop smoking.

NATIONAL TELEPHONE HELPLINES

The helplines below offer confidential services. If callers wish, they do not have to even give their name.

Professionals, parents and young people can also often access telephone information and advice through their local services (see above).

Childline
0800 1111 (24 hours a day)
Advice and listening service for children and young people up to 19 years old.

Drinkline
0800 917 8282 (weekdays 9am to 8pm, weekends 11am to 4pm)
Information and advice for people who experience alcohol problems.

Family lives

0808 800 2222 (7am to midnight)

General support and advice for parents.

Frank

0300 1236600 (24 hours a day, 365 days a year)

Information and advice about drugs for young people, parents and other relatives.

Release

020 7324 2989 (weekdays 11am to 1pm and 2pm to 4pm)

Information and advice about the legal aspects of drug use.

Samaritans

08457 909 090 (24 hours a day, 365 days a year)

Listening service that is especially useful in a crisis for young people and parents.

Stop Smoking (Smoke Free)

0800 022 4332 (weekdays 9am to 8pm, weekends 11am to 4pm)

Information and advice about giving up smoking.

Recommended Reading

Listed below are some of my favourite books about drugs. They have been an important part of my education over the past 30 years. Many of them challenge the myths and stereotypes that commonly surround discussion of drug use and place it within a wider perspective. They encourage us to question and think. If you are one of the fortunate people who still has a local bookshop, especially an independent one rather than the soulless national chains, please buy books from them.

All of them, even the older books, should be available through libraries and most can be purchased through Amazon. The more recent ones can also be ordered and purchased through good bookshops.

Aldridge, J., Measham, F. and Williams, L. (2011) *Illegal Leisure Revisited: Changing Patterns of Alcohol and Drug Use in Adolescents and Young Adults*. Didcot: Routledge.
Results from, and discussion of, a detailed, long-term study of young people's drug use between the ages of 14 and 27/28 years old.

Alexander, B.K. (2008) *The Globalisation of Addiction: A Study in the Poverty of the Spirit*. Oxford: Oxford University Press.
Examines the underlying causes of drug use and drug problems, and our failure to understand and control it.

Blackman, S. (2004) *Chilling Out: The Cultural Politics of Substance Consumption, Youth and Drug Policy*. Milton Keynes: Open University Press.
Wide-ranging discussion and critique of drug policies in the UK targeted at young people.

BMA (2011) *New Guide to Medicines and Drugs*. London: Dorling Kindersley.
Detailed information about medicines and also some information about illegal drugs.

Daly, M. and Sampson, S. (2012) *Narcomania: A Journey Through Britain's Drug World*. London: Heinemann.
A fascinating exploration of the current drugs trade in this country through the eyes of users, dealers, the police and policy makers.

Davenport-Hines, R. (2001) *The Pursuit of Oblivion: A Global History of Narcotics.* London: Weidenfeld and Nicholson.
Focusses on why and how drugs have had such an impact on Western society from the year 1500 to current times.

Davies, J.B. (1997) *The Myth of Addiction.* Amsterdam: Harwood.
A challenging and provocative book that explores and refutes the many commonly held myths regarding addiction.

Gardner, D. (2009) *Risk: The Science and Politics of Fear.* London: Virgin Books.
A sober, yet entertaining, examination of our contradictory attitudes towards different risky behaviours. Includes examples of how drug risks are often exaggerated.

Gossop, M. (1993) *Living With Drugs.* Aldershot: Ashgate.
Dispels the many myths about drugs and drug taking and places drug use within a broad social and psychological perspective.

Inglis, B. (1975) *The Forbidden Game: A Social History of Drugs.* London: Hodder and Stoughton.
Excellent and wide-ranging history of drug use.

Jay, M. (2011) *Emperors of Dreams: Drugs in the Nineteenth Century.* Cambridge: Dedalus.
If you thought that use of mind-altering drugs was a relatively new phenomenon read on. Focusses on use of nitrous oxide, ether, chloroform, opium, cannabis, cocaine, mushrooms and mescaline.

Jay, M. (2012) *High Society, Mind-Altering Drugs in History and Culture.* London: Thames and Hudson.
Fascinating history book that tracks drug use back to antiquity and across many cultures. Includes many revealing photographs.

Nutt, D. (2012) *Drugs Without the Hot Air.* Cambridge: UIT Cambridge.
Information about the effects and potential harms of using a wide range of drugs.

Peele, S. (1977) *Love and Addiction.* London: Abacus.
Provocative and challenging discussion of dependency in personal relationships and drug use.

Peele, S. (1985) *The Meaning of Addiction.* San Francisco, CA: Jossey-Bass.
A calm and reasoned critique of viewing addiction as a disease.

Peele, S. (2007) *Addiction Proof Your Child: A Realistic Approach to Preventing Drugs, Alcohol and Other Dependencies.* New York, NY: Three Rivers Press.
Excellent, myth busting explanation of addiction that includes advice for parents about how they can help their children avoid dependency and respond effectively to drug use and dependencies.

Power, M. (2013) *Drugs 2.0: The Web Revolution That's Changing How the World Gets High.* London: Portobello Books.
A detailed and eye-opening account of the advent of legal highs and the current availability of drugs over the internet.

Young, J. (1971) *The Drugtakers: The Social Meaning of Drug Use.* London: Paladin.
A wide-ranging exploration into the social meaning of young people's drug use. This book is over 40 years old but still very relevant today.

Zinberg, N.E. (1984) *Drug, Set and Setting: The Basis for Controlled Intoxicant Use.* New Haven and London: Yale University Press.
A key study that was a foundation for understanding the factors that influence people's experiences of drug use and for developing harm reduction advice.

References

ACMD Advisory Council on the Misuse of Drugs (2006) 'Further Consideration of the Classification of Cannabis under the Misuse of Drugs Act 1971.' London: Home Office.

ACMD Advisory Council on the Misuse of Drugs (2008) 'Cannabis Classification and Public Health.' London: Home Office.

ACMD Advisory Council on the Misuse of Drugs (2009) 'MDMA ("Ecstasy"): A Review of its Harms and Classification under the Misuse of Drugs Act 1971.' London: Home Office.

ACMD Advisory Council on the Misuse of Drugs (2013) 'Khat: A Review of its Potential Harms to the Individual and Communities in the UK.' London: Home Office.

ACPO Association of Chief Police Officers of England, Wales and Northern Ireland (2006) *Joining Forces. Drugs: Guidance for Police Working with Schools and Colleges.* Available at www.acpo.police. uk/documents/crime/2012/CBADrugsPsychoactiveNov2011.pdf, accessed 4 March 2014.

Alexander, B.K. (2008) *The Globalisation of Addiction: A Study in the Poverty of the Spirit.* Oxford: Oxford University Press.

ASH Action on Smoking and Health (2013) *Smoking Statistics: Who Smokes and How Much.* London: ASH.

British Medical Association (2011) *New Guide to Medicines & Drugs.* 8th edn. London: Dorling Kindersley.

Cohen, J. (2012) 'Drug Education or Drug Propaganda?' In R. Pates and D. Riley (eds) *Harm Reduction in Substance Use and High-Risk Behaviour.* Chichester: Wiley-Blackwell.

Davies, J.B. (1997) *The Myth of Addiction.* Amsterdam: Harwood.

Department of Health (2009) 'Guidance on the Consumption of Alcohol by Children and Young People.' London: Department of Health.

Department of Health (2011) 'United Kingdom Drug Situation 2011.' London: Department of Health.

Duffy, M., Schaefer, N., Coomber, R., O'Connell, L. and Turnbull, P.J. (2008) *Cannabis Supply and Young People.* York: Joseph Rowntree Foundation.

EMCDDA European Monitoring Centre for Drugs and Drug Addiction (2013) 'European Drug Report 2013: Trends and Development.' Luxembourg: Publications Office of the European Union.

ESPAD European School Survey Project on Alcohol and Other Drugs (2012) 'The 2011 ESPAD Report.' Stockholm: Swedish Council for Information on Alcohol and Other Drugs.

Forensic Science Service (2008) 'Home Office Cannabis Potency Study 2008.' London: Home Office.

Ghodse, H., Corkery, J., Ahmed, K. and Schifano, F. (2012) 'Trends in UK Deaths Associated with Abuse of Volatile Substances 1971–2009.' London: St. George's, University of London.

Global Drug Survey (2013) 'Mixmag's Global Drug Survey: The Results.' Available at www.mixmag.net/words/features/mixmags-global-drug-survey-the-results, accessed on 26 February 2014.

Hansard (2012) 'Drugs: Prosecutions.' Written Answers and Statements. 18 December 2012, col. 718W. Available at www.publications.parliament.uk/pa/cm201213/cmhansrd/cm121218/text/121218w0002.htm, accessed on 27 February 2014.

Health and Social Care Information Centre (2012a) 'Statistics on Smoking, England, 2012.' London: HSCIC.

Health and Social Care Information Centre (2012b) 'Statistics on Alcohol, England, 2012.' London: HSCIC.

Health and Social Care Information Centre (2013) 'Smoking, Drinking and Drug Use among Young People in England in 2012.' London: HSCIC.

Home Office (2013) 'Drug Misuse: Findings from the 2012/13 Crime Survey for England and Wales.' London: Home Office.

Lane, C. (2012) 'The Tranquilizer Trap.' *Psychology Today*. Available at www.psychologytoday.com/blog/side-effects/201210/the-tranquilizer-trap, accessed on 4 March 2014.

Lloyd, C., Joyce, R., Hurry, J. and Ashton, M. (2000) 'The effectiveness of primary school drug education.' *Drugs: Education, Prevention, and Policy 7*, 2: 109–126.

Manning, V., Best, D.W., Faulkner, N. and Titherington, E. (2009) 'New estimates of the number of children living with substance misusing parents: Results from UK national household surveys.' *BMC Public Health 9*: 377.

Meier, M.H., Caspi, A., Ambler, A., Harrington, H. *et al.* (2012) 'Persistent cannabis users show neurophysical decline from childhood to midlife.' *Proceedings of the National Academy of Science 109*, 40: E 2657–2664.

Ministry of Justice (2013) 'Criminal Justice Statistics Quarterly Update to September 2012.' London: Ministry of Justice.

National Treatment Agency (2012) 'Substance Misuse among Young People 2011–12.' London: National Treatment Agency for Substance Misuse.

National Treatment Agency (2013) 'National and Regional Estimates of the Prevalence of Opiate and/or Crack Cocaine Use 2010–11.' London: National Treatment Agency for Substance Misuse.

Nutt, D. (2009) 'Equasy: An overlooked addiction with implications for the current debate on drug harms.' *Journal of Psychopharmacology 23*, 1: 3–5.

Nutt, D. (2012) *Drugs Without the Hot Air.* Cambridge: UIT Cambridge.

Office for National Statistics (2013a) 'Alcohol-Related Deaths in the United Kingdom, 2011.' London: Office for National Statistics.

Office for National Statistics (2013b) 'Deaths Related to Drug Poisoning in England and Wales, 2012.' London: Office for National Statistics.

Peele, S. (1977) *Love and Addiction.* London: Abacus.

Peele, S. (1985) *The Meaning of Addiction.* San Francisco, CA: Jossey-Bass.

Peele, S. (2007) *Addiction Proof Your Child: A Realistic Approach to Preventing Drugs, Alcohol and Other Dependencies.* New York, NY: Three Rivers Press.

Power, M. (2013) *Drugs 2.0: The Web Revolution That's Changing How the World Gets High.* London: Portobello Books.

Rogeberg, O. (2013) 'Correlations between cannabis use and IQ change in the Dunedin cohort are consistent with confounding from socioeconomic status.' *Proceedings of the National Academy of Science 110*, 11: 4251–4254.

St John Ambulance, St Andrew's First Aid, British Red Cross (2011) *First Aid Manual.* 9th edn. London: Dorling Kindersley.

Sewell, R.A., Polling, J. and Sofuoglu, M. (2009) 'The effect of cannabis compared with alcohol on driving.' *American Journal of Addiction 18*, 3: 185–193.

Shapiro, H. (2010) *The Essential Guide to Drugs and Alcohol.* London: DrugScope.

UK Drug Policy Commission (2010) *Drugs and Diversity: Ethnic Minority Groups.* Crowborough: UKDC.

United Nations (2013) *World Drug Report.* New York, NY: United Nations Office on Drugs and Crime.

Wakeman, S. and Seddon, T. (2013) 'New age austerity highs.' *Druglink 28*, 5 (September/October): 14–15.

Zinberg, N.E. (1984) *Drug, Set and Setting: The Basis for Controlled Intoxicant Use.* New Haven and London: Yale University Press.

Index

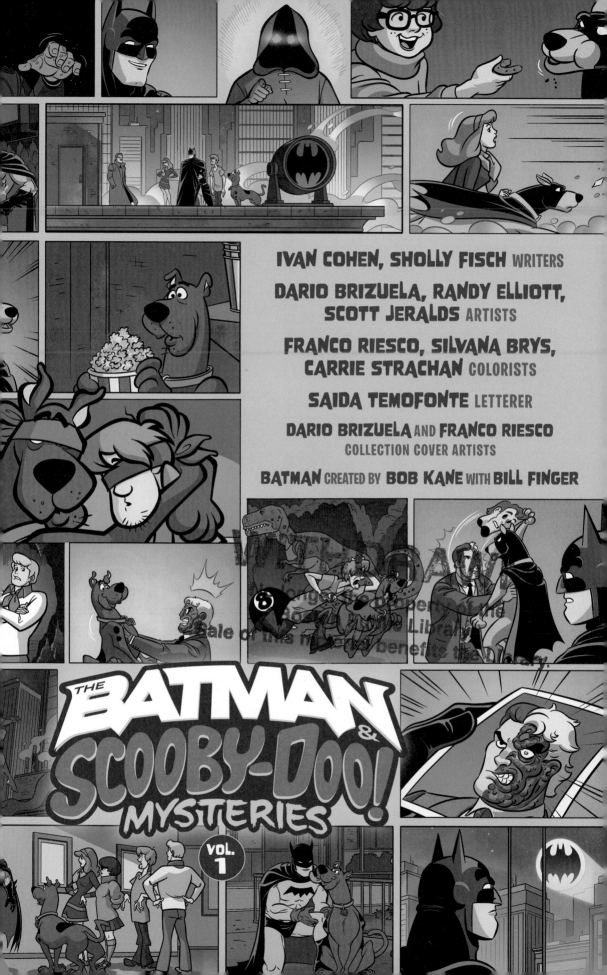

IVAN COHEN, SHOLLY FISCH WRITERS

DARIO BRIZUELA, RANDY ELLIOTT, SCOTT JERALDS ARTISTS

FRANCO RIESCO, SILVANA BRYS, CARRIE STRACHAN COLORISTS

SAIDA TEMOFONTE LETTERER

DARIO BRIZUELA AND FRANCO RIESCO COLLECTION COVER ARTISTS

BATMAN CREATED BY BOB KANE WITH BILL FINGER

THE BATMAN & SCOOBY-DOO! MYSTERIES

VOL. 1

MICHAEL McCALISTER Editor – Original Series & Collected Edition

STEVE COOK Design Director – Books

AMIE BROCKWAY-METCALF Publication Design

CHRISTY SAWYER Publication Production

MARIE JAVINS Editor-in-Chief, DC Comics

DANIEL CHERRY III Senior VP – General Manager

JIM LEE Publisher & Chief Creative Officer

JOEN CHOE VP – Global Brand and Creative Services

DON FALLETTI VP – Manufacturing Operations & Workflow Management

LAWRENCE GANEM VP – Talent Services

ALISON GILL Senior VP – Manufacturing & Operations

NICK J. NAPOLITANO VP – Manufacturing Administration & Design

NANCY SPEARS VP – Revenue

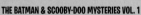

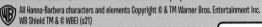

THE BATMAN & SCOOBY-DOO MYSTERIES VOL. 1

DC Comics, 2900 West Alameda Ave., Burbank, CA 91505
Printed by Solisco Printers, Scott, QC, Canada. 10/22/21. First Printing.
ISBN: 978-1-77951-307-6
Library of Congress Cataloging-in-Publication Data is available.

PEFC Certified

This product is from
sustainably manag
forests and control
sources

PEFC/26-31-02   www.pefc.org